An
American
Heroine
in the
French
Resistance

An American Heroin

a *the* French Resistance

The Diary

and Memoir

of Virginia

d'Albert-Lake

Edited,

with an introduction,

by Judy Barrett Litoff

FORDHAM UNIVERSITY PRESS New York 2006

World War II: The Global, Human,
and Ethical Dimension, No. 9
ISSN 1541-0293

Library of Congress Cataloging-in-Publication Data
Albert-Lake, Virginia d', 1909–
    An American heroine in the French Resistance : the diary and memoir of Virginia
d'Albert-Lake / edited by Judy Barrett Litoff. — 1st ed.
        p.   cm. — (World War II—the globa, human, and ethical dimension,
ISSN 1541-0293 ; 9)
    Includes bibliographical references and index.
    ISBN 0-8232-2581-X (cloth : alk. paper)
    1. Albert-Lake, Virginia d', 1909–   2. Ravensbrück (Concentration camp)
3. World War, 1939–1945—Prisoners and prisons, German.   4. World War,
1939–1945—Personal narratives, American.   5. World, War, 1939–1945—
Underground movements—France.   6. Prisoners of war—Germany—Biography.
7. Prisoners of war—United States—Biography.   8. France—History—German
occupation, 1940–1945.   I. Litoff, Judy Barrett.   II. Title.   III. Series.
    D805.5.R38A43   2005
    940.53'44092—dc22

                                                                2005034897

Printed in the United States of America
07 06   5 4 3 2 1
First edition

CONTENTS

ACKNOWLEDGMENTS

The making of *An American Heroine in the French Resistance* is the result of the aid and counsel of many thoughtful friends and colleagues. First and foremost, I would like to thank the journalist Jim Calio for introducing me to the diary and memoir of Virginia d'Albert-Lake. Jim had the good fortune to know Virginia during the last decade of her life. He visited her several times at Cancaval, the d'Albert-Lake family home near Dinard, Brittany, conducted lengthy interviews with both Virginia and her husband, Philippe, and wrote about Virginia's courageous wartime work with the French Resistance for the November–December 1989 issue of *Philip Morris* magazine. Although I did not begin work on this project until after Virginia's death in 1997, Jim shared with me his extensive knowledge of this remarkable woman. Virginia's son, Patrick d'Albert-Lake, graciously made the extensive d'Albert-Lake Family Papers available to me. My interviews and talks with him at Cancaval as well as our many e-mail conversations further confirmed what a remarkable woman his mother was. Patrick's son, Sebastien, Virginia's grandson, skillfully prepared the illustrations from the d'Albert-Lake Family Papers that appear in this book.

My dear friend and colleague, Suzanne Cane, took a personal interest in this project, and I can never thank her enough for her indispensable assistance. She translated numerous and vital French documents, traveled with me to France in the summer of 2003 to meet with Patrick d'Albert-Lake, and answered a multitude of questions about French life and culture. She also read and carefully commented on the entire manuscript several times. Her attention to grammar, syntax, and historical detail has greatly improved this work. Over the past several years, we have also had many lengthy and productive conversations about the life and work of Virginia, none more memorable than when we picnicked together that gorgeous July day in the beautiful gardens of Cancaval.

Once again, Bryant University has been enormously supportive of my work through the awarding of summer research stipends, course reductions, and, most recently, a sabbatical that allowed me to complete the project. The research staff at the Douglas and Judith Krupp Library at

Bryant University, in particular Colleen Anderson and Paul Roske, expeditiously fulfilled my numerous research requests. Linda Asselin, a faculty suite coordinator at Bryant, efficiently corrected errors, formatted chapters, and came to my rescue on numerous occasions when I became frustrated because of computer glitches. Without her help, this book would have been much longer in the making.

The research staff at the United States Holocaust Memorial Museum was enormously helpful in answering questions about Ravensbrück, Besançon, Vittel, Torgau, Königsberg Neumark, and Liebenau. In particular, I would like to thank, Dr. Peter Black, Senior Historian, and Severin Hochberg. Kenneth Schlessinger of the Textual Archives Services Division of Modern Military Records at the National Archives at College Park, Maryland, carefully answered my queries about RG 498 MIS and MIS-X series. Joe Rawson, librarian at the Providence Public Library, and Evelyn M. Cherpak, Head, Naval Historical Collection, Naval War College, Newport, Rhode Island, answered a number of puzzling historical questions that have been incorporated into the notes. Robert Oppedisano, Director of Fordham University Press, provided invaluable guidance, as did G. Kurt Piehler, professor of history at the University of Tennessee and general editor of Fordam's World War II Series. William C. Newkirk, graphic designer and faculty member at the Rhode Island School of Design, kindly prepared the maps. Thanks and appreciation also go to David J. Boardman, David E. Cane, and David C. Smith.

My adult daughters, Nadja Barrett Pisula-Litoff and Alyssa Barrett Litoff, continue to support my work with love, companionship, encouragement, and scholarly advice. They bring great joy and fulfillment to my life. This book is dedicated with love and affection to the youngest member of our family, my granddaughter, Dorothy Barbara Pisula-Litoff.

EDITOR'S NOTE

The handwritten wartime diary of Virginia d'Albert-Lake did not survive, but fortunately, Philippe d'Albert-Lake typed out the diary after the war. The original typescript is in the possession of Virginia's son, Patrick d'Albert-Lake. Occasionally, in order to enhance the diary's readability, spelling and grammatical errors have been silently corrected. In a few instances, the diary entry dates were not correct and they, too, have been silently corrected. Given the difficult conditions under which Virginia wrote the diary, it is not surprising that spelling and grammatical errors, although rare, did occur. Likewise, it is understandable that Virginia occasionally misdated her diary entries. Immediately following Virginia's reunion with Philippe in May 1945, she began writing a memoir of her last eleven months as a kind of letter to her mother, who had recently died. She completed her memoir in 1946. The original typescript is in the possession of Patrick d'Albert-Lake. Here, too, for the sake of readability, a few spelling and grammatical errors have been silently corrected. The chapter divisions for both the diary and memoir have been added and were not part of the original materials. Explanatory footnotes that provide historical context and identify key persons, places, and events have also been added to both. The documents in the appendixes are reproduced verbatim.

Women and the French Resistance:
The Story of Virginia d'Albert-Lake

Judy Barrett Litoff

Something broke inside me. I knew somehow that it was all
over. There was no more reason to hope. The sun that only a few
minutes ago was so bright and warm, now seemed eclipsed by
a grey fog. Disappointment and fear clothed me in a hot vapor.
Sweat started in my armpits; my scalp tingled; I had no choice but
to stand there in the center of the dusty road, grip my [bicycle]
handle bars, and wait.[1]

These were the thoughts of Virginia d'Albert-Lake shortly before her
arrest by German authorities on June 12, 1944, as she escorted downed
Allied airmen to a hidden forest encampment near Châteaudun, France.
Virginia's life was now at a crossroads; her important and dangerous
work with the renowned Comet escape line was over. She would spend
the next eleven months as a German prisoner of war, much of it at the
infamous Ravensbrück concentration camp for women, where she almost
died. Her incredible story, as revealed in her wartime diary and memoir,
is representative of thousands of unheralded and nearly forgotten escape
line resisters who, at great personal risk, protected, nurtured, clothed,
and fed downed Allied airmen. What distinguished Virginia from most
other resisters, however, was that she was an American citizen who had
the option to return to the safety of her native country. Yet she chose to
remain in France to be with her beloved husband, where her dangerous
work with the Comet escape line nearly cost her her life.

Born on June 4, 1910, in Dayton, Ohio, Virginia d'Albert-Lake was the
first of three children of Franklin and Edith Roush.[2] Shortly after World

1. Virginia d'Albert-Lake, "My Story" (hereafter "My Story"), p. 28. The original
typescript of this memoir is in the possession of Patrick d'Albert-Lake.

2. Biographical information on Virgina d'Albert-Lake has been culled from the
editor's interviews with Virginia's son, Patrick d'Albert-Lake, Cancaval, Dinard,
France, July 22–23, 2003; taped interviews by Jim Calio with Virginia and Philippe
d'Albert-Lake, Cancaval, Dinard, France, October 1989; and the d'Albert-Lake Family Papers, in the possession of Patrick d'Albert-Lake. Biographical information on

War I, the family moved to St. Petersburg, Florida, where Virginia's father established a medical practice and her mother founded a private country day school. After graduating from high school, Virginia attended St. Petersburg Junior College and eventually continued her education at Rollins College in Winter Park, Florida, where she received the B.A. degree in 1935. During the summer of 1935 she began graduate study at Columbia University, but in the fall she returned to St. Petersburg, where she taught at her mother's school. The following summer she traveled to England to attend an international convention on progressive education. She also made a side trip to France, where she met and fell in love with Philippe d'Albert-Lake, a young Frenchman who had grown up in Paris and at the family's château, Cancaval, near Dinard, Brittany. In a 1993 interview Virginia remarked that "my mother was devastated" upon learning that she intended to marry someone from France. "She stayed in bed for a week. She didn't want me to marry a Frenchman and move away."[3] Despite her mother's misgivings, the couple was married at the First Presbyterian Church in St. Petersburg on May 1, 1937. After honeymooning in New York City, they set sail for France, where they set up housekeeping at Philippe's apartment at 57, rue de Bellechasse, located in the seventh arrondissement of Paris.

With the outbreak of World War II in September 1939, Virginia began keeping a diary, written in pencil in four different notebooks. Inserted in the notebooks were postcards of where she traveled as well as newspaper clippings that she later described as "mostly German propaganda."[4] Her

---

Virginia d'Albert-Lake is also included in Margaret L. Rossiter, *Women in the Resistance* (New York: Praeger, 1986), pp. 204–211; Jim Calio, "Resistance and Remembrance," *Philip Morris*, November–December 1989, 36–39; and Thomas Fleming, "'Deliver Us from Evil,'" *Reader's Digest*, August 1991, 115–119. Relevant works in French include Catherine Rothman-Le Dret, *L'Amérique déportée: Virignia d'Albert-Lake de la Résistance à Ravensbrück* (Nancy: Presses Universitaires de Nancy, 1994). This work, however, contains a number of historical errors and inaccuracies. See also Rémy, *La Ligne de démarcation*, XII (Paris: Librairie Académique Perrin, 1964), pp. 131–173, and Rémy, *Mission Marathon* (Paris: Librairie Académique Perrin, 1974), pp. 137–181.

3. Laura Griffin, "An Unsung War Hero Gets Her Due," *St. Petersburg Times*, May 30, 1993.

4. Virginia d'Albert-Lake to Trudy Lowell, February 12, 1984, d'Albert-Lake Family Papers. The handwritten diary did not survive, but, fortunately, Philippe typed out the diary after the war. The original typescript is in the possession of Patrick d'Albert-Lake.

first diary entry, written on October 11, 1939, summarized the events of the previous eight weeks. She described how she had "adjusted myself to this new strange state of living, diving in a kind of suspension, just waiting and hoping, while time itself seems to have neither a yesterday nor a to-morrow."[5]

There is nothing in these early diary entries to suggest that Virginia's daring work with the Comet escape line in 1943 and 1944 would lead to her arrest and imprisonment at the Ravensbrück concentration camp. Indeed, her chief concern appears to be the fear that the exigencies of war would encroach upon the loving and pleasant life that she and Philippe had carefully carved out together in her newly adopted country.[6]

During this initial stage of the conflict, Virginia held out the hope that France would not find it necessary to become embroiled in a full-scale war. After attending church one Sunday, she expressed disappointment when the priest "said that the Mass was held for the victory of France"; she would have preferred him to say a Mass "for Peace."[7] Like many of her contemporaries, Virginia may have been swayed by the respite in the fighting that occurred following the rapid defeat of Poland in September. The "phony war" of October 1939–April 1940 lulled many people into a sense of complacency; they presumed that the Germans did not have the strength or the determination to invade Western Europe. The French, in particular, believed that the Maginot Line, a system of fortifications constructed between 1930 and 1937 and extending for 140 kilometers along the eastern border with Germany, would protect them. Moreover, the memory of the horrific battles of World War I and the 1.3 million French citizens who had lost their lives made the French especially reluctant to commit to war. Consequently, in October 1939 many people in France and elsewhere in Europe, including Virginia d'Albert-Lake, incorrectly believed peace to be a feasible alternative to total war.

Virginia's early diary entries tell of her adventures as she followed Philippe to his various military postings, the twenty-one-day agricultural leave they spent together at their country home in Nesles, a small village

5. Diary of Virginia d'Albert-Lake (hereafter Diary), October 11, 1939.

6. Although she considered France to be her adopted country, Virginia retained her U.S. citizenship.

7. Diary, October 11, 1939. For a discussion of how the French people hoped for peace even after war had been declared, see Julian Jackson, *The Fall of France: The Nazi Invasion of 1940* (New York: Oxford University Press, 2003), pp. 151–155.

thirty-five kilometers northwest of Paris, and the horrors associated with the German invasion of France in June 1940, followed by the June 22 armistice. She worried about her family in the United States, with whom she had only intermittent contact, and she wrote of the great relief she felt upon learning that Philippe was unharmed and with his unit in the Unoccupied Zone. She also included a riveting account of her unauthorized trip to the Unoccupied Zone, where she joined her husband; they then returned to Cancaval via a six-hundred-kilometer bicycle trip. As the war wore on, her diary entries focused on coping with food shortages and rationing, gas restrictions, and the scarcity of firewood. As an enemy national, she worried that she might be interned, and she also feared that Philippe might be conscripted to work in Germany.

Virginia's last diary entry, dated April 1944, was written after she and Philippe had become actively involved in the work of the Comet escape line, but she was careful to provide no clue about their clandestine activities. After witnessing a powerful bombardment of Paris from the window of friend's apartment, she remarked, "There were such powerful concussions caused by the explosions that my heavy skirt was wrapped about my legs!" During a stay at Nesles, she told of watching "a Flying Fortress fall in flames" and seeing "five men bail out." Well aware of the dangerous consequences of written records about escape work falling into enemy hands, she provided no indication that their home at Nesles and their apartment in Paris now served as safe houses for downed airmen such as the five she had seen bail out.[8]

Shortly after the war Virginia wrote a memoir, which she later titled "My Story"; it detailed her work with the Comet escape line, her capture and arrest by German police in June 1944, the horrors of her imprisonment at Ravensbrück, and her eventual reunion with Philippe in May 1945. Unlike many other personal narratives of this genre, often written long after the events occurred, this memoir is particularly valuable for its nearly contemporaneous perspective.[9] In addition, it is one of

8. Diary, April 1944.
9. During the late 1940s Virginia submitted the manuscript to several publishers in the United States and England. While they offered high praise for the memoir, they nevertheless rejected it because, as one publisher put it, "There is at the moment a great resistance to books dealing with any aspect of the war." Virginia's subsequent efforts to get the memoir published also failed. The letters to and from prospective publishers are contained in the d'Albert-Lake Family Papers. For a Resistance memoir

only a very few memoirs by a woman resister in France to be written in English.[10]

Virginia wrote the memoir as a letter to her mother, who had worked tirelessly for her release but who died of leukemia in mid-April 1944, unaware of the ultimate fate of her daughter. Writing the memoir helped Virginia to assuage her sorrow, and years later she commented, "It was easier for me this way, as I know that she would have wanted to know all that had happened to me."[11]

Virginia began her memoir with an account of how she and Philippe initially became involved in escape work with the Comet line, one of the largest of the escape lines; it extended from Brussels to Paris, southward to San Sebastian in Spain, and finally to Gibraltar. Although escape organizations had existed since 1940, the couple's first efforts to help downed Allied airmen did not occur until the late fall of 1943, when Marcel Renard, a baker at Nesles, contacted them and asked if they would serve as interpreters for three U.S. airmen whom he was sheltering. Inspired by this meeting and the delightful dinner that followed, Virginia and Philippe decided to join the Resistance.[12] As Julian Jackson has noted, "Until at least the end of 1942, the Resistance was too small to be a presence in the experience, even consciousness, of most people." By contrast, 1943,

-----

written in the mid-1990s by the head of the Code Service in Paris for General Charles de Gaulle's delegation, see Claire Chevrillon, *Code Name Christiane Clouet: A Woman in the French Resistance* (College Station: Texas A&M University Press, 1995). Written in French four decades after the war, this memoir lacks the sense of immediacy found in Virginia's narrative. Two other first-person accounts originally written in French by women are Germaine Tillion, *Ravensbrück: An Eyewitness Account of a Women's Concentration Camp* (New York: Doubleday, 1975; orig. Paris: Editions du Seuil, 1973), and Geneviève de Gaulle Anthonioz, *The Dawn of Hope: A Memoir of Ravensbrück* (New York: Arcade Publishing, 1999; orig. Paris: Editions du Seuil, 1998).

10. Two works written in English by American women who were active in the French Resistance include Devereaux Rochester, *Full Moon to France* (New York: Harper and Row, 1977), and Drue Tartière, *The House Near Paris* (New York: Simon and Schuster, 1946).

11. Virginia d'Albert-Lake to Daryl Frazell, April 5, 1985, d'Albert-Lake Family Papers.

12. "My Story," pp. 1–5; Philippe d'Albert-Lake, "Report from Philippe d'Albert-Lake," National Archives and Records Administration, RG 498, Records of Headquarters, European Theater of Operations, United States Army (World War II), MIS-X (a copy of this report is included in the d'Albert-Lake Family Papers; see Appendix 1).

the year that Virginia and Philippe joined the Resistance, represented the year of its "fastest expansion."[13]

Escape line work was of crucial importance to an Allied victory since it took significant time and considerable money to train new airmen. Moreover, every airman returned to England had what one escape line historian described as a "marvelous effect" on the morale of the Allied air forces, "who, in the later stages [of the war], had more than an even chance of return if they were shot down."[14]

The actual number of persons who worked for escape lines is difficult to determine. Airey Neave, a British escapee who served as the chief organizer of MI9 during the last two years of the war, estimated that at least twelve thousand persons helped downed airmen find their way to Spain or England. Neave also noted, however, that many occasional helpers who were not part of a regular escape line were not included in this figure. Although the names of many helpers have been lost to history, Neave concluded that they "formed an essential link in the whole machinery of escape."[15]

Work with escape organizations was especially dangerous, as the sheer size of the movement made it vulnerable to infiltration. Consequently, lines were broken many times. Anyone caught either directly or indirectly helping downed Allied airmen could expect severe punishment. Men were shot on the spot, whereas women were deported to German concentration camps.[16] Of the 500 who died in this cause, 150 were betrayed by traitors who worked with the Gestapo and other German secret police and security services. Although it is impossible to determine the exact number of servicemen who were assisted by escape lines during World War II, Airey Neave estimated that 4,000 Allied servicemen from France, Belgium, and Holland returned to England via organized escape routes before the June 6, 1944, D-Day landings.[17]

13. Julian Jackson, *France: The Dark Years* (London: Oxford University Press, 2001), pp. 240, 475.

14. Airey Neave, *Saturday at M.I.9* (London: Hodder and Stoughton, 1969), pp. 20, 24.

15. Ibid., p. 315. MI9 was the British intelligence organization established in 1939 to aid in the escape of British prisoners of war and the return of downed airmen to England. A very good memoir written by a downed American airmen is George Watt, *The Comet Connection* (Lexington: University Press of Kentucky, 1990).

16. Rossiter, *Women in the Resistance*, pp. 24, 31, 55.

17. Neave, *Saturday at M.I.9*, pp. 20, 23–24.

In her work, *Women in the Resistance*, Margaret Rossiter identified and discussed the activities of four women from the United States who worked for escape lines. She asserts that the work of Virginia d'Albert-Lake for the Comet escape line was "probably the most important" of those four.[18] Undoubtedly, there were other American women who provided both regular and occasional aid to downed airmen, but their names, like those of many of their French counterparts, remain largely unknown.[19]

Fortunately, Virginia d'Albert-Lake's important escape line work has not been lost to history. Her memoir provides vivid descriptions of the ingenious ways she offered aid and succor to downed Allied airmen, the valiant courage she demonstrated following her arrest, and her steadfast will to live even as she faced what appeared to be insurmountable obstacles during her frightful incarceration at Ravensbrück.

Virginia's memoir includes accounts of how thrilling it was to convoy downed airmen from the Gare du Nord in Paris to secret hideouts in the city. She wrote of how she and other escape guides sometimes "took the men sightseeing in Paris, which meant rubbing elbows with Germans, doing the same thing." While this was "dangerous sport," the guides nonetheless "sensed their [the airmen's] vital need of getting out of the house and stretching their legs." Some of the airmen were hidden at Nesles until train tickets and guides to the Spanish frontier could be arranged. In total, Virginia and Philippe provided sixty-six aviators with shelter and assistance.[20] To the downed airmen, their gracious American hostess was a godsend. In a 1993 interview Thomas Yankus, a pilot shot down over France in the spring of 1944, recalled: "There we were, walking into this apartment after some pretty hairy experiences and being greeted by this beautiful woman who said, 'Hi fellas, how're you doing?' . . . She had no fear whatsoever. . . . She showed us around even with the

18. The other three American women whom Rossiter identifies as working for escape lines were Drue Tartière, Rosemary Maeght, and Countess Roberta de Maudvit. She discusses two other American women, Virginia Hall and Devereaux Rochester, who were agents for Special Operations Executive, a British intelligence agency founded specifically to promote sabotage against the Nazis and to help the Resistance in Europe. See Rossiter, *Women in the Resistance*, pp. 189–219.

19. Ibid., p. 204.

20. "My Story," pp. 7–12.

Germans there. She took us to see the sights, like Napoleon's tomb. There were Gestapo everywhere."[21]

Because of heavy Allied bombing of railways in preparation for the June 6, 1944, D-Day invasion of Normandy, it became increasingly difficult to transport downed airmen via train to Spain. This situation led to the extraordinary decision to build an encampment in the midst of German-occupied France where the airmen would be hidden until the arrival of Allied troops. Located at the Forest of Fréteval, near Châteaudun, the encampment included adjacent open areas where the Allies could drop tents, stoves, plates, and saucepans by parachute, but the airmen received most of their support and supplies from local women and men who risked their lives to help and protect them.[22] D-Day marked the camp's official opening; the first 30 Allied airmen were brought from the nearby villages where they had been hidden to the encampment at the Forest of Fréteval. By the time of its liberation in mid-August, some 152 men were hidden at two camps located about nine kilometers from each other.[23]

During the month leading up to D-Day, Virginia recalled that "events were moving fast . . . and we sensed the Invasion was not far off." With more and more men to shelter, feed, and clothe, there was no longer time to take them to Nesles. Instead, they crowded the men, five or six at a time, into their Paris studio apartment. Rationing and shortages necessitated that they rely on "the black market and false ration tickets" for food and other supplies. Moreover, with gas on for only "an hour at noon and a half hour at night," cooking a meal for ten people on a two-burner stove proved to be a quite a challenge. For Virginia this "was an exciting but enervating period."[24]

Virginia and Philippe were in Paris on the morning of June 6 when a friend phoned to tell them that the invasion had begun. Thrilled to hear this news, they also knew that they would have to act quickly if they were to maintain the safety of the eleven airmen then under their care. It took three days, however, before the d'Albert-Lakes could make the necessary arrangements for the journey to begin. Two days later, on June 12, Virginia and a downed airman were arrested as they bicycled along the outskirts of Châteaudun.

21. Griffin, "An Unsung War Hero Gets Her Due." For examples of letters grateful airmen sent to Virginia, see Appendices 11 and 12.
22. Neave, *Saturday at M.I.9*, pp. 250–259.
23. Ibid.; "Report from Philippe d'Albert-Lake," pp. 2–3.
24. "My Story," pp. 13–17.

Virginia recalled that "once the game was up, I know that I appeared very calm and in perfect command of myself, but, inside, I felt a throbbing excitement and a kind of deep heavy misery, clutching and dragging me down." She described her horror when the police discovered in her handbag a list of the addresses of Resistance contacts in Châteaudun that Philippe had given to her the previous day as well as her amazement when they put the address list back into the handbag and returned it to her. She then explained how she discreetly tore the paper into tiny bits and inconspicuously, but with great difficulty, ate the bits of paper that had contained the address list.[25]

Virginia spent the next seven weeks in prison at Fresnes, on the southern outskirts of Paris. She recalled in her memoir that she "suffered greatly from my loss of liberty. It was very hard to go suddenly from the stimulating worthwhile life I loved, fraught with danger and excitement, to this stagnant one." Still, she made the best she could of prison life. With an illegal knife, she took out the bolts that held her cell's window shut so that she and her prison mates could enjoy "delicious cool air" each evening. She used several ingenious methods, such as tying strips of cloth together to send messages down the hot-air shaft, to communicate with neighboring prisoners. But what gave Virginia "the keenest satisfaction came each day at sundown when one of the prisoners possessing a lovely voice would sing out . . . Evening Song and Taps," followed by "the victory knocks systematically relayed from wall to wall and from cell to cell."[26]

Twice while at Fresnes Virginia was taken to Gestapo headquarters in Paris for questioning. Unlike other prisoners who were often brutally tortured, Virginia was treated "with perfect respect" by her interrogator. She wrote that she tried "to appear dignified, but not proud, confident, but not aggressive. . . . I told the truth whenever I considered it would be of no importance, but I lied about everything else." During the course of her interrogation, Virginia learned, to her great relief, that both Philippe and his mother had eluded capture.[27]

Aware that Allied troops were quickly advancing toward Paris, Virginia and the other prisoners at Fresnes held out hope that they might soon be

25. Ibid., pp. 29–35.
26. Ibid., pp. 44–53.
27. Ibid., pp. 57–58.

liberated. On August 1, however, Virginia was transferred to the prison at Romainville. This prison, on the eastern outskirts of Paris, served as a holding area for prisoners about to be deported to Germany. Still, the conditions at Romainville were far better than those at Fresnes, and Virginia wrote that it seemed like "a pleasure resort after Fresnes."[28]

With the sounds of advancing Allied artillery becoming louder each day and an assurance from the prison commander that Romainville would soon be liberated, Virginia was hopeful that she and the other inmates would not be deported to Germany. But on August 15, just ten days before Allied troops triumphantly entered Paris, the entire prison was evacuated. The prisoners were crowded into requisitioned city buses for a trip to La Gare de Pantin, where they would begin the long journey to Germany. On the way to the station Virginia managed to stand next to the sympathetic French bus driver, who whispered to her, "This job makes me sick. All day long since early morning I've been driving prisoners . . . to the station at Pantin." When the guard wasn't looking, Virginia cautiously handed the bus driver a number of hurriedly scribbled messages written to family members and friends that she had collected from prison mates and that she later learned were all delivered.[29]

Throughout this two-month ordeal Virginia had never revealed the true nature of her work with the Resistance to the German authorities, and the hideout at the Forest of Fréteval remained secure. On August 14, the day before Virginia was deported to Germany, Airey Neave of MI9 arrived at the encampment with a backup team to rescue the airmen, who now numbered 132. On the previous day 20 others had left and were presumably hiding out in villages or in the care of Allied troops. Almost all these men returned to flying; 38 were killed in action before the war ended. Virginia's courage and ingenuity in the face of grave personal danger helped to ensure that this daring scheme to hide 152 airmen "under the noses of the German Army and the Gestapo" was successful. Had she broken under questioning, the Germans would have assuredly captured the airmen, destroyed the camp, and arrested scores of resisters.[30]

28. Ibid., pp. 70–77.

29. Ibid., pp. 77–81. See Illustration 9 for a copy of the original note that Virginia sent to Philippe in care of his aunt Mme. de Gourlet.

30. Neave, *Saturday at M.I.9*, pp. 268–271. For a memoir written by a downed British airmen who was provided aid by the Comet escape line and later hidden at the encampment at the Forest of Fréteval, see Raymond Worrall, *Escape from France: The Secret Forest of Freteval* (North Yorkshire: Silver Quill Publications, 2004). See

As the airmen at the Forest of Fréteval celebrated their rescue, Virginia faced a harrowing 144-hour journey in an overcrowded, stifling boxcar that ended at the Ravensbrück concentration camp for women. In total, some three thousand prisoners, about six hundred women and twenty-four hundred men, traveled on this train caravan to Germany. It was one of the last convoys of deportees to leave France. During one of several stops the train made, Virginia made contact with a recently arrested woman she had known in Paris who had convoyed airmen for Comet and who had news that Philippe had made his way to England via Spain. This welcome information brought Virginia a great sense of happiness, and she recalled in her memoir, "I nearly danced back to my box car. . . . I had always heard that women supported prison hardships better than men, and I had more faith in my future than ever, now that I knew that Philippe was out of danger."[31]

At the time of Virginia's arrival at Ravensbrück on August 22, its population, including over seventy subcamps, was nearing its peak of between 45,000 and 65,000 women, 80 percent of whom were political prisoners accused of opposing National Socialism. According to the historian Jack G. Morrison, Ravensbrück and its subcamps constituted nothing less than a "Mini-Empire."[32] Established as a labor camp rather than an extermination camp in May 1939, Ravensbrück was ninety kilometers north of Berlin, just outside the village of Fürstenberg, a resort area situated along a beautiful chain of lakes. Although SS officials were responsible for the management of Ravensbrück, female overseers, often incorrectly referred to as SS women by the inmates, supervised what went on inside the camp. Morrison maintains, however, that "to a surprising extent, much of the

---

pages 56–57 for Worrall's discussion of the work of Virginia d'Albert-Lake. Worrall states: "The arrest of Virginia caused very great concern to the escorts and also to us in the forest. Sentries were reinforced and we were all tense and ready to flee at the least alert."

31. "My Story," pp. 81–95.

32. Jack G. Morrisson, *Ravensbrück: Everyday Life in a Women's Concentration Camp 1930–45* (Princeton: Markus Wiener Publishers, 2000), pp. 76, 207, 277. This is the best single-volume history of Ravensbrück. Another useful study is Tillion, *Ravensbrück: An Eyewitness Account*. See also Rochelle G. Saidel, *The Jewish Women of Ravensbrück Concentration Camp* (Madison: University of Wisconsin Press, 2004). Almost all the official records at Ravensbrück were destroyed by the Germans as the war waned. What we know about Ravensbrück, therefore, comes primarily from personal accounts and testimonials, such as Virginia's memoir.

actual day-to-day running of the camp was in the hands of the prisoners themselves."[33]

By the time French prisoners began arriving at Ravensbrück in significant numbers in late 1943 and early 1944, Polish and Russian women had already established themselves as prison leaders. Consequently, French inmates "were assigned to some of the worst jobs . . . [and] subjected to continued oppression, not only by the SS, but also by their fellow prisoners."[34] Although Virginia had retained her U.S. citizenship after she married Philippe, she was usually grouped with French prisoners and ordinarily did not receive preferential treatment because of her nationality.

As the six hundred new arrivals from Romainville marched from the Fürstenberg train station to the camp, they were initially struck by the beauty of the area. Virginia wrote of the "large, attractive, substantial-looking houses with broad cement terraces and green lawns, on which little children were running about" and a "lovely lake and great tall pines [that were] silhouetted against the sky." Entering the camp, however, she was horrified to see "the inmates, strange, gnome-like looking women, with shaved heads, dressed in blue and grey-striped skirts and jackets, with heavy wooden-soled galoshes on their feet." Following a humiliating and lengthy processing that included naked body searches and a vaginal exam to look for hidden valuables, the prisoners were assigned to a barracks, known as a block, where they lived in "overcrowded, unsanitary conditions." For the first ten days the new arrivals were kept in quarantine in a common room, "crushed one against the other; six hundred of us in a space suitable for one hundred." At the end of the quarantine, they were assigned to work details. Each was identified by a prison number sewn on her left sleeve; Virginia's number was 57,631.[35]

33. Morrison, *Ravensbrück*, pp. 19–24. The SS-*Schutzstaffel* was an elite, all-male military force within the Nazi Party. Morrison states (p. 24) that "technically . . . the overseers were not *bona fide* members of the SS, which was an all-male organization. They belonged to the SS Women's Auxiliary (*weibliche SS-Gefolge*)."

34. Ibid., pp. 94–98.

35. "My Story," pp. 96–105. Virginia may have been issued a second number on her return to Ravensbrück, for her demobilization form listed her number as 57,795. Whether she received a third number on her second return to Ravensbrück is unknown; d'Albert-Lake Family Papers.

With more and more prisoners arriving at Ravensbrück each day, the already overcrowded conditions became even more congested. Fortunate prisoners like Virginia slept in flea-infested, three-tiered bunk beds, three to a bed. The less fortunate slept on the floor of the block or were assigned to a huge tent, constructed in August 1944, where as many as seven thousand women were crammed together.[36]

For Virginia "the most terrifying sound" of Ravensbrück was the "weird, penetrating wail" of the sirens awaking the inmates at 3:30 A.M. A two-hour roll call followed at 4:15 A.M., when inmates were forced to stand at perfect attention while they were counted by the guards. Regardless of the weather or an inmate's state of health, roll call occurred every day.[37] Virginia wrote of how the "directing of prisoners by prisoners was successful psychological sadism" and that "lack of food" caused "the pitiful mental and physical deterioration of the inmates."[38]

Depending upon specific labor needs, prisoners were often moved from the main camp to one of the subcamps or rented out to private firms such as the nearby Siemens factory, which produced electrical equipment for the military. As the conditions at Ravensbrück deteriorated, Virginia "prayed constantly for one thing—to be allowed to leave."[39]

That opportunity came on the evening of September 11, when Virginia was among a group of five hundred French prisoners selected to be transferred to the Buchenwald subcamp at Torgau, located on the Elbe River about one hundred kilometers south of Berlin. Much to her consternation, she learned that Torgau was the site of a large munitions factory. As one of only seven Anglo-Americans, Virginia was initially spared the brutal work details demanded of women from other countries. Instead, she was assigned to kitchen work, preparing vegetables and peeling potatoes for eleven and a half hours a day. Later, in early October, she was assigned to the much harder task of digging potatoes. Nonetheless, digging potatoes was far preferable to laboring in the munitions factory, where the

36. "My Story," pp. 101–106. For additional information on the horrible conditions in the tent that was constructed in August 1944, see Morrison, *Ravensbrück*, pp. 278–282.

37. "My Story," pp. 102–103. Morrison states that the first sirens sounded at 4:00 A.M. and roll call, which usually lasted "at least an hour," began at 5:00 A.M. Morrison, *Ravensbrück*, pp. 110–111.

38. "My Story," pp. 103–105.

39. Ibid.; Morrison, *Ravensbrück*, p. 209.

work was especially strenuous and dangerous. Whatever the situation, life at Torgau was preferable to the horrors of Ravensbrück.[40]

Unfortunately, Virginia's assignment to Torgau lasted only a month, and on October 6 she and 250 other French prisoners were reassigned to the dreaded Ravensbrück.[41] This time the period of quarantine was abbreviated, and they were almost immediately put to work digging out sand dunes surrounding the swamps just outside the camp.[42]

On October 16, ten days after their second arrival at Ravensbrück, Virginia and the other 250 French prisoners who had been at Torgau were transferred to one of the subcamps at an airstrip near Königsberg Neumark, about eighty kilometers east of Ravensbrück.[43] Approximately 800 women, including 550 Polish and Russian inmates, labored chiefly at enlarging the airfield. Although Virginia didn't mind the work itself, she wrote that she did object to "the impossible conditions under which we worked, the cold and the damp, and the fact that we were under clothed and underfed." The first snows arrived in November, making work on the airfield even more miserable. Although never seriously ill, Virginia, like many other prisoners, because of her mistreatment and poor nourishment, stopped menstruating.[44]

In an effort to seek refuge from the extreme cold of the airfield, Virginia sought work in the forest, where the trees provided some protection from the bitter winds. The trade-off was that the march to the forest was much longer and the labor more strenuous. Work in the forest included digging out heavy stumps from a wide road that was to serve as a runway for planes and laying steel rails for a train track. Although Virginia took part in every phase of the road building, she acknowledged that the

40. Ibid., pp. 108–119.

41. The precise date of the Frenchwomen's return to Ravensbrück was provided by the Division of the Senior Historian, United States Holocaust Memorial Museum, e-mail communication, March 25, 2004.

42. "My Story," pp. 121–127.

43. Königsberg Neumark, about ten kilometers east of the Oder River, is now in Poland and is called Chojna. I would like to thank Dr. Peter Black, Senior Historian at the United States Holocaust Memorial Museum in Washington, D.C., for providing me with the precise location of the subcamp at Königsberg Neumark.

44. "My Story," pp. 127–142. On the lack of menstruation at Ravensbrück and its subcamps, see Morrison, *Ravensbrück*, pp. 173–174.

French prisoners did not have the same physical strength as their Polish and Russian counterparts, who "kept their flesh and color and strength far longer, as well as their bright, gay and brutal energy."[45]

As Christmas and the New Year drew near, the prisoners were aware that the holidays would be difficult, especially for those women who were separated from their children. They were thankful, however, that they would have six days off from work and the cold. Virginia told of how they brought back a "baby fir from the forest and decorated it with bits of cloth and paper." By carefully saving parts of their bread, margarine, and honey rations, they also made a delicious Christmas pudding. Despite their best efforts, which included caroling and a prayer service, Virginia wrote that Christmas day was "very sad" and "a heavy nostalgia settled down upon us." In addition, the "discouraging news" of the major German counteroffensive in the Ardennes Forest that had begun in mid-December had "seeped through" to the inmates.[46]

Virginia's memoir emphasizes that the weeks following the New Year were a desperate time for the inmates. The cold was unbearable and roll calls were "heavy with misery" as women were "constantly falling unconscious on the snow." The starving inmates rummaged through the kitchen garbage heap for potato peelings, rotten vegetables, wilted cabbage leaves, or anything else that was edible. As their hunger became more acute, "bread stealing" became all too common.[47]

By the last week in January conditions at Königsberg had become almost unbearable, and prisoners "were fighting not to lose their minds." They did know of the massive Soviet assault against East Prussia that had begun in mid-January as "the road to the forest was lined with over loaded vehicles of all sorts, heading West—German refugees running

---

45. "My Story," pp. 142–146. For an account of another French woman interned at Ravensbrück, Torgau, and Königsberg with Virginia, see David Ignatius, "After Five Decades, a Spy Tells Her Tale; Britain Gained Warning of Nazi Rockets," *Washington Post*, December 28, 1998.

46. "My Story," 147–151. The battle in the Ardennes, popularly referred to as the Battle of the Bulge, represented Hitler's last effort at driving the Allied forces out of Europe. It began on December 16, 1944, and ended on January 7, 1945. It was the largest battle fought on the Western Front during World War II and resulted in a decisive victory for the Allies.

47. Ibid., pp. 151–160.

from the Russians." Although the inmates' spirits were buoyed by these developments, they also worried that they might be evacuated before the Soviet army arrived.[48]

On January 31, with the Soviet army fast approaching, the panic-stricken German guards set the airplane hangars on fire and evacuated the camp. This led to two days of chaotic plundering of food, fuel, and other supplies by the prisoners. Fearful that the Germans might return, most of the inmates in Virginia's block did not take part in this "liberation." By contrast, Virginia demonstrated great courage, stamina, and determination as she brought back firewood, large tins of jam, fresh milk, bread, vegetables, blankets, and other supplies to her block of mostly French prisoners. The women were ecstatic, but the arrival of a German patrol from Könisberg Neumark tempered their excitement. Nonetheless, the plundering continued, as the patrol did not have the resources to restore order to the camp.[49]

On February 2, with the Soviet army reported to be only four kilometers away, SS guards from Ravensbrück arrived at the subcamp to lead the "horror-stricken" prisoners on a forced march back to the main camp.[50] The women, weak from malnutrition and dysentery, somehow "found the strength to keep going" as they stumbled along over the next two days. Sometime after midnight on the second day of their trek, with their strength rapidly failing, the prisoners made their way to a railroad

---

48. Ibid., pp. 160–161. On the Soviet assault against East Prussia and the final stages of the war in the east, see David M. Glantz and Jonathan House, *When Titans Clashed: How the Red Army Stopped Hitler* (Lawrence: University Press of Kansas, 1995), pp. 241–276; John Erickson, *The Road to Berlin: Continuing the History of Stalin's War with Germany* (Boulder, Colo.: Westview Press, 1983), pp. 431–529. Much has been written about the brutality of the Soviet army during the massive exodus of some two million East Prussians toward the German interior in early 1945. See, for example, John Keegan, *The Second World War* (New York: Penguin Books, 1989), pp. 512–514.

49. "My Story," pp. 161–174.

50. By the end of January the Soviet army was within eighty kilometers of Berlin and in the vicinity of the subcamp at Königsberg Neumark. The final advance across the Oder River toward Berlin, however, did not begin until April 16. Soviet troops reached the suburbs of Berlin on April 21 and completely encircled the city on April 25. Berlin surrendered to the Soviet Army on May 2.

yard and were crowded into boxcars for a slow, twenty-four-hour train ride to Ravensbrück.[51]

The prisoners' third arrival at Ravensbrück occurred toward the end of the first week in February. By this time, the admission system, including the quarantine period, had broken down, and they were sent directly to the large tent that had been constructed the previous August. The situation in the tent, notorious for its harsh conditions, had worsened with the onset of winter. With the bunk section of the tent already occupied by Polish and Russian prisoners, Virginia and her friends were forced to find a space on the already overcrowded floor.[52]

For eight horrific days, Virginia survived life in the tent, where immobile women, ill with dysentery, lay in their own excrement and dead bodies littered the floor. Whenever the tent occupants entered the washroom, they were looked at "with horror and disgust . . . the untouchables, the filthy lice-infested occupants of the tent."[53]

Just when all hope seemed lost, Virginia and approximately one hundred remaining tent women were moved to a block. A few days later, on February 16, she experienced the humiliation of having her lice-infected head shaved. As Virginia grew weaker with each passing day, she realized that she was "on the border line of life and death." Then, on February 25, she was suddenly singled out to be given antivermin powder and clean clothing. Three days later, on February 28, a guard informed Virginia that she would be leaving Ravensbrück later that day for a prisoner-of-war camp at Liebenau, near Lake Constance on the German-Swiss border. Released at the same time was the well-known and greatly respected *résistante*, Geneviève de Gaulle, the niece of General Charles de Gaulle. In her 1998 memoir, *The Dawn of Hope: A Memoir of Ravensbrück*, Geneviève de Gaulle Anthonioz remembered Virginia as a "terribly emaciated woman who look[ed] absolutely ancient. On her shaven skull, a rare tuft of hair ha[d] regrown here and there. She look[ed] like Gandhi at the end of his life." At the time of her release, Virginia's body was covered with lice and open sores, and she weighed only 76 pounds, 50 pounds under her normal weight of 126.[54]

51. "My Story," pp. 173–182.
52. Ibid., pp. 183–186.
53. Ibid., pp. 186–191.
54. Ibid., pp. 191–212; de Gaulle Anthonioz, *The Dawn of Hope*, p. 82.

Virginia's release from Ravensbrück had occurred largely because of the efforts of her mother, Edith Roush. Mrs. Roush had learned of Virginia's arrest from Philippe, who, after briefly returning to Paris and Nesles to warn friends of what had happened and to destroy incriminating documents, made his way to London in July 1944. On July 30 he cabled his mother-in-law with the alarming news that her daughter had been arrested by German authorities.[55] She, in turn, wrote letters to high-ranking officials at the War Department, the American Red Cross, and the Department of State in the hope that they might be able to secure the release of her daughter through an exchange of prisoners.[56] The State Department responded by sending a cable to Berne on August 30, 1944, requesting that the Swiss government ascertain Virginia's whereabouts and obtain a report on her arrest.[57] Eventually, Virginia's case was turned over to MIS-X, a secret section of the Military Intelligence Service of the War Department that dealt specifically with escape and evasion work of U.S. forces. During this difficult period Mrs. Roush's spirits were partially buoyed by letters of appreciation and praise that she received from grateful airmen whom Virginia had assisted.[58]

Meanwhile, Philippe, still in London, learned on September 1, 1944, that Virginia had been transferred to Germany before the August 25 liberation of Paris. With much of France no longer under German control, Philippe was especially eager to return to his native country. In late September he finally arranged to return to Paris, where he worked as an intelligence officer for the Free French forces for the remainder of the

55. See Illustration 8 for a copy of the cable. Philippe followed up the cable with a series of letters to Mrs. Roush, which are in the D'Albert-Lake Family Papers.

56. See the following letters: Mrs. F. W. Roush to Honorable Cordell Hull, August 24, 1944; Albert E. Clattenburg Jr., Assistant Chief, Special War Problems Division, Department of State, to Mrs. Roush, September 4, 1944; Richard F. Allen, Office of Vice Chairman, American Red Cross, to Mrs. F. W. Roush, August 26, 1944; Marion Rushton, Office of the Under Secretary of War Department to Mrs. F. W. Roush, August 15, 1944; Howard F. Bresee, Office of the Provost Marshal, to Mrs. F. W. Roush, August 15, 1944; Albert E. Clattenburg Jr., Assistant Chief, Special War Problems Division, Department of State, to Mrs. F. W. Roush, January 11, 1945; all in d'Albert-Lake Family Papers. See Appendices 2, 3, 4, 5, 6, and 7.

57. Clattenburg to Mrs. Roush, September 4, 1944.

58. M. R. D. Foot and J. M. Langley, MI 9: Escape and Evasion, 1939–1945 (Boston: Little, Brown, 1980), pp. 44–45. See, for example, Lt. Joseph Johnson to Mrs. Roush, September 10, 1944, d'Albert-Lake Family Papers (see Appendix 9).

war while also continuing in his efforts to learn the whereabouts and seek the release of Virginia.[59]

On January 28, 1945, with Virginia's status still uncertain, the military intelligence office at the Headquarters of the European Theater of Operations sent a memo to the Pentagon requesting that the State Department be reminded of the case and inquiring if Virginia could be released through a prisoner-of-war exchange. From time to time Major John F. White Jr., who worked for MIS-X, would write to Mrs. Roush about efforts to locate and secure her daughter's release. In a brief but welcome letter dated February 23, 1945, he reported to Mrs. Roush that Philippe had "at last had news" about Virginia and had learned that she was at Ravensbrück and "in good health."[60]

In February 1945 Virginia, of course, was not in good health, and the harrowing journey from Ravensbrück to Liebenau, a distance of approximately one thousand kilometers, did nothing to improve her fragile state. On the afternoon of February 28 Virginia, Geneviève de Gaulle, and three SS guards embarked on a six-day journey to Liebenau that took them through war-ravaged Germany. Traveling by train to Berlin, Munich, Ulm, and Stuttgart, Virginia witnessed the massive destruction caused by Allied bombing, survived several terrifying air raids, and walked many kilometers along bombed-out streets in search of functioning train stations. She wrote that she had never "known such fatigue," but that she "struggled on believing and living for one thing—my arrival at our destination."[61]

Arriving at Liebenau on March 6, Virginia knew from the moment she entered its gates that she had been "saved." Because Liebenau was an internment camp for enemy nationals, including American and British

59. Philippe d'Albert-Lake to Dear Muffy [Edith Roush], September 1, 1944; Philippe d'Albert-Lake to Dear Muffy, September 22, 1944; both in d'Albert-Lake Family Papers.

60. Memo from Colonel G. Bryan Conrad, Headquarters, European Theater of Operations, Office of the AC of S, G-2, to Colonel Russell H. Sweet, Pentagon Building, Washington, D.C., January 28, 1945; Johnny White to Mrs. Roush, January 14, 1945; Johnny White to Mrs. Roush, February 23, 1945; all in National Archives and Records Administration, RG 498, Records of Headquarters, European Theater of Operations, United States Army (World War II), MIS-X (copies of these documents are in the d'Albert-Lake Family Papers).

61. "My Story," pp. 198–210.

Commonwealth civilians, as well as prominent figures, it was, unlike concentration camps such as Ravensbrück, subject to international humanitarian laws governing prisoners of war that had been agreed upon at the Geneva Convention of July 27, 1929. This meant that the International Committee of the Red Cross was able to protect and assist the prisoners by regularly sending the camp supplementary food and other supplies, ensuring that proper medical care was available, and overseeing the mail. From Virginia's perspective, Liebenau was "paradise," but she also understood that for the enemy nationals who had been interned several years and had not experienced the appalling conditions of German labor camps, it was "a purgatory of mental suffering."[62]

While at Liebenau, Virginia received the medical care she so desperately needed. At first too weak to walk, she remained in the room that she shared with four other women, "eating anything and everything." Two weeks into her stay, she was transferred to the infirmary, where the German camp physician prescribed a special diet, medicines, and sunbaths that cured her dysentery and healed the open sores on her body.[63]

Although postal service was very limited, Virginia made her first direct contact with Philippe by mail since her arrest the previous June. In this letter, written on March 8, she began: "My own darling, how strange to be able to write to you. Last June seems so far away, that you and my past life seem a dream." In her typical solicitous manner, she continued by assuring Philippe that she was "very well off" and that there was "no reason to worry" about her.[64]

On the afternoon of April 21 Free French troops who had joined the Allied forces arrived to liberate Liebenau. Virginia observed that the liberation occurred without "the slightest opposition from any part of the camp and the soldiers drove in as if they had been invited." While the longtime internees went "nearly mad with joy and excitement," Virginia,

62. For a similar view of Liebenau, see Ruth Mitchell's memoir, *The Serbs Chose War* (New York: Holt, Rinehart and Winston, 1943). Mitchell, an American journalist, was arrested in 1941 for supporting the Chetniks. After spending months in German prisons, she was interned at Liebenau. Like Virginia, she described Liebenau as a "paradise." In 1942 Mitchell was released through a prisoner-of-war exchange. She returned to the United States on June 30, 1942.

63. "My Story," pp. 211–212.

64. Virginia d'Albert-Lake to Philippe d'Albert-Lake, March 8, 1945, d'Albert-Lake Family Papers (see Appendix 10).

by contrast, felt "a serene quiet happiness born in the realization that this most horrifying of wars was nearly over, and that soon I should find myself buried in the arms of those I loved."[65]

With millions of liberated prisoners and refugees to be repatriated, it would be another four weeks before Virginia received authorization to depart for the repatriation center at Strasbourg. Following a brief interval at Strasbourg, she arrived in Paris on May 27, 1945. Virginia was one of only 25 women of the original group of 250 who had been sent to Königsberg in October 1944 who survived.[66]

Miraculously, it took Virginia only a year to regain her health. On May 27, 1946, exactly one year after her return to Paris, she gave birth to her first and only child, Jean Patrick d'Albert-Lake. In November 1946 Virginia and Patrick traveled to the United States for an extended stay of six months. During this visit, Virginia gave more than forty highly acclaimed lectures to church and civic groups about her work with the Resistance. In St. Petersburg, Florida, where her father still lived, and in her hometown of Dayton, Ohio, she achieved celebrity status. Among the many honors and recognitions that she received during this visit to the United States was the Rollins College Decoration of Honor, awarded to its highly esteemed alumna at its midwinter convocation in January 1947.[67]

For her work with the Resistance, Virginia d'Albert-Lake received prestigious awards from the governments of France, Belgium, Great Britain, and the United States. Shortly after the war France honored her with the Croix de Guerre, and in 1989 she received that nation's highest civilian honor, the Légion d'Honneur. From Belgium she received the Medal of King Leopold; Britain made her a member of the Order of the British Empire; and the United States awarded her the Medal of Honor.[68] Just as important was the great personal testimony that came from her Ravensbrück prison mates who, after the war, praised her "generosity" and "courage" and singled out "her inspiration to the morale of her associates."[69]

65. "My Story," pp. 212–213.
66. Ibid., Epilogue, p. 7.
67. News clippings and other materials concerning Virginia's visit to the United States in 1946–1947 are located in the d'Albert-Lake Family Papers.
68. Copies of these and other award citations are in the d'Albert-Lake Family Papers.
69. Memo from Major John F. White, 6801 MIS-X Detachment, Military Intelligence Service, United States Forces, European Theater, to American Embassy,

Wartime veterans also heralded Virginia's work. The Veterans of Foreign Wars in France awarded her the Order of the Croix de Malte. She was also a highly respected member of the Air Forces Escape and Evasion Society (AFEES), and she attended AFEES reunions whenever possible. What Virginia most cherished, however, were visits from grateful airmen as well as the many cards and letters of appreciation that they sent to her after the war.[70]

Despite her arrest and the harrowing months that she spent in German concentration camps, Virginia never regretted her actions. Years later, when asked how she survived this horrible ordeal, she responded with steely resolve: "It was a matter of morale. You couldn't let them see you weep. The women who wept at night usually were dead by morning. You couldn't give in."[71]

Virginia was proud that she had assisted sixty-six downed airmen escape capture by the Germans and that she "had a share" in the "gallant career" of the Comet line and its "climactic success" at the Forest of Fréteval on August 14, 1945. As she often said, she did not join in the dangerous work of the Resistance because she thought it was her duty; she did it because it "was simply doing the right thing."[72] In a 1993 interview she remarked: "I believe firmly in doing the right thing, and that's what we were doing. . . . What right did the Germans have to invade, to make arrests, to make so many people suffer? . . . I wanted to do it and thought I should, and I had the opportunity to do it, so I did. . . . Once you come through something like that, you don't regret it. . . . I don't regret anything—except for those who didn't get out."[73]

Virginia d'Albert-Lake's wartime diary and memoir provide us with a new appreciation for the heroic deeds performed by thousands of escape line resisters who risked their lives to bring about the defeat of Nazi Germany. As an American citizen living in France, Virginia could have returned to the safety of her native country when war broke out in Europe in 1939, but she never considered that as an option. Remaining in France

---

2 Avenue Gabriel, Paris, October 10,1945, in d'Albert-Lake Family Papers (see Appendix 13).

70. Examples of these cards and letters are in the d'Albert-Lake Family Papers (see Appendices 11 and 12).

71. Calio, "Resistance and Remembrance," p. 39.

72. "My Story," Epilogue, p. 6; Calio, "Resistance and Remembrance," p. 39.

73. Griffin, "An Unsung War Hero Gets Her Due."

to be near her beloved husband, she gracefully and compassionately accepted the challenges of living in a war zone while defying conventional gender stereotypes on an almost daily basis. As she performed the traditional supporting role of loving and dutiful wife, she also put her life in jeopardy as she sheltered, nurtured, fed, and clothed downed airmen.[74] The toughness that she demonstrated after her capture by the Germans and the survival tactics that she adopted during her months of incarceration are further examples of her defiance of conventional notions of womanhood. Always modest about her courageous and daring work during World War II, Virginia continued to live in France after the war, where she enjoyed a fulfilling and quiet life with Philippe and their son, Patrick. Virginia d'Albert-Lake, an unassuming but valiant wartime heroine, died at Cancaval on September 20, 1997, at the age of eighty-seven.

74. Several historians have emphasized that Resistance women challenged conventional gender stereotypes as they made political choices that endangered their lives as well as those of their families even as they performed "traditional supporting roles" such as sheltering, feeding, and clothing those in need. See, for example, Margaret Collins Weitz, *Sisters in the Resistance: How Women Fought to Free France 1940–1945* (New York: John Wiley and Sons, 1995), especially pp. 7, 10–11, 287–288, 301, and Paula Schwartz, "Redefining Resistance: Women's Activism in Wartime France," in *Behind the Lines: Gender and the Two World Wars*, ed. Margaret Randolph Higonnet, Jane Jenson, Sonya Michel, and Margaret Collins Weitz (New Haven: Yale University Press, 1987), pp. 141–153.

Remembering My Mother

Patrick d'Albert-Lake

My mother never thought of herself as a hero. In wartime, of course, there are many opportunities to become a hero. Almost everyone has a chance. But when you talk to people who have actually done something heroic, they say, "Well, no, I'm not a hero. I just did what I did because it is normal." As we all know, however, heroism is not normal. My mother never talked about what she did as being heroic. She genuinely thought it was normal.

For years my mother rarely talked about what had happened to her during the war. Of course, I knew some things—they came out in bits and pieces—but there was never a discussion about it in my family. We never actually sat down and talked about it. It was taboo, a way for my parents to protect themselves from what had happened. They just put it out of their lives. Besides, the attitude in France after the Second World War was "Let's keep all of this sad history out of the way because it's not going to help." A lot of people just wanted to forget what had happened.

Also, we have very high expectations of people we call heroes. We somehow think that they will be different, and indeed their actions make them so, but they don't think so themselves. Thus, when you approach someone with the attitude that he or she is a "hero," a wall automatically goes up between you and conversation shuts down. My father had a friend who was taken prisoner by the Japanese. He didn't want to talk about that experience either.

The war's impact on my mother came out in indirect and subtle ways. We could be gardening and it would be cold outside and maybe it was difficult to dig a hole. My mother would say, "Oh, that's nothing, I can handle that," and she'd go ahead and dig a hole in the frozen earth. And, in fact, it was nothing for her. After all, she had built airstrips during one of the coldest winters on record when she was a German prisoner.

Even as a child, I knew something had happened to her. I remember that there were airmen who would come through Paris, and my mother and father would go out to dinner with them. I remember going to one or two of these dinners. Although it was years after the war, the airmen wanted to go back and see where they were shot down and who had rescued them. It was a kind of pilgrimage. But I was a small child, so I don't remember much about the conversations except that these people were very, very nice to me.

I suspect they talked about some of the funny things that had happened in Paris when they were hidden by my parents. Of course, when you are in the kind of situation that they were in—the Germans occupied the city and my mother and father were taking great risks—you have to find some humor to survive. Otherwise, you'll go crazy.

When I was about fifteen or sixteen, I read my mother's memoir. But at that age, it was hard to imagine what she had been through. You don't understand suffering and courage as well as you do when you're older. I do remember that she couldn't stand to be in the same room with a German. She would go crazy. It was physical. She would just shake and start to sweat and we'd have to leave.

Because my parents were young, they were not conscious of how dangerous their work with the Resistance truly was. My mother and father and the airmen would go into the Métro and travel all over Paris and there would be Germans everywhere. I think when you are young you are much less conscious of danger and the value of life than later on. You don't believe in bad luck when you are young; you think you are immortal. It's only natural.

In my mother's case, however, there was something more. She was also very strong willed. She married my father in 1937 deliberately against the advice of her family. She then left Florida and went to France to live with her husband because, for her, this was an adventure into the unknown.

My mother was very determined in her decisions and how she wanted to live her life. She was also strong and could be quite stubborn as well. You can see how her strong, determined nature affected her actions during the war. When the war broke out in Europe in 1939, my father wanted her to go back to the United States, where he felt she'd be safe, but she refused. She wanted to remain near her husband. Later she made the dangerous decision to join the French underground. When she was captured, she risked death by refusing to reveal the names of other Resistance fighters. That takes a lot of guts.

My father was very proud of my mother. He was very impressed with her. He told me many times how brave and strong and wonderful he thought she was. Because of her strong will, however, it was sometimes a little difficult to get along with her. My father always said, "Yes, but that's why she's still around. She's strong-minded." And he was right.

I don't think my parents decided to join the Resistance because of any deep political conviction. A lot of people did, but not my parents. During the first three years of the war, my mother and father, like most other people in France, struggled to survive the German occupation as best they could. Not until 1943 did my parents feel they had to act, to do something, but not for political reasons. It just made sense for them to join the Resistance. It was the right thing to do.

They were together in this dangerous and exciting underground life. They were doing exactly the same things, taking the same risks. Had my mother not been arrested, they would have been just like a lot of other people who did their job during the war. But because she was arrested and sent to a concentration camp, the light shone on her. My father always thought of their lives as intertwined. He said, "This is the story of both of us." He was right, except for one important difference: my mother was caught by the Germans and almost died at Ravensbrück.

I think that from 1945 on, after she was released from Ravensbrück, my mother thought she had been given a second life. She didn't take it for granted. She knew that she had come very close to dying, and she was conscious that her postwar life was a gift. Her attitude toward life was different from other people's. She was very strong, as I've said. And you would think that after what she'd been through, she would not tolerate weakness in other people. But she was very forgiving, very compassionate.

Sometime in the late 1970s or early 1980s she went back to Ravensbrück. My parents had gone to various wartime commemorations throughout the years, to cemeteries in Normandy and things like that. This time, however, she went without him. She took a bus trip to Ravensbrück with some other Resistance fighters. I don't know many details. She never talked about it much, but later she said it was a mistake and that she shouldn't have done it. She was shaken by the experience.

My mother had a very strong sense of her duty, of her responsibility to behave in a certain way. She felt she could never show any sign of weakness. When you think of people like my mother who have had these enormous obstacles to overcome, you see that they always find the strength to cope with them. There's always hope. There's always a positive side to things. Even today if I am feeling a bit discouraged or depressed, I think of what she always said: "Lift up your thoughts." That was her expression: "Lift up your thoughts." It was typical of her to be very positive.

Interestingly, my mother said she never had nightmares about her time in the prison camps. It seems amazing; it must have been a kind of self-defense. I would think if you had nightmares about it all the time, the experience would never go away. I'm sure she must have had nightmares when she first came back. But then they stopped. And that's true of any major pain. You bury it. Of course, if you talk about it, it all comes back up to the surface.

I don't want to paint a sad picture of my mother, because she wasn't that way at all. We tend to be sad when we think of her today because she's gone. In fact, she was full of life. She loved life. She had a fantastic sense of humor. It was very sharp, very American. And she loved having fun.

My children are now interested in what happened to my mother. They have read her diary and memoir, and they appreciate that there is something very special about their family. For many French people, World War II is ancient history. But I think my children are increasingly sensitive to this period. They now realize how precious this knowledge of their grandmother is and what a heroic woman she was.

When you go through a life like my mother's, you have to be able to have faith in humanity. You've got to believe that it's possible for things to improve. That may be the great lesson of her life: the more faith we have in humanity, the better chance we have of not slipping into chaos again.

I think my mother would be very happy that this book is being published, especially in the United States. After all, she was an American. And I think Americans should be proud of her.

The Diary

OCTOBER 11, 1939–APRIL 1944

1 Outbreak of War to the Fall of France

OCTOBER 11, 1939–JUNE 23, 1940

Vincennes—Paris[1]

....

October 11, 1939

In commencing this story—"my" story of the war, I plan that it be a diary of personal experiences, reflections and impressions. It should have had its beginning on Sunday Sept. 3, the day that the war was declared, first by England, then a few hours later, by France.[2] But I was not in the mood to write then—it was even difficult to write meager post cards home. Now I have adjusted myself to this new strange state of living, diving in a kind of suspension, just waiting and hoping, while time itself seems to have neither a yesterday nor a to-morrow. Time is standing still.

At this writing I have the one with me who gives my life its real fullness. Since the international tension first started on August 22nd we have been separated only once during a period of two weeks.[3] One cannot complain at that! When I think what it may have meant or what it might be, even at this early stage of the war, I realize how unbelievably fortunate we are to be together.

To deal briefly with a bit of past history, in order that this record may be more complete, I will add that Philippe was mobilized Wed., Aug 23rd. When he came home to Nesles[4] the evening before he felt uneasy about international conditions, and the foreboding increased when we heard over the air that French men taking part in sport events at Monte-Carlo

1. Vincennes is on the western outskirts of Paris.

2. Following the German attack on Poland on September 1, 1939, Great Britain and France declared war on Germany on September 3. This marked the official beginning of the Second World War.

3. Virginia is referring to the signing of the Nonaggression Pact between the Soviet Union and Germany in Moscow on August 23, 1939.

4. Nesles-la-Vallée is a small village thirty-five kilometers northwest of Paris where Virginia and Philippe were building a rustic country home.

were being called back. On Wed. morning I went in to Paris with Philippe, to learn the news immediately, that he was mobilized and called to Vincennes.[5] He went the next morning, and tho I was without him for the next two nights, I had him after that from 5: PM until 6:30 AM, until Sat, Sept 2nd, the day I left for Cancaval.[6] On Friday the day before, general mobilization was called, and Sunday Sept 3, when Hitler would not withdraw his troops from Poland, war was declared.[7]

Cancaval—Dinard.

At Cancaval we were quite a party, Grandmère, Mum,[8] Miss Sparrow (a lovely woman who lost the man she loved in the last war), Jeanne Clarck, whose husband was mobilized with the requisitioning of his business house in Paris, Louise Lobitz, an American girl from Cincinnati who has been studying and teaching in France for the past year, and myself. At Cancaval it was so beautiful and we had such perfect weather. It was impossible to believe that war existed. Philippe and I had always said it would be that way. We started knitting, all of us except Mum, in order to pass the time and employ it to some advantage. We had offered our services to the Red Cross in Dinard but had not yet been called. However, some days later we were called to a meeting at the Gallic Hotel which was being transferred into a Hospital and it was then I felt for the first time, the realness and horror of war. In the same building, which six weeks before we had seen full of gay people, holiday makers in sports attire, we now saw instead, hospital beds with boards for springs, mattresses piled ten feet high, medical officers striding nervously about, and all this climaxed by the rumor that two hundred wounded were expected the next weekend. But I was not on hand to see whether or not the rumor became fact for that same evening I received a telegram from Philippe saying, "Try to come and see me at Dammartin-en-Goële, Seine & Marne, 35 Kms from Paris. I can put you up"!!![9]

5. Virginia stayed at their Paris apartment at 57, rue de Bellechasse.

6. The d'Albert-Lake family owned a château, Cancaval, near Dinard, Brittany.

7. The general mobilization of Frenchmen between the ages of eighteen and thirty-five began on September 1, 1939.

8. Philippe was of English and French ancestry. His mother, Violet Elizabeth Lloyd Whitmarsh, was English and his father, Jean Amédée d'Albert-Lake, was French. Hence, Virginia uses the British term "Mum" when referring to her mother-in-law.

9. Dammartin-en-Goële is thirty-five kilometers northeast of Paris.

It was as if an armistice had been declared! I was so happy. Everyone said that I suddenly lost ten years off my looks, which of course left me practically a child.[10] To think that it could be really true. I was afraid to believe it until I really had arrived. The mail had been so bad all this time. I had had no word from Philippe until I had been away from Paris ten days. Then two days later word came that he was being sent to Dammartin. But it never seemed possible that I could really go to him.

So the next day the adventure started! Certain papers were necessary.

October 14th a "sauf conduit" or "laisser passer,"[11] and my fingerprints taken with the indexes. By inquiring at one of the Dinard Hotels I was fortunate in finding a ride to Paris with several Americans. We spent the night in Alençon[12] which was crowded with mobilized men. We reached Paris the next morning at 10:30, and I caught an afternoon train to Dammartin. Paris seemed quiet and empty, but nevertheless gave a certain impression of gay fantasy all due to the geometric designs traced by paper stripping on every show case window and glass store front. The paper keeps the glass from splintering when bombs explode. Philippe's office, the P & O, had been unusually clever and artistic in the use of paper stripping.[13] They had designed boats and palm trees on their windows; it brought them newspaper publicity which is very rare in France.

My train coach was crowded with newly mobilized men, middle-aged men recruited for the building of trenches and fortifications. We hear that a new Maginot line is being built to encircle Paris, within 60 Kms of the City itself. They indeed will need men . . . ![14]

The train stopped at a station 3½ Kms. from Dammartin, and the only way to reach the town at that hour of the afternoon was either by foot or

10. Virginia was born on June 4, 1910, in Dayton, Ohio. The family moved to St. Petersburg, Florida, shortly after World War I. Virginia was twenty-nine years old at the time of the outbreak of World War II.

11. This is an official pass needed for travel.

12. Alençon is about midway between Dinard and Paris.

13. Before his mobilization Philippe had worked for the Peninsular and Oriental Steam Navigation Company, a British firm that either went out of business or was requisitioned by the Germans following the German occupation of northern France in June 1940.

14. The Maginot Line was a system of fortifications constructed between 1930 and 1937 and extending for 140 kilometers along France's eastern border with Germany.

by "the" taxi, across from the station. By calling and rapping I finally unearthed my driver from some place behind his "bistro"[15] and was driven in state to D[ammartin], for a fee of 10 Frs. Having no idea as to what D[ammartin] would turn out to be in the way of a town, and not knowing just what to do to find Philippe, I was a bit unsettled, but it did not last long. As I descended from the taxi in the center of what turned out to be a small town with one main street, I found myself in front of the town hall. Soldiers seemed to be every place, and I was conscious of their faces being turned toward me in friendly interested welcome. One rather independent soldier stepped up to me, as I'm certain I looked quite bewildered, and started conversing. "Bonjour Madame. Est-il assez large, assez gros, et un peu roux ?" (Is he rather tall, rather stout and rather red headed?)[16] I laughed an answer in the affirmative, because he was in a gay mood too; and when he said, "Follow me," I did so with much eagerness, and there down the street 100 yds. I found my honey on guard. He never looked so big and good to me in his life! He had a huge khaki colored coat on, one of immense dimensions, which fell in great folds from his belt! But oh that smile!

Some one took his place at guard and he took me "home" on down the street, past the soldiers' monument, up a little rutty road, and there, protected by two huge walnut trees and an old blind dog 10 yrs. old, was a cute little house.

Thus commenced my month's stay in Dammartin-en-Goële, Seine & Marne, 35 Kms. from Paris.

The little house was owned by a widow, who only occupied the one room in which she slept, as all during the day she managed a little notions store in the village. Hence we were free to use the kitchen, a fact that meant a great deal! Our bedroom was really the "salon,"[17] the one other bedroom being occupied by another soldier, André Delille, and for the present his wife too, who had arrived just the day before. Christine and I managed beautifully together, and as long as she was there (approximately a week) we took turns planning and cooking the dinners.

At Vincennes, Philippe had been requisitioning trucks, cars, and motorcycles, here he was mobilizing workmen, the kind I had seen on the

15. Small café or bar.
16. Philippe was six feet tall and at the time weighed about 185 pounds.
17. Sitting room.

train. Dammartin was the center of mobilization and from there the men were sent to different points. Philippe's regiment, C.S.M.C. 21. (*Centre Secondaire Mobilisateur de Cavalerie*),[18] consisted of approximately one hundred men, who were living in various buildings and private homes where they had considerable freedom. I saw Philippe often twice a day, and had him every night also. He had lunch with the men (and wonderful lunches too, even turkey and rabbit) but dinner at home. There was always Delille, and very often Donald Tritsch, a boy half English, half French and who used to work for the Canadian Pacific in Paris, also from time to time, Steilhin, a lawyer from Dieppe. Other men came in for Apperitifs or coffee, so we had some happy evenings crowded into that gay little red and white kitchen.

Christine returned for two short stays, once bringing her fifteen-year-old sister, Jacqueline, and Donald's charming sister, Betty, spent several days at the time. Mum too came for a couple of days, sleeping in a lovely old 15th century Château now become a hotel. The Château had belonged to the Prince de Sax and had recently been used as the setting for an historical moving picture of him and his time.

So I loved my four weeks in Dammartin. The day I left I felt very sad. The town in itself was not very significant but its setting was on a hilltop set in the center of a flat fertile country side. There were lovely views from many angles, and one was from our bedroom window. It was harvest time, but there were not enough men to work, and as a result the sugar beets were being neglected, and the apple, pear, and peach trees were bending with the weight of their fruit unpicked. A few days before leaving, a truck loaded with blank sad faced Algerians arrived. They were to help harvest the beets, while as Delille said "It's they, the French, who must go to the front."

In doing my shopping every day at the same time, I became quite friendly with those who ran the little shops. They were always sweet and friendly, and seemed to get a certain amusement out of talking with me and trying to understand my highly accented French. The lady butcher always gave me the best meat "bon marché,"[19] the produce lady gave me the freshest, biggest eggs which she kept hidden under the counter, the bakery lady lent me her umbrella the day of a downpour, the cute little

18. Secondary Mobilization Center of Cavalry 21.
19. Good price.

old man in the grocery always ground my coffee and gave me an onion when I only needed one. The last day at Dammartin, a neighbor gave me two baskets of peaches, and a cabbage as large as two basketballs. The milk lady who honked her presence and that of her cart and donkey all over town was so sweet, and sat in front of me at church on Sunday. I loved all these people; they were always so cheerful, friendly and honest.

Speaking of honesty. One day the husband of the produce lady greeted me with, "I took 45 centimes from you yesterday. I only realized my mistake after you had gone." (45 centimes is about 1½ cent!!)

But better still: I missed a thousand francs note one day! I knew that the last time I had opened my bill purse was the evening before at a restaurant. We went there at once, and yes, the proprietor had found it. The amazing part was that it had been found many hours after we had left, besides the table, and in the meantime the room had received many clients including soldiers! What luck it had been overlooked by all except the owner of the place who was honest! But to have proven time after time the honesty of the French is not unusual. This story traveled quickly all over town, and turned up in amazing places and from the mouths of people I had never seen! I don't suppose that there are many folks in that town who ever see a thousand francs note. (about $30!)

We went to church on Sunday. It was full of town people, officers and soldiers. The kindly faced white haired old priest was a picture, but I was disappointed when he said that the Mass was held for the victory of France, and I was not the only one. We would have preferred him to say "For Peace."[20]

Philippe was always thrilled, and I must say I was too, by the magnificent fighter planes that flew over Dammartin. The strength of their pulsating motors, the beauty and grace of their design would thrill anyone. On the edge of Dammartin was a battery of anti-aircraft guns, and one of these planes, evidently flown by an ace judging from the way he handled his ship, came very often to practice attacking anti-aircraft machinery. From a height he would dip and roar down upon these guns at terrific speed, seeming just to miss touching the ground, and then climb again suddenly at a steep angle that dived over the main street of the town, and once over our little house that seemed to settle a bit to avoid being struck. I easily saw the pilots.

20. See the Introduction regarding the sense of complacency felt by many in France.

Having seen these planes disappear into the landscape and hearing that they were kept tunneled under the ground we decided to go exploring, so one day Philippe, Donald, Delille and I started off across the fields. When we were so tired of walking and not yet having found our destination we almost gave up, but a little rise showed us it was only a bit farther. There we found the planes, 22 of them dotting a field, the pilots being harbored in buildings connected with a beet refinery. We talked with the pilots, and "my" soldiers seemed to envy them their dangerous but free life, and the cleanliness of that branch of the army. Then we started back, stealing a ride in a beet wagon for a bit of the way, but the going was so rough over the cobble stones that we were not relieved of our fatigue. On reaching Dammartin we found that we had walked nearly ten miles.

I did not feel war or see many serious signs of it at Dammartin. At first, all night long it seemed, trains in the valley passed, going, as we were told, to the front loaded with armaments and supplies. Planes passed too at intervals of fifteen minutes from the N.W. to the S.E., making us think they were English planes coming from Britain to an aviation center perhaps at Meaux where there are said to be English planes.

My only air raid warning up to date was experienced one morning, or hardly experienced because being shut up in the kitchen and on the edge of the town, I did not even hear the sirens! Philippe arrived suddenly and breathlessly to get his gas mask as required, and announced the warning. Mum was there then, so we went out in the garden to scan the North Eastern horizon to no avail, and the end of the alert was announced thirty minutes later. In the paper the following day I read that a reconnaissance plane had crossed the frontier; that was all!

I have said practically nothing of the attitude of the soldiers toward the war. Every night at dinner there were deep discussions on all sorts of subjects but the present war always poked its nose in sooner or later. I think the morale of the men wonderful, especially in considering that they are going into this war with their eyes open. They do not hate the Germans and would kill only in self-defense. Philippe said that if he saw a German come out of a trench to go to the "Johnny" he would give him the wound that he himself wishes in the leg! The men laughed at the newspaper propaganda because they recognize it so easily, they are not being taken in! An American journalist at the front writing for the "Paris Soir" told how a lone Frenchman attacked forty Germans all by himself, killing some of them, and receiving three wounds himself.[21] Guillon, the humorist of the group, remarked dryly, "He forgot to say that all the Germans had for defense were spades." The men go into detailed explanation and discussion on wounds, the horror of war at the front, etc. calmly and without display of fear, apprehension, or alarm. Philippe, who presumably has to face war in an armored car knowing that shells are made these days expressly for cars and tanks, shells that pierce the metal sides and explode in the interior, blowing everything to pieces, is the perfect example of calmness and fortitude. He has overcome all fear of death, to the point when he can say frankly, "It does nothing to me to think of having one of my legs blown one direction, the other in another, and my head someplace else!" I think that is wonderful. I really can't say what my reaction would be were I in his shoes. Delille is the pessimist, the fatalist. Where Philippe knows in his heart of hearts that he is coming back, André is just as sure that he himself is not! André is not fighting for any worthwhile reason, whether it be false or no, nor has he an ideal of any kind. He believes that the whole state of things, war included, is caused by the Jews. He loves to argue and is intelligent as well as being gifted in expressing himself, but he is an extremist. What the others are seeking is some sort of equilibrium, in this topsy-turvy world; hence André makes himself unhappy and unpopular. He is to be pitied.

Donald Tritsch is a nice fellow, kind and a gentleman. In discussions he has fixed ideas, almost stubborn ones, and hence is incapable of arguing broadly and intelligently. He is not a thinker. Steilhin is always gay, seeing both sides of a question and perceiving clearly when it comes to evaluation of ideas.

Philippe may be my cute husband but I can see his abilities in an unprejudiced light, believe it or not. He is the sanest man I know. If in a discussion he takes part as he usually does and seems to enjoy, he is just and well balanced in his judgement. If he stumbles upon a prejudice, he says so at once! How many people do that, or can do it? What a pair he and André make, André lacking idealism, Philippe full of it.

We loved listening in on these men's ideas. I have taken little part, chiefly because to express my opinion in French is still rather difficult. I have considered it a privilege and an honor to have been present at these round table talks, not only because I am a woman but a foreigner as well.

21. *Paris Soir* is a popular French newspaper.

I have wanted to be accepted without fuss, without bother, to be a friend and another "soldier," so I was happy the other evening when Donald without thinking, called me "mon vieux"!![22]

I believe I have about completed my story of Dammartin. If experiences or remarks occur to me later I will add them. I was happy there, and life was almost normal, because Philippe got up each morning and went to work, I rose later to make the bed, clean the room, wash the dishes, plan the dinner and do the shopping. Then Philippe came home to dinner and we went to bed together. I felt I could go on living there and be happy, if need be. But after the weeks rolled around we began hearing rumors of the men leaving "in a week," "next weekend," "next Tuesday," and finally "next Thursday" which was the last and true statement. They were to go to Vincennes or Rambouillet or to both. It was the unknown, but it was not "la haut" (the front). So I might be able to follow.

Rambouillet[23]

....

Sunday, October 15, 1939

So on October 12th the squadron marched to the station while Christine and I followed in a bus. (Christine had come the day before to see André who had had his knee badly injured in a friendly scuffle with Philippe). The train was crowded with civilians, but we managed to crowd in. On arriving in Paris the men were hurried into the Métro as they had to change stations, going from the "Gare du Nord" to the "Gare Montparnasse." As many women had met their men at the "Gare du Nord" I followed along in the Métro too. On arriving at the station the men were given two hours of freedom until train time at 7:32 P.M. So Philippe and I grabbed a taxi, went to the apartments at Vaneau and Bellechasse.[24] Philippe said he felt as though he were coming home to stay! How I wish that that were a fact.

We had dinner at "Dupont's" across from the station. Paris seemed crowded in this part of the city and almost gay. In fact, there were some civilians in the restaurant who were too gay, and we resented them. There

22. "Mon vieux" is a friendly French term that means "my old one."
23. Rambouillet is fifty-six kilometers southwest of Paris.
24. Philippe's mother owned an apartment at 1 bis, rue Vaneau.

is such a thing as showing good taste in wartime, more than in peacetime. The night began to fall, and at once great blue curtains were dropped over the huge window. In leaving the place I was stirred by the blackness of the city, really ghost-like with the tiny blued light of the traffic adding to the unrealness. We hurried to the station, I bought my ticket while the men were gathering and being checked, and as each woman was saying "au revoir" to her man, I was boarding the train with mine! I found myself the only woman in the car! It was a modern electric train lighted dimly by tiny blue bulbs.

The men in the regiment seemed highly amused by the way I follow Philippe about. One of them remarked that this was married fidelity, as he conceived it! They speak of giving me a uniform and taking me to the front as "Cantiniere."[25] I know many of the men now, and never are they other than polite, friendly and respectful.

On arriving at Rambouillet it was pitch black, and not a person on the streets. We could not even see each other's faces. We had no idea where the "Caserne"[26] was, where a hotel could be found, or anything! The soldiers started marching and I fell in step. We passed few houses, and avoided the center of the town entirely. I felt that any moment we might reach the "Caserne," Philippe would have to enter, and I would be left alone in all that blackness to do what I did not know exactly. Suddenly the great iron gates did loom up in front of us, and as if by magic a little hotel, "Hotel de la Biche" appeared exactly opposite! A noncomissioned officer out in front encouraged our relief by saying that the hotel was full of officers and he doubted that I would obtain a room. But he was wrong, there was one! And exactly across from the gates, and I watched my honey disappear into his prison. I was so happy though that I danced, to have had such luck and to feel Philippe so near. But I was not undressed when Philippe appeared at the door!! They had not been expected and so he could spend the night out and he has managed to be free every night since! As long as he is present for the last call at night and at the first in the morning, he is alright.

I cannot say that we sleep very well here however. We are on the main route to Paris and being opposite the gates of the "Caserne" which are always clanging open and shut there is much noise. There must be hundreds or perhaps thousands of men here, there is so much activity. The

25. A *cantinière* is a woman manager of a military canteen.
26. Barracks.

bugle is always blowing, trucks and wagons constantly passing in and out, companies of soldiers marching, and due to this being a cavalry post, men on horseback passing in and out over the cobblestones, also planes flying over head.

"My men" are not very happy here. They had so much freedom in Dammartin that they furiously resent these high stone walls and iron gates. It is easy to understand, but they knew it was just temporary, and only this morning news came that they were to be moved eight Kms. from here to some little village.

They left only about an hour ago, in a big open truck, my Philippe towering above the others.

We talked over what I should do before he left. Since we heard that the village lacked most everything, we thought it better that I continue here until we surveyed the possibilities of my staying there. If it is a hopeless proposition, I plan to go to the "Montcel" (Philippe's old school) where I will be comfortable and not alone, and where he can come when he is free.[27] Now there is nothing but to wait for perhaps a couple of days. But we have been so fortunate up to the present that we have great faith in the future, in a future with our being together as long as possible.

There is not a great deal to do here. Rambouillet is just a bit too large, and with so many men here it is not very enjoyable going out walking alone, though the countryside itself is very inviting. There is a lovely forest full of autumn colors, and a charming "Château" where President Lebrun spends his summers.[28]

I have been busy catching up on my diary, and writing cards and letters. Philippe has been leaving me at 7:00, I have breakfast at 9:00, lunch in the dining room at noon, and then Philippe joins me after 5:00. Last night we dined alone in Rambouillet, the night before with six other soldiers including Donald and Steilhin (André is in the "Caserne" infirmary).

There are officers of very high rank staying in this hotel, and I have opportunity to study them in the dining room at noon. They are well over forty, and two or three of them must be in their sixties and still another

27. The Ecole du Montcel is in Jouy-en-Josas, a small town on the southwestern outskirts of Paris.

28. The head of state of France was the president, elected by Parliament for seven years and largely a ceremonial figure with little power. In 1939 Albert Lebrun held the post.

must be more than that. Splendid, honest, noble looking in their uniforms. Most of them have iron grey hair. I wonder how it feels to them to be going in to another war?

I will be happy when Philippe goes ahead in rank, not only the fact of going ahead but so that he can have a good looking khaki uniform. He is unhappy in his old blue misfit, which was probably taken from a dead soldier in the last war. He is a "Brigadier" (Corporal) now. The next step is noncommissioned officer. He would have that rank now if he had not finished his military training in Syria. In going there he had to start from the foot again.[29]

I like my little room here, warm and comfortable with its grey walls and red hangings. Just before my arrival it had been occupied by a soldier who has now been sent to the front. He left tacked on the walls three huge maps, one of Central Europe, one of the Mediterranean Basin and the third of a region in the Loire Valley. He has traced his voyages on these maps, and he must have been in a very sad and depressed state to leave them behind. He must have wondered if he were off now on his last trip! He must have loved his trips. He appears to know well England, Italy, and Spain. He knew Prague and Vienna too; Switzerland and Southern Germany. He has been to Tunis, Egypt, Palestine, Greece, Albania, Yugoslavia, and Morocco, Crete and Sicily. There is so much to see in this world. I wonder how much of it Philippe and I have yet to explore together.

When I look across at those gates, realizing that one day Philippe will have gone without my knowing where or how soon I shall see him again, I have that awful depressed feeling of uncertainty, especially in times like these, it is not very enjoyable.

....

Monday, October 16, 1939
Well that awful depressed feeling did not last very long after all! The "femme de chambre"[30] came in as I was completing the last sentence, to clean up the room, so I decided to go for a walk and get a bit of fresh air.

29. Philippe completed his required eighteen months' active military service with the French army in the late 1920s. He spent part of this time serving in what was then the French protectorate of Syria.
30. Housekeeper.

It was raining, but I did not care; went to Rambouillet and bought some stamps, cards and paste. I had just turned back when I heard Steilhin call to me, "I have your husband in my car." Well, did I jump and run prepared for the worst when things are uncertain, but it never happens. Of course it could, but it has not, and we are so thankful. It gives us more and more faith in the future.

But, all the same, some problems have arisen over Philippe's change of quarters. He is with 120 other men in a deserted farm, in the center of a flat plain, and the nearest town is 3 Kms. away! They may stay there and they may not. The town is small and off the main route. Philippe and some of the men are anxious on finding a little house in the town, where I shall keep the home fires burning, a place for them to come when they are free. I am sure they will have definite need of such a place if the farm is as they say, completely deserted, a court yard full of mud, and the buildings abounding in rats! Why do they have to put men in a place like that, and what will they do all day? So today I guess I am back where I was yesterday, all at loose ends!

But we did have a jolly evening. Philippe and I went to the cinema and afterward met Steilhin and Rendu for dinner in a little restaurant. They all spent the night in town, and Steilhin drove them back to the farm at 6:30 AM. Of course farmers do have to get up early!!

....

Tuesday, October 17th 1939

Well, it looks as if the war may have started! Hitler made two definite offensives, on the front east of the Moselle, and an aerial raid near Edinburgh in an attempt to destroy the economically valuable Bridge of Forth.[31] Up to now there has been comparatively little activity at the front

31. On September 7 French troops crossed the Moselle River near Saarbrücken and moved a few miles into German territory. By October, however, the French had retreated and both sides had assumed defensive positions along the border. There was no serious German attack into France until May 1940. According to John Killen, the German Luftwaffe's first attack on Great Britain occurred on October 16, 1939, when British warships in the Firth of Forth in Scotland were bombed. Two German planes were intercepted by Spitfires and shot down. This "marked the first enemy aircraft to be destroyed over Britain since 1918." John Killen, *A History of the Luftwaffe* (Garden City, N.Y.: Doubleday, 1968), p. 109. The strategically situated Bridge of Forth, in the western environs of Edinburgh, was a railway bridge approximately 2.4 kilometers long that spanned the River Forth.

and no aerial raids. There has been more activity on the seas, a considerable number of German submarines destroyed, and several English and French ships sunk. A few days ago, the splendid British Battleship "Royal Oak" was destroyed with a loss of 800 men! I believe this is to be the greatest single catastrophe to date.[32] We were told that after three weeks of war that "only" 281 men had been killed on the French front. But the war had not really commenced. I dread to think of the future.[33]

Today I read this:

MORTS

au Champ d'Honneur:

—Le lieutenant pilote de chasse Marius Baize

—Le Maréchal des logis Georges Hadamar, age de trente ans.[34]

It shocked me deeply because it is the first definite mention of casualties that I have seen.

I have not felt war yet really. Life, except that all the men are in uniform, goes on much as before. There is plenty of sugar and good butter, the bread is as white as before. I know no bereaved family, I have seen no wounded. There have been no air raids. But today it is in the air—War has started.

After Hitler entered Poland and divided it with Russia, he acted as though England and France, since they had not been able to save the

32. The Battle of the Atlantic began as soon as war broke out on September 3, 1939. During the first two months of the war, fifty-six thousand tons of Allied shipping were lost. On October 14, 1939, a German submarine (U-47) sank the battleship *Royal Oak* within the British base of Scapa Flow in the Orkney Islands of Scotland. All 785 crew, including the admiral, were killed. Gerhard L. Weinberg argues that during the early stages of the war "German efforts [in the Atlantic] did indeed have a substantial impact with the sinking of several hundred thousand tons of Allied shipping, but on balance it must be noted that the greater strength of the Allies at sea gave them an advantage the Germans could not yet overcome." Gerhard L. Weinberg, *A World at Arms: A Global History of World War II* (Cambridge: Cambridge University Press, 1999), p. 70.

33. In September 1939 almost all fighting was concentrated in Poland and in the Atlantic Ocean. French casualty rates remained low until the German offensive into Belgium in May 1940.

34. DEAD / on the Field of Honor / —Lieutenant fighter pilot Marius Baize / —Sergeant Georges Hadamar, age thirty.

country for which they went to war, would be ready to demobilize their troops and sign a peace![35] For this reason he had not taken an offensive step towards war with us. But he did not know the French and the English!! Without a liberated Poland the war would advance. So now Hitler knows, but he is not the kind to back step. He would lose his face, so, the war carries on, and probably in not so mild mild a fashion as up to October 16th.[36]

Why is one man permitted to bring such suffering? Why don't we go straight to him as other criminals are treated? That will come one day, but human beings progress so slowly. However, since it is as it is, I am thankful that we are fighting on the right side. The Allies tried desperately every means of conciliation through diplomacy. Nevertheless, Hitler would only answer with force of arms, and so we must take up arms too.

Philippe came up again last evening, late, and could only stay until 9:30. We dined with Steilhin and two others. From what they had to say, I understood the men were terribly unhappy at the farm and that their morale was going down and down. Hours earlier I had seen Donald looking abject, tired and miserable; he said the place was terrible and that he wanted to make himself sick so that he would not have to stay! But as Philippe says, they do not mind the physical discomfort so much, that can be borne, but the atmosphere is unkind and depressing. They have fallen on a superior officer who is severe and lacks understanding. He believes in treating his men as if they were children and had never experienced any military life. He told the Brigadiers that it was their responsibility to see that the men were clean. Cleanliness is certainly a personal

---

35. The August 23, 1939, Nonaggression Pact between Germany and the Soviet Union included secret provisions for dividing Poland and other parts of Eastern Europe between the two powers. Like many of her contemporaries, Virginia often referred to the Soviet Union as Russia.

36. With the defeat of Poland, Hitler initiated peace feelers with Great Britain and France in public and in private. On October 12, 1939, British Prime Minister Neville Chamberlain delivered a speech that emphasized that neither the British nor the French would accept what had happened to Poland and that "there was no alternative to fighting on until the European countries which had lost their independence had had it returned to them, the Hitler regime had been removed, and such restrictions had been imposed on Germany as would prevent her from attempting to conquer Europe and dominate the world a third time." Weinberg, *A World at Arms*, p. 93.

thing, and when demanded of men living in mud where they must wear wooden shoes in order to keep their feet dry, it seems a bit farcical![37]

Of course there is no place for me at a farm full of soldiers, but I can stay here where Philippe can come when he is free to do so. I would not think of going further away, even to Jouy-en-Josas, when he is so unhappily situated. I felt so sorry last night I wanted to cry. Of course the farm is not the front, but that is coming no doubt and in the meantime why can't they live like men not beasts? There are 40 of them sleeping in a drafty attic, side by side, on straw with only slates above their heads.

The nearest town is Gazeran, 5 Kms. from here, 3 Kms. from the farm. I walked there this afternoon in order to see if there might be a room for me there. It is a dear little town off the main highway, on a little winding road that encircles a hilltop. It is very tiny, and as there is already a squadron of men there, all the vacant rooms have been rented by officers. Perhaps it is better so as it might be depressing to spend the winter months ahead there. After all Rambouillet is a fairly large town and a woman does not feel so conspicuous. I loved my walk though. This is rolling forest country, and now with the autumn leaf tints and the grey haze that comes often with the fall, it is so very beautiful. I followed the highway going in order not to lose my way, but coming back I cut across the forest. The trees are magnificent; there is a lake and little streams, a rocky grotto, statues and benches. It is a fairy forest, full of ducks, swans, and little birds. The Château is beautifully situated on a lake, with charming gardens about it and a wonderful vine clinging to its walls, a vine that turns red with the autumn.

I have made a successful attempt to see Delille. I entered the "Caserne" gates and was accosted by a soldier on guard to whom I presented my demand. He called me an escort who led me past the stables to the infirmary. I waited for André in a cold, bare, ugly room. I wonder what the rest of the building is like? I hear that the walls are painted dark brown and the atmosphere is most depressing! André is better and seemed cheered by my visit so I am glad that I went. In leaving the infirmary I found that my escort had left, but I headed for the gate anyway, as I knew

37. Julian Jackson describes this period as that of the "Phoney War Blues." He states that during the winter of 1939–1940 French troops experienced "a growing sense of lassitude and boredom after months of forced inactivity." Jackson, *The Fall of France*, pp. 152–153.

the way now. In passing the stables I heard a large voice call "a woman in the Caserne" and suddenly the doors were crowded with soldiers laughing and calling, a woman, a woman.

....

October 26, 1939

Again we have moved but to our advantage and happiness. We are at Nesles. Philippe has obtained a "Permission agricole" of 21 days.[38] Of course our little "Baumées" does not offer anything at present in the way of harvesting, but there is a great deal to do anyway to prepare the ground for early spring planting which was planned for next year.[39]

We left Rambouillet on Sunday, the last days were without special significance other than that of meeting Pamela Saint Georges, an English girl who was also at the Hotel de la Biche. We met in the hall, the proprietor having told each of us about the other. We had lunch together and were still in the dining room at 3:00, just talking! Pam's husband is French, and a student officer at the 4th Hussards. Philippe and I both liked him at first meeting, but after dining together one evening, and getting his point of view concerning the war, we feel that there could be a certain irritation between us. He glorifies war and patriotism, I fear he was born a century or so too late. He and Steilhin who was also having dinner with us had a terrific argument. Philippe kept fairly quiet in order not to fan the flames.

Saturday was a day of terrific uncertainty. (There seems to be so many in such times as these.) Philippe on Friday evening was not certain to get his leave so we were unable to make any definite plans as to time of departure, means etc. Should Philippe be able to leave, he was to take the train in Gazeran with other men on leave. I was to catch the same train at Rambouillet after being certain that he was aboard, but he was not and I was left on the station platform with two valises, a gas mask, and a package of laundry. A lone figure on a deserted platform!

So Philippe was not on that train. Did that mean he was unable to get his leave or was he simply late and boarding another train? What to do? Hang around the station or go back to the Hotel? I decided to remain at

38. This is an agricultural leave.

39. Baumées is the name of the cottage that Virginia and Philippe were building at Nesles.

the station until some time later I met one of Philippe's comrades who told me that I was being searched for all over the place and that Philippe at that moment was in a certain Restaurant with Steilhin! Oh me, what next, so I literally ran for fear he would have left, and there he was, together at last and entitled to leave! However, after such a strenuous day, we decided not to leave that night, we felt we now had all the time in the world. We spent the night at the Hotel and missed the morning train! In the afternoon we managed to reach Marly-le-Roi near Versailles where "Grandmère" was staying at the time and after having spent some time with her we finally reached Nesles-la-Vallée where we found everything in order and spent a wonderful leave.

Here, it was hard to realize that there was a war at all; we were surrounded by peace and beauty. Three weeks of work and rabbit hunting but three weeks of happiness added to all those we have already been allowed.

....

February/March 1940

This diary is like the war, it does not seem to be getting anywhere![40] Philippe's permission seemed to throw me off!

After that marvelous break, Philippe returned to Rambouillet and I this time to Paris to stay with Mum who had come back from Dinard. Philippe found the farm had improved, the ingenuity of the men had done a lot. The roof had been repaired, stoves put in, and they now had a community room with bar and stage. Even the muddy courtyard now had stone paths.

Donald Tritch had become an interpreter and was sent to Le Mans. Steilhin had also gone. Delille while on leave left a vacant place in the squadron's office and Philippe was able to fill it. Since that lucky day, he remained in the office. For a while he was at Gazeran, now he is back in the Caserne of Rambouillet, always with the Seventh Squadron. He had made new friends too, those that work with him, Christian Neucheze, a tall kind young fellow from Paris, Pierre Pruvost, a short amusing man, also from Paris, and Thibault, an older man, frank and friendly.

40. This is a reference to the "phony war" of October 1939–April 1940.

After Philippe returned to Rambouillet, he had a room with Christian in the "Hotel de la Gare," where the two of them were warm and comfortable. At this epoch I spent some time there too, at various intervals. Now they had taken full pension in the "Vieux Moulin," a little establishment run by a widow and her three young attractive daughters. Pierre and Thibault have a room there too, and at this writing I am also present having come down especially to celebrate Philippe's promotion as non-commissioned officer, "Maréchal des logis"[41] in the French Cavalry. Out of a depot of 18,000 men, 50 names were put forward for promotion, and five only were chosen! Philippe says it is luck, I say it is an honor he deserves. It is probably both, but more credit is deserving to the latter.

My Maréchal des Logis has a beautiful new cap, light blue with a red top, and a silver stripe on each sleeve. I might mention that long ago he discarded his hideous blue uniform to wear a new khaki uniform that he had made. The clothes certainly helped the man to look like a fine soldier.

Of course the promotion had to be celebrated by a gala dinner in a nice restaurant, with all the members of the office including the commanding officer. It was a lovely gay party and the food and drinks the best we had had for a long time.

Philippe now has considerably more freedom and is treated as an officer. Under the present circumstance he is no longer required to sleep and eat with the rest of the men, and is free to eat and sleep in town if he will it. Before, he always had to be so careful not to miss a call.

The members of the office take turns in order to guard the premises each weekend, so that Philippe has been free to come to Paris almost every weekend from Saturday to early Monday morning. This has meant a happy winter for me. When he is on guard, I come to Rambouillet. He was free both for Christmas and New Year!

In the meantime "Les Baumées," our future little house in Nesles-la-Vallée, continues to be built and should be completed this spring. It has been delayed all along by the unprecedented cold and lack of workmen, but it is coming along. Nesles fills our thoughts night and day. It is so good for our morale to have something like that to hang on to in a period like the one we are living.

41. Sergeant.

There is no spectacular news from home. Franklin, because of his serious illness in the fall, was forced to discontinue his studies until next summer. Eleanora has recently had a visit home in St. Petersburg.[42]

Between my happy days with Philippe, my time has been full and has passed quickly. Mum and I take weekly turns with the meal planning, working and cleaning up. Otherwise she is busy with her church work, and I read, visit Jean,[43] and prepare to move little by little from our Bellechasse flat to Nesles when the time comes. I have experienced no more alerts so life has been quite calm.

Now rationing is starting in earnest; 70 liters of petrol allowed per month; no meat on Mon., Tue., Wed. of each week, fancy breads prohibited, pastries, alcohol, aperitifs, chocolate on certain days only. But we accept these restrictions very easily somehow, which proves that peacetime essentials are not wartime ones.

We have bought a practically new Simca 8, a lovely little car, grey metallic color, neat and modern. Unfortunately, after having had her for a few days, we crashed into an unlighted military wagon one night, causing 9,000 francs damage to the car, but none to us fortunately! Though it was not our fault, we had to pay because our insurance did not cover that risk, and to fight military authority in time of war is a losing battle. But she is all fixed now, and we are enjoying her again.

Michel de Gourlet (Philippe's first cousin) who was mobilized in Versailles and has been there ever since, is leaving for a place near Verdun. His wife Nicole is staying in their little flat in Paris. Grandmère and Tante Germaine[44] are together in the latter's apartment, also in Paris.

Now a few remarks on the war and international affairs. The war still refuses to become a bloody affair, also there have been considerable losses on the sea, especially in ship tonnage. The blockade is presumably enforced, but Germany has been mine laying all winter and the neutral countries have been suffering as well as the Allies.[45]

42. Franklin and Eleanora were Virginia's younger brother and sister. Her parents, Franklin and Edith Roush, still lived in St. Petersburg.

43. This is probably a reference to Jean Clarck, mentioned in the October 11, 1939, entry. Jean had stayed with the d'Albert-Lakes at Cancaval after her husband was mobilized and his business in Paris was requisitioned.

44. Germaine de Gourlet was the sister of Philippe's father and the mother of Michel de Gourlet.

45. The Battle of the Atlantic intensified during the winter of 1939–1940.

Germany suffered criticism in the eyes of the world from the viewpoint of traditional warfare, when she scuttled one of her battleships, the *Graf Spee*, off the Montevideo coast instead of meeting the enemy in combat. The Commander committed suicide a few days later.[46]

The worst tragedy lately has been the Russian-Finnish war of some two months duration, which ended a few days ago. The Russians attacked the little country, an act of pure aggression, without reason. The Finns proved to be splendid soldiers, and with very little means and the aid of the unbearable cold, held the Russians for a few weeks. We are given to understand that the Finns lost 27,000 men in battle, the Russians 200,000. Thousands of the latter froze to death. The Finns short of matériel were aided considerably by the Allies and neutral countries, but they were short of men and in this respect they received practically no help. (If we are fighting aggression why don't we fight it?) Norway, taking a firm neutral stand, refused to allow allied troops to pass through her territory to reach Finland, and has been criticized for this. I consider that a poor excuse, however, for our not helping the Finns with more men. Why did we not attack Russia from the south? We have already sent 100,000 men out there.[47]

46. On December 13, 1939, the German warship the *Admiral Graf Spee* was damaged during a naval battle with the British off the coast of Argentina and Uruguay. Fearing defeat by the British and the loss of his crew of more than seven hundred, Captain Hans Langsdorff transferred the crew of the *Graf Spee* to a German merchant ship and, on December 16, blew up and sank his ship. Two days later Captain Langsdorff committed suicide.

47. The Soviet-Finnish War began on November 30, 1939, when the Soviet army attacked Finland after Finland refused to cede to the Soviet Union a large strip of the Karelian Isthmus leading to Leningrad (now St. Petersburg). Fighting continued until March 1940. Some two hundred thousand Soviet troops and twenty-five thousand Finnish troops were killed during this "winter war" of 1939–1940. While Finland earned worldwide admiration for its courageous resistance to the Red Army, Allied support was primarily limited to matériel rather than men. The only Europeans who fought for Finland were volunteers from Britain, France, and Italy. The French, however, did provide the Finns with "145 planes, 496 heavy guns, 5,000 machine guns, 200,000 hand grenades, 400,000 rifles and 20,000,000 rounds of ammunition." Martin Gilbert, *The Second World War: A Complete History* (New York: Henry Holt, 1989), p. 34. Not wanting to antagonize either Germany or the Soviet Union, neither Norway nor Sweden allowed Allied troops to cross their lands to Finland. The peace treaty was agreed upon on March 12–13, 1940, with the Soviet Union demanding and receiving more than it had originally requested. Virginia's statement about attacking Russia from the south is a reference to the French troops stationed in the

This war is making me more of a pacifist than ever. Our actions appear so inconsistent with the ideal of a world without aggression, for which we are supposed to be fighting. We harpoon Germany and yet when Russia takes the prize, for unwarranted aggression, we say and do nothing, and only when the attacked country begins to weaken do we make a half-hearted offer of assistance. As a result, Finland pleads for peace and has it, but on Russia's unfair terms, and to think that 27,000 if not many more died for that! What a feather for the cap of our enemy![48] And now Russia is free to continue her supplying of raw materials to Germany. Another break for us!

The final stir has been caused by Sumner Wells, President Roosevelt's ambassador, who has just completed a tour of the belligerent countries with Italy thrown in! He has conferred with Hitler, Mussolini, Daladier, Chamberlain and the others. However, we know nothing of what has been said or done. . . . Many hope there is a possibility of peace.[49] How glorious if true! But the Allies are holding out for destruction of the Nazi regime, and as no one can trust Hitler, due to past experiences, how can

---

French protectorates of Syria and Lebanon, just south of Soviet oil fields near Baku in the Caucasus.

48. On February 5 Britain and France "agreed to intervene militarily in Finland, and to send an expeditionary force of at least three divisions." By early March, however, with Finnish troops exhausted and peace talks under way in Moscow, Anglo-French plans to aid Finland were abandoned. Gilbert, *The Second World War*, pp. 42, 47. According to Gerhard L. Weinberg, "The Finnish government saw no alternative to accepting what it considered a very harsh peace. They had fought hard and lost; they had no real prospects of effective aid; and though they had retained their independence, their position for defending it in the future was geographically weaker than before." Weinberg, *A World at Arms*, p. 105.

49. Early in 1940 President Franklin D. Roosevelt sent U.S. Under Secretary of State Sumner Wells to Europe to meet with political leaders to determine whether a U.S.–negotiated end to the war might be possible. Among the leaders with whom he met were Adolf Hitler, Benito Mussolini, the French prime minister Edouard Daladier, and Neville Chamberlain. Mussolini and Hitler had signed a secret protocol on October 21, 1936, that promised a coordination of their foreign policy. On September 27, 1940, Germany, Italy, and Japan signed a treaty, known as the Tripartite Pact, which stated they would provide military assistance to each other in case of attack by any nation not yet in the war. This marked the completion of what was known as the Axis alliance.

a decent peace be arranged?[50] I do not know. I have a feeling that Nazism is another word for German mentality and how can our waging a war destroy that? That change of mentality must come from within not from without. Why destroy ourselves in such an attempt? And yet countries cannot be allowed to bully the weak. What will be the result? Will they bring about their own destruction sooner or later? I believe so, but is that an excuse for our sitting idly by in the meantime? I don't know. We have never tried before. We have always gone to war. What would happen if we turned the other cheek, over and over, as Christ commanded? Up to the war we tried it, not because we were trying Christ's methods, but because we were unprepared for war. As a result Abyssinia, Albania, Austria, Czechoslovakia, Poland, and now even Finland have been victims. Would we too be included one day if we did not make a stand of force? I do not think so. There are too many unhappy people under one flag to not revolt sooner or later. Could I be happy as a Nazi? I doubt it, but I would rather be alive to try it than dead and not be able to try anything.

....

March 22, 1940

Well, things are still happening, politically and personally! Daladier, the French Prime Minister has been forced to resign! There was distinct opposition brought about primarily by his inaction in the Finno/Russian affair. He continues to hold a position however as a Minister of National Defense. Paul Reynaud, the Finance Minister, is taking his place.[51] He has

50. This is a reference to the September 1938 Munich Pact, in which Chamberlain and Daladier agreed to give Hitler the Sudetenland, the German-speaking region in northern Czechoslovakia, in an effort to avert all-out war with Germany. The Munich Pact became a symbol of appeasement, and, rather than stopping Hitler, it emboldened him to take over most of what remained of Czechoslovakia the following March, which further set the European stage for the Second World War.

51. Edouard Daladier was forced to resign as prime minister on March 20, 1940, in part for failing to bring effective help to Finland during the Soviet-Finnish War. With the bloodshed of World War I still fresh on the minds of French citizens, many had hoped that a Finnish victory would keep the fighting away from French soil. Daladier's successor, Paul Reynaud, a strong anti-Nazi, was one of the few conservatives during the 1930s who had opposed the appeasement of Germany. A week after becoming prime minister, he met with Neville Chamberlain in London, and they signed a joint declaration stating that the two countries would not make a separate peace with Germany.

made several changes in the Cabinet, putting in some men of little or no value and drawn from the "Front Populaire."[52] This I hear from Philippe and the others who think such radical changes at this time, really dangerous.

Philippe has been sent somewhere else too, but not far away. He is to be in the village of "Le Perray" five kilometers from Rambouillet on the route to Paris. He has been changed for the better, as he now is personal secretary to the Commandant. Poor Pierre was not so fortunate. He has been sent to a wretched farm in the vicinity with no special duty attached. Christian and Thibault are still at the Caserne. At Le Perray, distinct new units are being formed of very young men of around twenty years old, who are there for instruction.

As I have a feeling things are going to be different from now on, I feel it is time to mention something that happened when Philippe was at the farm just before he got his three weeks leave and consequently was not recorded in my diary at the time.

Philippe was sent on guard for a week at the Power Station in Gazeran along with Steilhin and ten privates. Receiving an "I would love to see you" note and my feeling the same, I decided to surprise him. I knew nothing about the Power Station or even where to find it, but back in my mind I imagined it a small place with Philippe the only guard! Was I surprised, in getting off the train, I found the Power Station in front of my eyes, a huge modern building with stout poles and power lines, a high wire fence about it all, and an armed guard pacing up and down who was not Philippe! However he was most gracious, called to an upper window, through which suddenly poked the surprised, pleased, concerned face of my cutie! So I was escorted into the booming, whistling, high ceilinged interior, crowded with immense clean shining power machinery.

I found Philippe and Steilhin the "high in command" sharing a steam heated room with hot and cold running water. When I saw how complicated the whole affair was, I planned to hurry back to Paris, but was urged

52. Concerns about the rise of Adolf Hitler in Germany and the economic effects of the Depression had led a broad coalition of leftists, including Communists, Socialists, and members of the Radical Party, to form the Popular Front in 1934. The Popular Front did well in the 1936 parliamentary elections, and Leon Blum became the first Socialist prime minister of France. By 1938, however, political dissension between the Communists and other leftists resulted in the dissolution of the Popular Front coalition. Virginia is referring to the fact that significant support for Reynaud came from the antifascist left.

by everyone, including the other men I met to stay to dinner. That was really fun. We all sat around a long wobbly table, on rickety benches, and ate soup, rabbit, and fried potatoes, toppling it all off with coffee "served in my honor." We sang a lot and those with special aptitude "rendered" solos! I offered that boy my congratulations. He did not need atmosphere and perfect working conditions and equipment to produce his art. Afterwards, I really had to go I thought. But no I was to spend the night!! So I did, on the floor with Philippe in the glass office of the power engineers! Only one sleeping bag for the two of us, and all night long the machines hissed and banged and grumbled and lightning. I did not sleep much! But what fun and another interesting experience to be added to my collection.

....

April 1940

My feeling was that things were going to happen, but up to date they have not, at least as far as we are concerned.[53] We are in Le Perray, staying in a nice house on the main street. The owner, Madame Fénié, first took Philippe in when the Commandant Vialet decided that the Squadron's office should be there, and later on myself. She is a charming woman and does everything she can to give us pleasure. Life goes on more or less like it did in Rambouillet with new friends and weekends spent in Paris or at Nesles. Spring is upon us and nature is at its best. Mrs. Fénié has a small garden and a dog. Philippe sometimes helps her in the garden. She is also

53. Given her interest in the politics and progress of the war, it is curious that Virginia did not report that on April 9, 1940, Germany invaded Denmark and Norway. This marked the end of the "phony war" and the beginning of the spring blitzkrieg, or "lightning war." Within twelve hours Copenhagen had fallen, and by the end of the day all of Denmark was under the Nazi yoke. Despite the German occupation of Denmark, the Danish Resistance remained strong throughout World War II, and Danish citizens undertook heroic measures to protect the country's Jews. In Norway the fighting proved to be more difficult, but much of Norway had fallen under German control by the end of the month. On April 29–30 the royal family, with Norway's gold reserves in tow, escaped to London, where a government-in-exile was established. From September 1940 until Germany's surrender on May 7, 1945, the Norwegian traitor Vidkun Quisling headed up a puppet fascist government that sent thousands of Norwegians to German concentration camps. After the war Quisling was arrested, put on trial, and convicted of treason, murder, and theft. He was executed on October 24, 1945.

a very good cook and takes good care of us. How lucky we are to have found someone as nice as she is!

The French say "Le calme avant la tempete" calm prior to storm. Le Perray is certainly calm and lovely at this time of the year. Let's hope the storm does not fall on our heads!

....

May 1940

This time, the war has really started . . . The Germans have invaded Belgium, we retaliated and sent troops there and now the battle is raging all along the front.[54] The news is not good. It does not seem as if we are able to hold our ground. The morning paper says that a pocket forced by the enemy into our lines is being pushed west and northwest, presumably with the intention of dividing the allied troops: those in Belgium from those in France. Anvers and Bruxelles have been abandoned by our troops.[55]

Refugees are starting to pass our windows. Two horses pulling a farm wagon with a family of four plus possessions just went by. We will see more and more of that. They need more time en route than the cars.[56]

Early this morning at about 5, Philippe was woken up by several bangs on the office door. It was a high ranking officer that said he had driven down from the front and could not understand how military staff could still be asleep as if nothing was happening. He looked worn and dirty and said "it is complete hell up there," nobody has any idea of what is going

54. Early on the morning of May 10, 1940, Germany launched a land and air attack on Luxembourg, the Netherlands, and Belgium. Luxembourg, lacking a sizable army, quickly fell to Germany. The Germans found the recalcitrant Luxembourgers difficult to rule, however. On May 15, after only five days of fighting, the Dutch surrendered. Dutch Queen Wilhelmina, along with leading members of her government, escaped to London and established a government-in-exile. Following the May 10 attack, both France and Britain sent troops to help the Belgians.

55. On May 16 British and French troops, who only days earlier had been sent to Belgium, began to retreat from Brussels (Bruxelles in French), the capital city of Belgium. On May 17 German troops entered Brussels. Anvers is the French name for Antwerp, the important port city located in northeastern Belgium on the Scheldt River. On May 18 German troops overtook Antwerp.

56. Following the German invasion of Luxembourg on May 10, more than forty-five thousand refugees fled to France.

on. Philippe took him to the premises of Commandant Vialet who was also asleep. By then we knew what we were more or less in for!!!

The number of refugees increase steadily every day, night and day, wagons and wagons full of people and their belongings. Most wagons pulled by four horses. I saw four people walking, one leading a bicycle. One could spend the day watching the poor souls go by.

....

Tuesday, May 21, 1940
We are in the war zone now. An armed soldier paces by the office front constantly and most men are armed.

"La patrie est en danger" (The country is in danger) so pronounced Prime Minister Paul Reynaud, over the air late this afternoon. The Germans have taken Arras and Amiens!![57] If they once cut us off from our troops in Belgium and in taking the ports on the Channel, cut us off from England too, it looks as if we'll be lost! The country is in danger!

Most of the day up to the present hour there has been a steady file of military cars, trucks, ambulances, heading away from Paris towards the southwest! Why? There have also been trucks full of air force, and cars of officers, both cars and officers giving the impression that they had just come from the front. Gasoline, airplane parts etc., all pass by here.

There was an air raid alert in this vicinity this afternoon. It was uneventful and only lasted 20 minutes. During that time, all the cars on the road were commanded to stop. The refugees continue to go by. Today, we saw countless wagons pulled by tired horses. Some of the horses were being led by people on foot. To see an old man or woman leading a tired horse, they themselves practically dead with fatigue is not pleasant to watch. Madame Fénié stopped a particularly exhausted looking group in a wagon with lots of children and gave them coffee.[58]

57. On May 13 the Germans poured across the Meuse River at Dinant and Sedan through the heavily wooded Ardennes Forest into northern France. This was north of the famed Maginot Line. Early on the morning of May 15 French Prime Minister Paul Reynaud telephoned the newly elected British prime minister, Winston Churchill, to inform him, "We are beaten; we have lost the battle." Jackson, *The Fall of France*, p. 9. By this time the Germans were advancing so fast that they were overtaking the French in retreat. Fighting in the region of the northwestern French towns of Arras and Amiens began on May 20, 1940.

58. On the significance of the "devastating psychological impact of witnessing, and being swept up in, the great wave of civilian refugees," see Jackson, *The Fall of France*, pp. 174–178.

Philippe was just called to quieten disorder taking place in a restaurant in Le Perray. There he found two hundred air-force men, who have been brought back from the front, all low, discouraged, and flinging remarks about the country, the army etc.; the result of five nights without sleep; abandoned by their officers, and having been ordered to go and they don't even know where! They are sleeping in the forest tonight the poor fellows. What disorganization. No wonder the Germans are advancing.

....

Wednesday, May 22, 1940

A large part of the French army is in retreat and it is retreating right by here: troops, cannons, trucks, everything. The expression on the men's faces proves that they have seen hell let loose. Their features are twisted. They come from the Belgium border and are to reassemble in this vicinity as they are completely disorganized.

As far as we know, the battle continues to rage, near Arras and Amiens. We are told that the enemy knows about this massing of troops and matériel around here, and that we will be bombarded! I am glad there is a cellar in this house! The Commandant Vialet says all the women should leave. I have just filled up the car anyway.

The Parisians are leaving the city also. At this moment there is a steady stream of cars along with the military fleet. I cannot seem to get panicky. All I know is that I am so happy to be by Philippe and that as long as I am not ordered to leave, I want to stay.

....

Thursday, May 23, 1940

We are told we have retaken Arras! One result of this is that the situation has calmed slightly, and the Commandant thinks that perhaps I need not go after all.

A part of the Army which was scattered by the Germans in Belgium, has come to Le Perray. 1400 arrived last night and they are still coming in. There are almost 3,000 now. There is not enough room for them all. Every vacant barn or space has been requisitioned, but so many officers and men are unable to be billeted. On the whole, the population of Le Perray shows little understanding and sympathy in respect to what is happening and we have heard many remarks regarding this fact from retreating men and officers! On the other hand, it is understandable that a population does not appreciate a retreating army and the first thought that came to us all when the first men retreating arrived here was that they had fled from the field of battle and were to be punished.[59]

....

Sunday, May 26, 1940

A few days ago General Gamelin was removed from his post without explanation, and General Weygand put in his place. We understand that 15 generals have been removed! Will that help any?[60]

A good part of the men sent here have already been moved on; regiments of which some Cavalry have passed through here in the other direction. It is said they have been removed from the border and are being sent where they are most needed.

Men from the 1st and 9th Army, those that retreated as far as here have been granted leave today. Commandant Vialet considers that such permission is unwise. Why should the men who fled from the field of battle be given privilege? Philippe says that while he was with the Commandant today not once was he saluted by these men! It proves their lack of discipline and respect. Because they were at the front, they believe they have every right but they forget they turned back and ran! If every one ran, where would we be?

....

Monday, May 27, 1940

A friend, Mrs. Kaufmann, and I drove to Nesles today. En route, we were stopped six times and were asked for our identity papers! I found a great change in the tranquility of the place; soldiers and enormous trucks everywhere. In the close-by town of l'Isle Adam, sand bags and cannons blocked the main street.[61] No one was allowed to park. As the town is on

59. Julian Jackson argues that French soldiers fought "bravely . . . when they were properly led and equipped," and that "the failure of 1940 was above all the failure of military planning" that included sending the best troops to Belgium when the "brunt of the German attack came further south" through the Ardennes Forest and across the Meuse River. Jackson, *France: The Dark Years*, p. 118.

60. With French forces in disarray and rapidly retreating, Prime Minister Reynaud recalled seventy-three-year-old General Maxime Weygand from the Middle East to replace General Maurice Gustave Gamelin as commander of the French forces. Weygand assumed his new position on May 20, 1940.

61. Nesles is just northwest of l'Isle-Adam.

the Oise River and has three bridges, it is strategic. When the Germans made their spectacular advance after invading Belgium, panic struck the population, and now the fair sized town seems empty! Neither Nesles nor l'Isle-Adam have been bombed directly but near by places have been, Beauvais, Meru, the railroad, adjacent factories, all have had bombs. There have been raids every day since I last came. Nothing has disturbed the tranquility of "Les Baumées" however. The Iris are blooming and I found the exterior doors and windows installed, which made me very happy. In the evening we were safely back in Le Perray.

....

Tuesday, May 28, 1940

King Leopold the Third of Belgium, Commander in Chief of the Belgium army, capitulated at 4:00 this morning without being forced to do so by the opposing German army!! He had not even warned the British and French before doing so. Again we have been betrayed. This news came over the air by Paul Reynaud at 8:30 this morning. What a shock! This means that the allied forces in Belgium may be annihilated.[62]

Today is Philippe's 31st birthday. Leaving aside all other events, we celebrated with a good dinner at the "Coq de Bruyère," inviting the Kaufmanns. We ended up with a bottle of Champagne and did not leave until 11:00.

....

Wednesday, May 29, 1940

In spite of the treason of the king of Belgium, parts of the Belgium army are still fighting. But that country too has been mined by German propaganda and spies. Heaven knows how many Belgiums sincerely support the Allied cause? Nevertheless it is awful to think that the king who begged Allied help when his country was invaded, and who recently gave a speech in which he proclaimed his duty and pledged himself to follow in the steps of his admired father, has done such a thing. What is going to happen next? The battle is raging in the N.W. but we seem to be

62. Without consulting the French and British, King Leopold surrendered early on the morning of May 28. Julian Jackson states that "on hearing the news of Leopold's capitulation, Reynaud went 'white with rage.' He told the French people in a radio broadcast that 'there has never been such a betrayal in history.'" Jackson, *The Fall of France*, p. 93. Virginia evidently heard this broadcast.

holding our own, and are fortifying our positions in the Somme. The RAF is doing its best to protect the Allied forces in Belgium.[63]

It is quiet in this vicinity. Many of the troops have left, and though refugees and war matériel continue to go by, the number cannot be compared to what it was before. We see more French planes however, a good sign. The railroad between Paris and Chartres is finally being guarded too! The French seem at last to be taking things seriously.

....

June 2, 1940

I am eight days late with the curse plus other baby symptoms! I cannot think that it might be time, so I will say no more until I am absolutely certain![64]

The army in Belgium that seemed doomed due to the capitulation of King Leopold has been disembarking in England from Dunkerque, but under constant attack from the enemy. What a dramatic escape! Fortunately the Channel is calm and every boat available, even the smallest type came over to help in the rescue. The Gods even sent a fog, unusual at this time of the year to protect the troops from serious aerial bombardments. But how heavy are the losses?[65]

We are expecting Italy to enter the war on Germany's side from one day to the next. The front is quiet in the Somme, but when will the next

63. By the time of King Leopold's surrender, British and French forces in the north had been cut off from those in the south by Germany's rapid advance toward the Channel. In a desperate effort to save the cut-off northern forces, a cross-Channel evacuation from Dunkirk, know as Operation Dynamo, was launched on May 26. In the meantime French forces dug in along the Somme River around Amiens in northwestern France in preparation for the anticipated German assault southward. RAF stands for Royal Air Force.

64. Since their marriage in 1937, Virginia and Philippe had very much wanted to have children.

65. Dunkirk (Dunkerque) is a small town on the Channel near France's border with Belgium. Between May 26 and June 4 more than 335,000 Allied troops were evacuated from the beaches of Dunkirk to England. About 110,000 of these troops were French. This massive evacuation used British ships and boats of all sizes, but in the process a vast amount of armament had to be left behind. A remarkable achievement, Operation Dynamo succeeded in part because on May 24 Hitler ordered German troops to stop their advance toward the Channel for three days. On June 4 the Germans marched into Dunkirk and captured the remaining 30,000 to 40,000 French soldiers.

German attack take place? They control the coast from Narvik to Dunkerque.[66]

....

June 4, 1940
My 30th Birthday!
(Whew, getting old!)
To celebrate I have the curse! Hence no baby; have had symptoms of a miscarriage.

Yesterday was some day and mostly unlucky. I went to Paris and chose the day of the first bombardment of the city. We are told 240 German planes and 1,087 bombs dropped.[67] At the time, I was at "Chez Bosc" Restaurant, having lunch. Everyone continued eating undisturbed, following the suggestion of Madame Bosc, when the sirens sounded. People in the street hastened to cover. From where I was near the window, I could see them looking up at the sky from doors and protected spots. There was a terrific din of airplane motors plus heavy flack from the DCA.[68] The alert lasted about an hour and most of that time we could hear planes above. I had no idea what was actually going on until later in the afternoon when I met Mary Louise Antonio whom I was to bring back to Le Perray. At the time of the alert, she was at the "Sacré Coeur" at "Montmartre."[69] Through the heat haze she saw the German planes at high altitude plus smoke and fire at the right of the Eiffel tower. Later we were told that the Citroën plant had been hit.[70] On our way out of Paris we went in that direction, found the plant half destroyed and smoking. We crossed to the right bank of the Seine River, opposite the plant where we had a splendid view, parked the car and went exploring. What we did not see! Not only the Citroën factory was badly damaged, but the fronts of

66. On June 10, 1940, Italy declared war on France and England. Narvik is a coastal town at the northern tip of Norway.

67. Paris was first bombed on June 3, 1940.

68. DCA refers to Defensive Counter Air, a system of defense against air attacks that includes the use of very noisy artillery fire.

69. Construction on the basilica of Sacré Coeur (Sacred Heart) on the Montmartre hill of Paris began after the 1870 capture of Paris by the Prussians. It was constructed in devotion to the Sacred Heart of Jesus following the 1870 disaster and the bloody civil war that ensued.

70. Citroën is a well-known French automobile maker.

several houses completely demolished. Broken windows every place, huge shell holes in the streets, lamp posts bent double, roofs collapses etc. etc.

We had seen enough misery; we returned to the car and started for home. For a while everything seemed alright but from Versailles on we saw the result of more bombing; smoke and fires in many places, burned cars and trucks along the road. Excited people standing in groups and so it went on until we reached Trappes.[71] From there on everything was quiet and peaceful. I felt no panic although we were anxious to reach Le Perray and be sure things were O.K.

I can hardly believe I saw all this, now it seems I had a dream or saw a movie. We heard this morning that 47 were killed, 200 injured and that 16 planes had been brought down. That does not seem much out of 240. . . . In any case, how can one trust official figures during wartime?[72]

....

June 5, 1940

Winston Churchill gave a remarkable speech to the Commons yesterday. He admitted that the battle of Flanders was a tremendous defeat, but contained a miraculous victory in that of the Allied army being safely brought to Britain.[73] The BEF is said to have lost 30,000 men and practically all its matériel including 1,000 cannons.[74] The defeat has given great

71. Trappes is on the main road to Le Perray, about twenty-five kilometers from Paris.

72. In total, 254 people were killed; 195 were civilians and the remainder were soldiers. Gilbert, *The Second World War*, p. 85.

73. This is a reference to Winston Churchill's famous June 4, 1940, speech, "We Shall Fight on the Beaches." Churchill concluded this speech with the following well-known passage: "We shall go on to the end, we shall fight in France, we shall fight on the seas and oceans, we shall fight with growing confidence and growing strength in the air, we shall defend our Island, whatever the cost may be, we shall fight on the beaches, we shall fight on the landing grounds, we shall fight on the fields and in the streets, we shall fight in the hills; we shall never surrender, and even if, which I do not for a moment believe, this Island or a large part of it were subjugated and starving, then our Empire beyond the seas, armed and guarded by the British Fleet, would carry on the struggle, until, in God's good time, the New World, with all its power and might, steps forth to the rescue and the liberation of the old." A copy of this speech is at "The Churchill Centre," www.winstonchurchill.org/i4a/pages/index.cfm?pageid=393.

74. BEF stands for British Expeditionary Force. In his June 4, 1940, speech, Churchill stated that thirty thousand British soldiers had been lost during the fighting in Belgium and France. In actuality, British casualties totaled more than sixty-eight

strategic advantage to the Germans now that they are in control of Channel ports and we may expect a new attack either in England or in France, from one day to another.

Already it seems to have come!! This morning the enemy started an intense new offensive on the Somme front from the sea to Soissons. It is now 4:30 P.M., but there is yet no news in detail.[75]

A message came to the office this evening stating that all noncommissioned officers are to leave here not later than tomorrow. Philippe is first on the list. My poor honey lost his appetite and I babbled of trifles. I refuse to think of it until I have to. What a life we are living, and if this war continues, the darkest days are ahead.

....

June 6, 1940

The radio says the Allies are able to sustain their new front. German tanks are said to have been pushed back in several points. Nevertheless, owing to the latest enemy offensive, a fresh string of refugees have been filing past here today along with all types of vehicles, tanks and horses.

Have just heard that Paris suffered an intense bombardment at 3 P.M.[76] It is now 5:00, glad I am here this time. Mum fortunately is here too, arrived at noon and brought part of her belongings with her. Seeing Paris full of stationary buses ready to evacuate the population gave her a bit of fright, so she decided to join us.

....

Saturday, June 8, 1940

Philippe is still here, I do not know how or why, nor does he, all I can do is to thank God.

------

thousand killed, wounded, or taken as prisoner during the Battle of France. Almost all heavy military equipment had to be abandoned at Dunkirk.

75. The anticipated attack across the Somme River began on June 5, 1940. There was especially heavy fighting between the coast and Amiens. Although the French had made some defensive preparations, they were not able to hold back the Germans, who broke the French line along the Somme between the coast and Amiens on June 6.

76. In actuality, Paris did not suffer an air bombardment on June 6. This was one of numerous war rumors that were circulating.

There wasn't even an alert in Paris on Thursday, much less a bombardment! How false alarms get around! The German tank advance has pushed through our lines at Forges-les-Eaux.[77] When I think that the front is only about fifty miles from Nesles!

People are fleeing Paris again today, almost a steady stream.

Last night we had some real sleep, but the nights before very little. There was cannon and sound of bombardment. We watched for some time the play of searchlights in the sky but could see no planes. When Philippe called me at six this morning, to come and see a parachute come down, there was real excitement. The parachute was floating down westward, but by means of field glasses we easily ascertained that it was minus a parachutist! Do not know how to explain its being there! There are many things we cannot explain, light flashes and gunshots are being heard and seen in the forest around us but the forest is too extensive to be searched.

Both Le Perray and Rambouillet are preparing to meet the advance units of the enemy. There are stone barricades across the roads at the entrances of the two towns.

We are having the most beautiful weather. As I sit in this garden scribbling these notations, I cannot believe that seventy miles away a most horrible battle and a decisive one, is raging.

....

Sunday, June 9, 1940

The battle is more intense than ever. The Germans are throwing in more Divisions and we have been forced to fall back. The enemy has succeeded in crossing the river Aisne, at Soissons, at which point they are exerting the greatest pressure. That is at the east of the Oise [River]. Nesles is on the west of the river!

An enemy plane dropped flares on the forest last night. Philippe received orders to go and warn the men in Le Perray security outposts. He said he drove along the country lanes, with his revolver in one hand, steering wheel in the other, wondering if he would fall on an enemy parachutist! It is known that several fell, but they have not been traced or tracked down.

77. Forges-les-Eaux is a small town just northeast of Rouen that was taken by the Germans on June 7.

....

June 10, 1940

The exodus continues. It is almost unbelievable just like a parade, with as much distance between each vehicle. The military and civilian all mixed together. Paris city buses full of refugees, wagons, trucks, soldiers and civilians all mixed together. Cannons, anti aircraft guns, horses, bicycles, army kitchens, where are they all going, where will they stay?[78] The news reports say we are holding the Germans although their advanced mechanized units have come to Gizor, Mantes, Rouen![79]

Out in front, there is a funny little car, topless and of the last century; all held together by pieces of wood. They are buying a new tire from the garage across the street. Gasoline is running out now, cars are having to stop when their tanks are empty.

Saw a car pass a bit ago with a big sheep in the back seat, calmly sticking his head out of the window for a bit of air. Also met a harassed looking woman in the grocery store, she had just come from Beauvais.[80] Her house had been demolished by bombs.

Ambulances of wounded are passing by, all driven by women! Later, just as dusk was setting in, saw more ambulances going toward the front. That is what I want to do, drive an ambulance.

More red signal flares were seen over the forest last night. Philippe was out until 2:30 this morning. I could not sleep until he came. There was so much noise of passing vehicles in the street and trains passed every five minutes.

Paris has evacuated the children. Have seen huge busses full of them passing by.[81]

78. Julian Jackson notes that "the scale of this extraordinary population movement, christened the Exodus, astonished contemporary observers. . . . Living through the Exodus was to experience a total disintegration of social structures. Thousands of children became separated from their families, and for months afterwards local papers contained poignant advertisements from parents trying to contact them. . . . Millions of people . . . were plunged in hopelessness and despair. Against this background, it is easy to understand why many people would greet the news of an armistice with such relief." Jackson, *France: The Dark Years*, pp. 120–121.

79. On June 9 German forces captured Rouen on the Seine River, the coastal town of Dieppe, and Compiègne. On June 10 the Germans crossed the Seine River west of Paris. The German advance toward Paris from the east was equally rapid.

80. Beauvais, north of Paris, was directly in the line of the German advance.

81. Beginning on June 6, frightened Parisians began leaving the city.

I am so full of excitement and various emotions, urging me to write, but to do so is very difficult. An official note arrived shortly ago stating that enemy tanks had crossed the Seine at Pont de l'Arche, a place east of Rouen. Now they are expecting them to come here, and we will just have to go! I have packed everything and am ready.

....

Afternoon

A friend of ours, just arrived from Paris, says all the Ministries have been evacuated today, including that of War. They are terribly fearful of what is to happen and say that Paris will be taken![82]

Paul Reynaud just announced over the air that Italy did declare war on the Allies!! The nasty low down trick, just when we are down, I hope she pays for this!

This ceaseless exodus is really nerve wracking.

I have no idea of leaving today. To go out on this road crowded without description does not appeal to me one bit. If the Germans machine gunned the fleeing refugees in the north, why should they not do it here? Nevertheless, we have to leave tomorrow whether we want to or not. The Commandant insists on my leaving.[83]

....

June 11, 1940

The refugees and military trucks passed all night. Up until midnight I was with Philippe out in the street, while he signaled cars to extinguish their lights. What a choice prize this route would be for the enemy at this moment, but I suppose all the roads going south or southwest are suffering identical conditions.

Cancaval

....

June 13, 1940

Here we are at last after a most strenuous trip. We had a delayed departure from Le Perray due to the blue baby car having engine trouble. We

82. On June 10 government officials were evacuated to various châteaux in the Loire region. The following day, Paris was declared an open city, free of military activity, and given immunity from attack or bombardment.

83. German planes sometimes attacked the refugees, thereby adding to the panic.

only left at 4 PM, joining the endless stream of traffic, and in so doing, becoming a part of it. I drove the Simca 8, loaded with baggage in the back, a mattress, blankets plus a bicycle on top, and on the trunk rack, 14 rabbits, 5 chickens and a canary!! With me, I brought as far as Rennes, Madame MacGrath, the nice young wife of an officer at Le Perray, Madame Fénié our landlady, and Pax our dog. Mum, who had not driven a car for years followed me in the blue baby Fiat loaded down too. With her was Marie-Louise, the daughter of people who have a grocery at Le Perray, plus Bobby, Madame Fénié's dog.

My goodbye to Philippe was very brief, fortunately perhaps. These last days have been so hectic and hard, our being together could barely be appreciated. But it gave us a source of strength, which now I miss terribly. Philippe is wonderful and seems to grow in wisdom all the time.

The route was so crowded that from Rambouillet to the other side of Chartres which we skirted, there were two steady lines of cars and we were forced to drive in first and second gear all the time. I lost mum in the scuffle and did not see her again until she arrived here four hours after I did, a miracle.

The Germans bombarded Chartres while we were only five miles away. We could see smoke rising across the flat plains, appearing from where we were to come from behind the cathedral. The enemy planes were too high for us to see but we witnessed the shell explosions from the anti-aircraft guns.

At 10 PM, it was nearly dark and we were only a short distance from Chartres. We had done so little mileage and there was no question of finding a room to sleep so we parked off the road in a field where there was a huge haystack. Madame Fénié and I made a comfortable bed in the side of the haystack, with blankets for warmth, while Madame MacGrath slept in the car. Around 1 AM however, it started to rain and we all had to crowd once more in the front seat of the car where we managed to doze off and on until 4 AM when we started off again. It was just light enough to see and there was little traffic on the minor road we were now following. We did beautifully for a while and were happy to make better time.

Near Le Mans, we had to go back to the main road and the terrible traffic again. We were in need of gasoline, but all the stations along the road had run out of it. There was not a drop to be had. At Le Mans, however, there was a long queue before a garage and we took our place in it. When we were the fourth car from the pump, it ran dry! We dashed to another and waited half an hour, but with success this time, being able to get ten liters, the last of my ration coupons. We continued towards Laval and then Rennes. East of Liffre we were again deviated and I was running short of gas again. At a little town I stopped at the Town Hall and asked for another ration ticket. They gave me one for five liters, so I went again for a pump. I was luckier than ever as they gave me the gas and forgot to ask me for the coupon! As a result and as I needed five more liters to finish my trip, I used the coupon in Rennes when we got there.

Around noon, we were all so tired we stopped off the route for a bite to eat and a rest. At Le Mans, Madame Fénié had bought cheese, cream and razberries, so we feasted like Queens. We fed the farm stock as well and then took a bit of a nap before going on.

At Rennes we left Madame MacGrath at her friend's house and then continued on toward Cancaval. We arrived at 7 PM. A trip that ordinarily takes six hours stretched in to 27 hours.

At every village there were barricades made of great tree trunks, huge stones, old farm machinery; farm wagons, and even in one place an old car was across the road filled with rocks. Always enough space was left for a single car to pass. We were always delayed by congestions near the towns, due to the barricades.

Although we were constantly asked to show our identity papers, we never experienced any difficulty and were greeted with extreme patience and politeness. Starting at Le Mans, we began seeing English soldiers. They were all so gay, laughing, smiling, and flirting, thumbs up in salutation.

On arriving at Cancaval, on the right of the little road leaving Pleurtuit, we found anti-aircraft. Just across the estuary there is more as we discovered last night when an enemy plane flew over and a huge search light shot its beams which reflected in the Rance and made a beautiful sight.[84]

I certainly slept last night and am still tired today. It takes time to get over nerve wracking days such as those we have lived. When I think that for my darling, they are still going on! The Germans are still advancing. Today's paper says they are fighting in the lower Oise—that is where Nesles is!! They are trying to surround Paris.

When I left Philippe, his final words were, "I have a feeling that we will be together again soon. Be a good girl and take care of the others, as

84. Cancaval is on the Rance, a one-hundred-kilometer river that extends through a long estuary to the English Channel.

you have more guts than all combined." He could not have said a thing that would give me more confidence. I cannot seem to remember what I said? It could not have been much. I wired him upon arrival here, but heaven knows if a wire can reach any place today?

....

Sunday, June 16, 1940

No news of Philippe. The enemy occupied Paris on Friday, but we hear that it is peaceful and "proud."[85] No material destructions, all the public facilities are working and food supplies continue. The Germans have advanced to the south, east and west of Paris, so of course Philippe is no longer at Le Perray. I wonder where and how he is, but there are thousands of women who wish to know the same thing. I am not afraid.

I started work this afternoon at the Crystal Hotel hospital in Dinard. I worked in the bandage room making all sorts of compresses. During the afternoon young women came and went, but we never were more than eight. Some were nice, but one in a very loud voice, argued in favor of capitulation and finally became so ardent in her ideas that the women in charge asked her to change the subject. Very silly and unwise that sort of talk, it arrives at nothing except a general depression.

All the hospitals in Dinard were to be evacuated today to make way for wounded men coming directly from the front but at 6:30 they were still there waiting. If the newly expected wounded arrive to-night, I don't know what will happen?

We were working in a room overlooking the beach and the sea. It was so beautiful. I could not imagine that the world was so miserable and that so many destructions were taking place not far away. I wonder if my darling is taking place in the battle. The beach was covered with sun bathers, the water full of swimmers, further out naval vessels were entering and leaving the St. Malo harbor no doubt evacuating British troops.[86] There also was a hospital ship, and RAF planes in the sky. The wounded

85. The Germans occupied Paris and its environs on June 14. Because tens of thousands of Parisians had fled the city, the Germans found Paris to be mostly a ghost town. Following the armistice, however, Paris resumed much of its prewar cultural activity.

86. Saint-Malo is located on the opposite side of the Rance estuary from Dinard. On June 13 the British abandoned attempts to rebuild the BEF in France and began to evacuate the remaining British and Canadian troops. More than 21,000 Allied troops were evacuated from Saint-Malo on June 16 and 17. Evacuations also occurred at other French ports along the Atlantic coast. Between June 16 and 24 approximately

were on the balconies watching the passing show, sometimes they sang or whistled. The majority have splendid morale.

Madame Fénié and Marie-Louise, our refugees, are now comfortably installed in a peasant house. We even painted the walls, a dusty rose. With the canary flowers and cretonne drapes, it is all very charming. If only we could do something to the dirt floor!

....

Monday, June 17, 1940

After two days of debate, the Paul Reynaud government has resigned. Maréchal Pétain, a glorious old man of 80 or more, has become Prime Minister and has named a new cabinet. All of this proves the seriousness of the situation.[87]

The Germans this morning are at L'Aigle on the West, have crossed the Seine near Fontainebleau, and have reached Chalon-sur-Saône![88] It is just unbelievable. Mum says that prophecy predicts a reversal the 25th of June when all seems lost! Roosevelt has promised all possible help to the Allies except the actual declaration of war. This response came after a frantic appeal for help before it is too late, by Paul Reynaud to the American Government. If the United States had not stayed neutral all this time, the situation would probably be very different.[89] The French Government is now at Bordeaux having abandoned Tours.[90]

160,000 mostly British troops were evacuated. A few days earlier, June 10–13, some 11,000 troops had been evacuated from Le Havre.

87. Having lost the support of his cabinet, Paul Reynaud resigned on June 16 and was replaced by the eighty-three-year-old Marshal Henri-Philippe Pétain, the famous World War I military hero.

88. Following the capture of Paris, German troops continued their advance into the center of the country.

89. On June 10 Reynaud had appealed to Roosevelt for American intervention in France. Roosevelt responded with great sympathy and praise for the resistance of the French and British armies, and he assured Reynaud that "this Government is doing everything in its power to make available to the Allied Governments the material they so urgently require." With Roosevelt seeking an unprecedented third term as president, however, American intervention was out of the question. Reynaud received this reply on June 16. Robert Leckie, *Delivered from Evil: The Saga of World War II* (New York: Harper and Row, 1987), p. 176.

90. In an effort to protect themselves from the advancing German army, government leaders who initially had been evacuated to Loire valley châteaux regrouped at Tours, and on June 14 they moved farther south to Bordeaux.

Last night there was an alert at Dinard, but nothing occurred. Airplanes woke me up this morning at 5 AM; they were flying very low over the house and dipping over the Rance, allied planes. St Malo is very likely to be bombed; the town is so crowded with troops, ships, petrol supplies, etc. We thought that we would always find safety and peace here, but it is a nightmare.

Maréchal Pétain just announced over the Radio that he has asked for an armistice, that we cannot continue the fight!!! Can it be possible, after but one month of hostilities?[91]

Nicole and I went to the hospital to find practically all the men evacuated, but instead of expecting more wounded, steps were being taken to close the hospital!

Everyone is terribly serious and depressed. It is just terrible to think that we have had to capitulate after so brief a struggle, however I thank God as long as it had to be, that at least lives have been saved. As far as we know, the fighting still continues. The Germans are at Caen, have crossed the Saône River south of Dijon, are at Avallon, and practically on the Swiss border, thus cutting off the Maginot Line.[92]

England announces that she will continue the war to the victory, how I hope she does![93]

What is Hitler going to demand of us? He has already stated that he will confer with Mussolini regarding peace terms.

The Germans are rejoicing on the air, we cannot avoid tuning in on stations ringing with German songs of victory.

What some people fear now is a revolution in France. Considering the number of Communists, it is possible.

Where is my darling? If only we could find each other again and stay together, I would not mind what happened. I am living years in weeks,

91. On June 17 Pétain announced that France was seeking an armistice with Germany.

92. German forces had advanced against the Maginot defenses on June 15.

93. On June 18 Churchill addressed the House of Commons and somberly reported: "The Battle of France is over. I expect that the Battle of Britain is about to begin. . . . Let us therefore brace ourselves to our duties, and so bear ourselves that, if the British Empire and its Commonwealth last for a thousand years, men will still say, 'This was their finest hour.'" "The Churchill Centre," www.winstonchurchill.org/i4a/pages/index.cfm?pageid = 418.

days in hours. Has there ever occurred in history such amazing changes in so short a time? For me it is still an unbelievable nightmare.

....

Tuesday, June 18, 1940

Mussolini left Rome last night at 8:30 to see Hitler.[94] Will we know today the armistice is granted? The reason for us demanding an armistice is because the Germans have managed to cut our army in several parts and are in a position to destroy it.

England has offered a plan to France whereby England and France would act as one nation putting all their resources together, but is it not too late now?[95]

At lunch time, we were told that St. Malo had been bombarded. We ran out to see great clouds of smoke rising but later realized that there had been a direct hit on a petrol dump or that such a dump was on fire for some reason. Many boats have come up the Rance and are anchored near us. It seems evident that it is to escape the eventual bombing of St. Malo which they fear.

....

Afternoon

We have just heard from Mr. de Jessey of the Montmarin that the Germans are at Dinan![96] So in the last thirty minutes everyone has gathered their valuables together and Nicole and I have buried them in the garden! This seemed to me as funny as it may sound tragic to others.

Since Nicole and I are the young and attractive ones in the house, we are to hide on the beach on the other side of the point if the Germans come here. They are said to be famous for attacking women, so here I sit,

94. Mussolini and Hitler met at Munich on June 18 to discuss the terms of the armistice with France. Mussolini had hoped to get some of France's possessions in North Africa, but all he received was a small zone of occupation in southeastern France.

95. On June 16, in an effort to thwart French plans for an armistice with Germany, Britain proposed a complete political union between the two countries, but this proposal was soundly rejected by the French. Why, asked Pétain, would France want to "fuse with a corpse"? Plans for the armistice moved forward. Jackson, *The Fall of France*, pp. 137–138.

96. Dinan is located at the head of the Rance estuary and is not to be confused with Dinard, situated along the eastern side of the Rance.

writing, thinking that at any moment I might have to grab my coat and bag and flee from the invader! It has come to this!

Just heard terrific bomb explosions. A bombardment must be taking place not far away!

....

Wednesday, June 19, 1940

I am so happy! I have news of Philippe! From the parents of Marie-Louise who arrived this morning, having left Le Perray Friday morning. Philippe left with his unit and the commandant on Thursday last. He said that they might be going to Orleans and then further south. This news is balm to my soul and I pray God that it is true. I am given to understand that we left Le Perray just in time, and Philippe too, as the place was bombarded and machine gunned by planes. Six people were killed and many wounded. Marie-Louise's parents experienced bombing and machine gunning during their entire trip. They also were caught up by German tanks and troops, but said that they found them considerate towards the French. The Germans say it is the English they are after!

The story about the Germans being at Dinan was a false alarm, though they may be there by now! They are at Rennes, Cherbourg, Avranches, which is near enough. It is amazing; they seem to be flooding the country.

Practically all the English have now left, even the Air Force, we have not heard one single plane since last night and as a result I slept beautifully!

No response yet from Hitler as to the terms of the Armistice, but I believe the decision has been made. The Radio says we cannot expect to hear anything before this evening.

I cannot express how I feel since having news of Philippe, meager as it is; it brings much relief, hope and confidence. Poor Nicole, I wish she knew as much regarding Michel.

....

Thursday, June 20, 1940

No response yet from Hitler, that is for the public. The Germans are at Lyon and Nantes! They are also a mile from us at La Richardais . . .[97] A

97. The Germans were continuing their advance both eastward to Nantes on the Loire River and beyond and southward to Lyon. La Richardais is 1.7 kilometers south of Dinard.

gasoline barge has anchored on the beach and was selling gas at 3 Frs. the liter instead of 4.85. When we heard of this, we decided to fill up, but we got there too late and fell on five Germans that had arrived on motorcycles well armed and that had taken over the barge! They were in their grey green uniforms and helmets leaning on their rifles, looking dead tired, and not at all like triumphal invaders. We went up to them all the same and asked if we could have gas. Of course they said "no." This is my first experience meeting the enemy. Not very dramatic, fortunately! It only disgusted me to see those ruthless "Bosche" in this gorgeous country.[98] That was my reaction.

The post has completely stopped, so I can expect no word from anyone, nor can I send any. At Dinard, the people are emptying the stores, because they know that once everything is sold there will be no replacements, at least for a certain length of time. We were able to stock up a bit too.

There have been no French broadcasts for the first time today. Thank goodness, we can get news from England. Otherwise we would not know what is happening.[99]

....

Friday, June 21, 1940

We do not yet know Hitler's terms. Although we do know that the French parliamentaries met Hitler, Ribbentrop, etc. in the same railway carriage in which the Armistice was signed in 1918 in the forest of Compiègne. Hitler thus occupied the chair which had been occupied by Maréchal Foch in the day when the Allies had won the war. What a blow to the pride of the French![100]

98. Bosche is a denigrating term for German that was in widespread use by the French during the war.

99. Following the defeat of France, the BBC regularly directed forbidden broadcasts to the people of France.

100. The terms of the German armistice were given to the French on June 21. The formal signing of the armistice at Compiègne occurred on June 22 in the same railway carriage in which Germany had surrendered to French Maréchal Ferdinand Foch on November 11, 1918. Among those present were Hitler's minister of foreign affairs, Joachim von Ribbentrop.

Saturday, June 22, 1940

American journalists' eyewitnesses at Compiègne have reported that the Armistice has been signed between France and Germany. However, it will not become effective until France has also signed with Italy where French plenipotentiaries are flying today, to meet with Mussolini. Is France selling her soul? She has said repeatedly that she would not sign a dishonorable peace, but what is a dishonorable peace from her point of view? It seems to me that we are in no position to dictate what we will or will not sign! This suspense is terrible and in the meantime the battle of France continues but with less intensity.[101]

Four hundred German soldiers have arrived in Dinard and have taken over the Hotel Royal, they would . . . First they have thoroughly examined the Rance to make certain that we have not hidden any boats that they can use for invasion purposes. Up to the moment, they have been very polite and do nothing out of the way except to empty people's gas tanks! But . . . how long can they remain gentlemen?

Sunday, June 23, 1940

France has capitulated, and according to the English broadcast, it is shameful capitulation which the French would never have made, had they not been forced to do so. The terms allow Germany to utilize the resources and land of this country against their present enemy Great Britain! Fighting will cease six hours after Germany has been notified of the signing of the Italian terms.[102]

Already we are able to feel the enemy pressure. Today in going to Dinard, we found all the clocks advanced one hour to German time (Central European). In passing the Hotel Royal where most Germans are, I was passed by and audaciously stared at by two officers. All of this makes my blood boil.

The Germans are encouraging the refugees to return to their homes, and those who go are given gas and have the best routes mapped out for them. We hear that certain trains will start running again tomorrow, and

101. French forces that had been driven from the Maginot Line continued to fight until finally surrendering under orders from General Weygand.

102. The Franco-Italian armistice was concluded on June 24. The following day, June 25, the Franco-German armistice was put in force.

that soon, all services in Paris will be working again. We are warned to be very careful in what we say in public as Germans in civilian clothes are all over the place listening. Thus we have begun a new existence under the Nazi regime! We are beginning to experience those regulations that have shocked us for the last few years knowing of their existence in Germany! What a blow for France and for the whole civilized world.

2 Life after the Fall of France

JUNE 24, 1940–AUGUST 29, 1940

Monday, June 24, 1940

France has to hand over all her army matériel and resources to Germany, plus the greater part of her metropolitan land area; all to be employed against her ally. She has now no independent government, and will be allowed only a small armed force in the unoccupied region south of a line drawn from Geneva to Tours. All the west coast is to remain under German control. Our army is to be demobilized at once except those who were taken prisoner. These will not be released until peace is signed. Hitler does not mention peace terms at this point, so it could be in years! Also the cost of the occupation is to be supported by the French in the meantime! These are the terms of the Armistice that France has signed in the forest of Compiègne.[1]

In London, the French General de Gaulle is organizing a Committee of France, which will be legal, in cooperation with the British Government. This organization will represent independent France in opposition to the Government put in place by the Germans and will uphold the treaty obligations of France with her ally. General de Gaulle has been deprived of his military rank for all of this by the French German-controlled Government

---

1. The terms of the armistice created a zone of occupation that included Paris, northern France, the Atlantic coast, and French borders with Belgium and Switzerland. The southern part of France remained unoccupied; a collaborationist government, headed by Pétain, was established at Vichy, a famous spa some 320 kilometers southeast of Paris. Unoccupied France, along with French colonies, was administered by the Vichy government. French prisoners of war, estimated at 1.8 million, remained in German hands. Except for a small "Armistice Army" of one hundred thousand that was maintained to help keep domestic order in the Unoccupied Zone, the French army was demobilized. The French fleet was to be disarmed, and France was required to assume the cost of occupation, which would total about $2 billion a year.

but that matters not a penny! Thank goodness there are men with still some fight in them!!²

....

Tuesday, June 25, 1940

Today is the day that prophecy marked to stop the invaders on the Loire river, but it seems that we are the ones to be stopped. We handed down arms yesterday evening at midnight, six hours after Hitler was notified of the signing of the Franco/Italian Armistice in Rome. We still do not know the terms of this Armistice, but it is disgraceful to think that we had to sign it with a country who has up to date suffered practically nothing of the fighting, much less reduced us to a state of surrender.

Today is also National mourning day as proclaimed by the Pétain Government. At 11 AM there is to be a minute of silence in honor of the dead, many of them useless dead.³ Why on June 13th, when Pétain decided we could resist no longer, did our men continue to fight? Why this waiting of six hours after the signing of the Italian Armistice? I know nothing of strategic tactics, but I feel we have been duped badly. The selfish side of

2. In a June 18, 1940, BBC Broadcast from London, General Charles de Gaulle delivered a stirring speech in which he told the French people: "This war has not been settled by the Battle of France. This war is a world war . . . whatever happens the flame of resistance must not and will not be extinguished." He also appealed to French officers, soldiers, and workmen in the British territories to join him in the fight against Germany. Quoted in John Keegan, *The Second World War* (New York: Penguin Books, 1989), p. 86. Evidently Virginia heard this broadcast. De Gaulle founded the Free French, an anti-German and anti-Vichy movement that included French forces who had been evacuated to England. On June 28 Britain recognized de Gaulle as the "Leader of All Free Frenchmen" and gave financial support to the Free French. For his actions de Gaulle was charged with treason and condemned to death by the government at Vichy. While de Gaulle argued that the Vichy government was illegal, he "was technically a dissident and rebel," which made "his position [in London] more precarious than that of the formally constituted governments in exile." Jackson, *France: The Dark Years*, p. 134. Jackson argues that "the radio was his [de Gaulle's] most powerful weapon. The Free French had fives minutes on the BBC every evening." In addition, "French broadcasts of the BBC . . . increased from two and a half hours daily in 1940 to five hours in 1942." Ibid., p. 398.

3. Julian Jackson puts the number of French soldiers killed during the Battle of France at between fifty thousand and ninety thousand. Jackson, *The Fall of France*, p. 180.

me wants my darling back here with me and yet I would have wanted the remaining French forces to be able to escape to Algeria, England, in order to continue the fight. It does not make much sense.[4]

....

Wednesday, June 26, 1940

We are becoming more "Nazified" every day. No one is allowed to be away from home after 10 PM. That is no one in the streets or in public places. It is forbidden to walk at any time in the street; people must remain on the sidewalks. What does one do when there is no sidewalk?! Public places are not to dial their radios to English broadcasts, and we, the people, are recommended to listen to the German broadcasts "as the English tell us only lies." Private owners of cars are forbidden to use them except for business, not for traveling or for personal needs. Special permits are to be given to those that can prove that they need a car and they will receive a gasoline allowance, and a special windshield sticker. If one breaks the law, the fine will be 5000 Frs. What a life!

Marie-Louise's parents and Madame Fénié, our refugees, must leave for home within 24 hours. They went to Dinard to ask for a gasoline allowance, and when it was discovered that they were refugees, they were commanded to leave for their home and handed the necessary papers. There are very upset as they are happy here and so in need of a rest.

All these German regulations and restrictions were printed in a newspaper published at St. Malo.

....

Thursday, June 27, 1940

We have been cutting roses, and enjoying their loveliness and the fun in arranging them. I completely forgot about the war and the aftermaths

4. On June 13, at a meeting of the French cabinet held at Château de Cangé, Pétain, having joined Reynaud's government on May 18, read a statement in support of an armistice because this was "the necessary condition of the durability of eternal France." Quoted ibid., p. 125. It was on June 17, the day that Pétain took office as prime minister, that he announced that he would seek an armistice with Germany. As many as half of the 1.8 million French prisoners of war captured by the Germans during the Battle of France were captured during the six days between Pétain's June 17 announcement and the actual signing of the armistice on June 22. For an examination of how French wives coped during the absence of their prisoner-of-war husbands, see Sarah Fishman, *We Will Wait: Wives of French Prisoners of War, 1940–1945* (New Haven: Yale University Press, 1991).

of the Armistice. Thank God there is such a thing as nature, which in its seasonal manifestation, always the same, gives us something stable on which we can lean and in which we can lose ourselves.

We have difficulty in getting the English broadcast. They are being blotted out, especially those in French emanating from "The French committee under British control" as the Germans say.[5]

Yesterday we learned the conditions of the Italian Armistice. The French colonies on the Mediterranean must be demilitarized, all arms and equipments handed over. This includes the ports in the south of France and also Djibouti.[6]

....

Saturday, June 29, 1940

I wonder where my Philippe is. Oh how I wish he would come! Some of the family think that he may be in the Unoccupied Zone and not allowed to come here. I do not believe this. I know of no soldiers who have come home yet. It takes time to demobilize a large number of troops and with almost no trains running how can a poor soldier get home in a hurry? It is all a call for patience.

Life is almost too beautiful and easy here. The days are summer ones full of roses and blue skies. The Rance is gentle and of the most beautiful coloring. With the two Yvonnes doing the cooking and house work, the rest of us have little responsibility. I feed the twenty rabbits that Madame Férié had to leave behind, work in the garden, read, write, gather flowers, etc. The days pass easily as long as I have no time to think of my separation from Philippe. There is so much to enjoy, I must take advantage of what I have.

I often think of my poor family in the United States, they must be craving news of me, and at this point I do not know when I will be able to write? Letters from here go no further than Rennes. I miss Mother's letters, but it is a different thing, they are not in a war torn German infested country![7]

5. The French section of the BBC broadcast programs were intended to undermine and destroy enemy morale while supporting and stimulating the resistance.

6. These areas remained under Vichy, not Italian, control. Djibouti, in eastern Africa bordering the Gulf of Aden and the Red Sea, was at that time a French colony.

7. Virginia's communication with her family in the United States remained sporadic during the war.

Nicole went to Dinard to ask for a permit and gas allowance in order to return to Paris. She had to wait three hours in a long queue, but the men contacted finally were very polite, helpful, and even conciliatory!! One must not forget however that Nicole is an attractive woman.

We are very careful with the Radio, closing all doors and windows, also keeping it tuned very low when we listen to London, which is several times a day.[8]

....

Tuesday, July 2, 1940

Still no news of Philippe, but I consider it is still too early to expect any.

We hear all sorts of rumours, and because I mention them does not mean that they are true! Hitler is to enter Paris on July 14th, France's Independence day![9] Himmler, the chief of the German Gestapo, has established his headquarters in Paris.[10] The population there is having difficulty in getting supplies now; one must stand in line to get potatoes!

At Dinard, more Germans seem to be arriving, and the town is to be a center of high command. An Admiral is already there. It seems that the Germans are very pleased with the population at Dinard. Hence folks can stay out until 11 PM. But at St. Malo, they must be in by 9: PM as they have not welcomed the enemy in the same spirit! The Germans are buying sugar and coffee to send home. German planes fly over us continually at Cancaval, so low that we easily see the black and white crosses on the wings. That always gives me a shock.

Even from England we get very little news of what is going on in France. Germany and England continue to make air raids on each other,

8. Although it was forbidden to listen to British radio, the BBC remained popular throughout the war.

9. Hitler made only one trip to Paris and that was for a few hours during the early morning of June 23, 1940.

10. It appears that Virginia has confused the Gestapo, Geheime Staatspolizei, the Secret State Police, with the SS, Schutzstaffel, the elite military force within the Nazi party. Heinrich Himmler was chief of the SS; his responsibilities included overseeing the Nazi concentration camp system. The Gestapo was the main investigative body of the SS and was headed up by Reinhard Heydrich. According to Julian Jackson, "The Nazi power-brokers—Goebbels, Goering, Himmler, Ribbentrop—all had representatives in France." However, he provides no evidence that Himmler was in Paris. Jackson, *France: The Dark Years*, p. 170.

but as yet there has been no offensive, although the Germans are now occupying all the Channel Islands.[11]

....

Thursday, July 4, 1940
Independence Day in the United States! Vive les Etats-Unis![12]
The English are taking under control the warships of the French navy which had taken refuge in the port of Alexandria. The French admiral wanted to comply with the terms of the Armistice so the British used force.[13]

Germans in Pleurtuit this morning stopped all cars in order to verify they had the right to be on the road.[14]

German planes constantly flying over us. It seems there are more and more!

In the meantime we are dashing about with sugar, bread, and food ration cards, but there is no sugar to be had even with ration cards. Gas is shut off part of the day, electricity also.[15]

11. German troops invaded the long-demilitarized British islands of Jersey and Guernsey, located ten to thirty miles off the French coast, on June 30, 1940. The islands were the only British possessions occupied by Germany during World War II.

12. Long live the United States!

13. According to the terms of the armistice, the French fleet was to be disarmed, but the Vichy government was allowed to retain custody of the French fleet docked at Toulon. Fearful that French ships docked outside Toulon might fall into the hands of the Germans, the British, without major incident, took control of French warships that were docked at British ports, the British base of Alexandria, and several French African ports. On July 7, following four days of negotiation, the French commander at Alexandria allowed the British to take control of his ships without any fighting. By contrast, at Mers el-Kébir in Algeria, where French warships were also docked, a peaceful accommodation was not possible, and on July 3 the British navy attacked and disabled four ships as they tried to leave the harbor. Seven other ships succeeded in getting away and crossing the Mediterranean to Toulon. In the process, more than sixteen hundred French sailors were killed or wounded. The events at Mers el-Kébir brought forth an angry anti-British reaction in France. Similarly, on July 7–8 a British carrier damaged a French battleship at Dakar Harbor on Africa's west coast. A French ship docked at Casablanca was also attacked by the British.

14. Pleurtuit is a small town near Dinard.

15. Following the defeat of France in June 1940, German requisitioning almost immediately led to food and fuel shortages. On how French women coped with shortages and rationing, see Hanna Diamond, *Women and the Second World War in France, 1939–1948* (Essex, Eng.: Longman, 1999), pp. 49–70.

No news from occupied France, no news regarding the rest of the French Army. The only newspapers available are those under German supervision and full of lies of course. No mail, few trains. No way of sending news home to the States.

The Germans I have seen certainly conduct themselves discreetly. They may be ordered to do so! But they play the part with seeming ease and natural inclination. One in a café yesterday in struggling French was saying, "Français, bons camarades. Nous ne voulons pas la guerre, c'est affreux, terrible."[16] But it is always the simple soldier in no matter what country that is sincere and sympathetic.[17]

I wonder if the calm unperturbed way that the French in Dinard are accepting the invaders is not more a spirit of not caring than one of fear. It may be another sign of the decline of this country. People fired with love of country and possessing a sense of national unity and consciousness would never treat the traditional enemy as if they were no more than tourists butting in to their peace and every day freedom. That is all I can see besides a visible childlike curiosity they have for these newcomers.

On the other hand what would pride and stubborn will bring, other than unfortunate incidents that would be cruelly punished. Perhaps the individual Frenchman does not hate the individual German, but sees him as a poor fellow, like himself dragged into war against his will and separated from home and those he loves?[18]

....

Friday, July 5, 1940
The post office tells us that from now on mail is back to normal. Nicole has had a letter from Michel. I am simply dying to have one from

16. French, good friends. We don't want war, it's awful, terrible.

17. Virginia's wartime observations about the conduct of German troops here and elsewhere in her diary support the findings of Robert Gildea, *Marianne in Chains: In Search of the German Occupation, 1940–45* (London: Macmillan, 2002), especially pp. 65–88, 414–422. Gildea concludes (p. 415) that "ordinary French and Germans . . . learned to live together. German atrocities feared by the French population in the summer of 1940 never took place."

18. These observations also support Gildea's conclusions; he disagrees with those historians who have portrayed the French as "passive victims of the Occupation." Although acknowledging that the country was in a state of shock, he focuses on how ordinary people adopted strategies, created networks, and subverted institutions "in order to negotiate the tricky passage through the Occupation." Ibid., p. 414.

Philippe. When no mail deliveries were made and no one was receiving letters, it was easier to wait. Now I am going to live for the postman!!'[19]

The English did a drastic but necessary thing when they fired on the French fleet yesterday in order to prevent them from falling into the hands of the enemy. However it is a real tragedy and I fear the French will resent this. One can understand the French not wanting their fleet to join allied forces thus breaking the terms of the Armistice and risking having the entire country worse off than it already is. On the other hand, could the British be sure that the Germans would not lay their hands on these ships sooner or later? England has a mighty navy, but with the German, Italian, and French fleets against her, she would face great difficulties. Thus she has decided to face this menace although it meant killing Frenchmen and destroying part of the fleet. I do not believe she had any other alternative. What can one expect; war seen from any angle is a beastly atrocity.[20]

....

Saturday, July 6, 1940

There has been an amazing movement of planes since early this morning. To see these powerful bombers fly in formation over the house gives me a feeling of hopelessness and desolation. It is like being in a chair, chained, and watching someone you love being strangled to death. That is an attitude of the present however. When looking up to the final issue, the sun comes out from under the cloud.

....

Monday, July 8, 1940

The French (Pétain) government is to change its constitution and will become totalitarian in principle.[21]

In their hurried departure from St. Malo, the English dumped hand grenades in the sea. In an exceptional high tide yesterday some were

19. According to Robert O. Paxton, by August 1940 "only three hundred letters a day were allowed to cross [the demarcation line] at a moment when millions of Frenchmen were trying to locate their families." Robert O. Paxton, *Vichy France: Old Guard and New Order, 1940–1944* (New York: Columbia University Press, 2001), p. 53.

20. This is a reference to the events of July 3 at Mers el-Kébir in Algeria.

21. On July 4 the French cabinet approved a plan to give Pétain the power to revise the constitution.

washed up on the beach at St. Servan.[22] Innocent children were delighted to find such a strange toy, threw them against rocks, and as a result three of the children were seriously wounded!

Went to Dinard yesterday and never once was out of sight of Germans! They are everywhere; many of them race about in high speed owned cars, sport types. Others were having tea at "Le Bras," the most famous pastry shop in town, and many many were on the beach.

Whew! While writing those last words, five Germans arrived here!! Asking for the stables to put as many horses as possible and several men. I must move the car, the rabbits, etc. No more time to write now.

....

Tuesday, July 9, 1940

Well, we are now sharing Cancaval with five Germans and eight of their horses. They say they are to be here for several days. Tante Germaine and Grandmère who both speak German, conversed with them a bit. In asking them where they had been before coming here, they said: "Holland, Belgium, France, Paris and would soon be in England." They are tired, as they go to bed at midnight and are up at 4: A M always. Here however they hope to be able to rest a bit.

They come to the kitchen to ask for coffee, cider, wine, but Azeline, the cook, always replies that we have none! Up to now they have accepted her answers.[23] They all are young and very simple, of the most ordinary class, but certainly are behaving themselves.

There are more at the Château du Montmarin, our neighbours, than here and they are on top of the de Jessey's, as the courtyard is directly back of the house. Here we are more fortunate and we do not see very much of them.

....

Wednesday, July 10, 1940

Just received an airmail letter from home written on the 17th of June! Parts of my letters are being published! Am I thrilled.[24] The Pétain

22. St. Servan is just south of Saint-Malo. More than twenty-one thousand Allied troops were evacuated from Saint-Malo on June 16 and 17, 1940.

23. Gildea argues that this type of "non-cooperation" was the principal response of rural communities to "repeated [German] demands for meat, milk, eggs, potatoes, wheat and oats." Gildea, *Marianne in Chains*, p. 128.

24. Virginia's letters to her parents were published in the *St. Petersburg Times*. See, for example, Lillian Blackstone, "Tragic Story of French Defeat Is Told in Local

government has succeeded in having a favourable vote on the new constitution by 569 votes to 80.[25]

At present the war is continuing between England on one hand, Germany and Italy on the other. German air attacks are getting heavier every day and I am afraid the English are in for a heavy attack this morning! For the last half hour our German bombers have been heading north and they are still passing. Also, I cannot tune in to an English radio station, all this seems to prove it!![26]

The plot is thickening! Two noncommissioned officers have arrived and requisitioned a room in the house! What next?

....

July 14, 1940
France is mourning today. The 14th of July is "La Fête Nationale" here but after the defeat it is not a day of celebration but one of remembrance and prayer.[27]

For me, it is celebration and how! My darling is safe. Received two cards yesterday and three letters today! He has had no news from us, so in expressing his concern for us he says little about himself; except that

---

Girl's Letter," *St. Petersburg Times*, July 10, 1940; Lillian Blackstone, "Local Girl Becomes a Refugee, Sees Horror of War Bombing," *St. Petersburg Times*, July 15, 1940; and "Life in France Is Being Germanized, Former St. Petersburg Girl Writes," *St. Petersburg Times*, August 6, 1940.

25. On July 10 the French parliament, by a vote of 569 to 80, gave Pétain full powers to revise the constitution. The following day, July 11, Pétain terminated the Third Republic, declared himself to be head of the French State, and dismissed parliament until further notice. This meant that "Pétain now had more power than any French leader since Louis XIV." Jackson, *France: The Dark Years*, p. 133.

26. This was the first phase of the air battle that came to be called the Battle of Britain. The main phase of the battle began on August 13 and did not end until October 31. The German air force, the Luftwaffe, lost 1,733 aircraft to British fighters and antiaircraft guns and failed to gain aerial superiority over Britain. The RAF lost 915 fighters.

27. July 14, a national holiday in France, commemorates the storming of the Bastille by angry citizens during the French Revolution on July 14, 1789. The event became a symbol that power no longer resided in the king but in the people. Few French people were in a mood to celebrate on July 14, 1940. France had suffered a resounding defeat by the Germans, and just three days earlier Pétain had abolished the Third Republic.

he had been very fortunate. His unit had belonged to the "arrière garde"[28] in the retreat and all they did was to fall back constantly. Now they are at Bussière-Galant, a small town in the Haute Vienne, about 30 Kms south west of Limoges.[29]

Twice he mentions that perhaps I should go back to the United States. Knowing that he loves me deeply, he has expressed the greatest unselfishness in suggesting it. But I can't. I love him too much to leave him, and besides I see no real reason to do so. If America entered the war, perhaps, but I will not take such a serious decision in the face of a future so undecided. No, it is here I belong and it is here that I stay.[30]

....

July 15, 1940

I appear to have a German admirer. While going to La Richardais on my bicycle I passed him riding horseback. By means of sign language he asked me to mount too! When I returned he was in the courtyard of the Montmarin, saw me, and shortly after came to the house. We talked more sign language. It was so funny; but I understood that he had no wife or children, and would like me to go swimming and boating with him. I described with great force the attributes of my husband, and replied "NEIN" to all the rest. This particular German is more distinguished than the others we have here. He is tall, has a moustache, a good athletic build, and does not look like a duck when he walks. He is up in 30 someplace. Nicole says she never could try talking to a German, and I understand it is solely because he is German. I think it is fun and interesting from many points of view. As far as going boating, swimming, and horseback, that is something else!![31]

28. Rear guard.

29. Bussière-Galant and Limoges were in the Unoccupied Zone.

30. When war broke out in Europe, more than eighty thousand American citizens lived abroad. The State Department urged American citizens living in danger zones to return to the United States. It sent five ships to Europe in 1939 and four more in 1940 to bring home U.S. citizens living in the European war zone. Mitchell G. Bard, *Forgotten Victims: The Abandonment of Americans in Hitler's Camps* (Boulder, Colo.: Westview Press, 1994), pp. 7–8.

31. Gildea devotes considerable attention to the relations between French and Germans under the occupation and argues that these relationships "cannot be reduced to German oppression confronted by French patriotism. Despite the obvious inequality of power between the parties, interactions between the two were multifaceted, subtle and often complex." Gildea, *Marianne in Chains*, p. 67. Certainly, this is

July 18, 1940

Indirectly we learn that Philippe has news of us!

There are more and more Germans at Dinard. We hear that Goering is being expected there.[32] At that rate it will soon be Hitler. Yesterday we heard three bombs fall not far away, followed by cannon and anti-aircraft fire. It gives me a strange feeling knowing that we are in the midst of our enemy and enemy firing at our ally.

All civilians living near Dinard airport have been evacuated.

Received Mother's June 3rd letter.[33] She says my May 10th letter from Nesles was published on the front page of the [St. Petersburg] *Times*. Whew. She mentions several opinions of people on my present situation. One was that my husband should have forced me to come home, but Philippe and I look at things very differently. Our love makes us as one. I know that because of it Philippe encouraged me to go home when the situation became serious. While I, because of it, refuse to go. His love for me expresses itself in his desiring my safety above all else, while mine refuses to let me run away from the danger that is ours to endure together, not for us to run away from home. Some one would probably say that Philippe would feel happier knowing I were safe, but I know Philippe better than that and myself too. Apart, life for us ceases to matter. We would both be sick with unhappiness. Suppose I had returned home. Being American when would I be allowed to return to France, and how? Instead I am here, not far from the only one in the world who really matters to me, with the certain prospect of having him soon again in my arms. All of this time with death and danger all around, not once have I been in a situation desperate or frightening. I lay it all down to feeling no fear. If I had been afraid, I would have gone home long ago. Without it I have been able to think and act deliberately for it is in fear that people

---

an accurate description of the relationship between Virginia and her admiring German soldier.

32. With the outbreak of World War II, Adolf Hitler appointed Hermann Göring in charge of the Luftwaffe. Göring took credit for the quick defeat of Luxembourg, the Netherlands, Belgium, and France in the summer of 1940. He also organized the German war effort during the Battle of Britain and the London Blitz. Nonetheless, the Luftwaffe failed to gain aerial superiority over Britain. No evidence was found that Göring visited Dinard.

33. It would be almost six months before Virginia would again hear from her family in the United States.

act foolishly. But it is not that I avoided having it by refusing to acknowledge it. It is because of a faith I have of God's goodness and his protection over us. It sounds trite to express it, but it is a belief that lives in my heart.

....

July 19, 1940
Daddy's 63rd birthday!

Well after Nicole and I spent a day and a half cleaning and arranging the billiard room, the Germans have come to claim it as theirs. This morning a splendid looking officer, and two subordinates came to ask for a room to be used as reading, writing, and play room, a general foyer. Grandmère encouraged them to use the pavilion on the Rance, but they found it too far away, too damp and without electric light. Always they were very amiable and polite, like the young and pretty wife who gets everything she wants by the same agreeable methods! However, we know that nothing can prevent them from taking over the entire house if they wish to, so long as they last we appreciate their good manners.

In returning to Cancaval this morning by the back entrance I saw the Germans leading their horses to pasture. Just as I entered here came one of them that had broken away coming in behind me at a lope! He did not have a bit nor bridle, only a rope around his neck, which I grabbed. He dragged me half the way across the lawn to the kitchen. He was under control just as two of the men arrived with smiles of admiration on their faces! I was amused. Fifteen minutes later here came the famous noncommissioned officer who Nicole tells me came several times yesterday to the house, seemingly to meet me! He told me that he had heard what I had done and that I was not to attempt such a thing again! Then he remained to repair the fish net that I was working on.

....

July 21, 1940
Another Sunday, and rain all day! I do not know what the Germans are going to think of our climate!

Letter from Philippe yesterday dated 15th of July. He has no direct news of us yet, no letters. He says he may be sent to Nesles when he is demobilized. I would like nothing better! We are both feeling the urge to start work again. We have wasted enough time on their war.

No special news here. We hear rumours all the time, but do not know which are true and which are not. Goering is said to be in Dinard and a member of his air-force was found hung in Pleurtuit after he had expressed his displeasure at risking his life in going to bombard England. The Germans in the same town buy Champagne but empty it at once from the original bottles into various containers, that is while they are still in the store. Such sacrilege!

My admirer, the noncommissioned officer came hunting again, but this time he met Mum. She knows and understands some German so they conversed. He was born in Dresden, the same year that Mum was there 1905! Now he lives in Leipzig. Before the war was an engineer, is not married but has the intention to do so upon returning to Germany, up to now he has not had time for that. Says England is a little place that will easily be conquered, Germany is BIG!! Says the Jews should work in the fields, manual labor etc, not in commercial enterprises! Mum told him that I was her daughter-in-law, hoping to discourage him. He does not seem to be in the mood however! The privates have their horses to groom, but he has nothing to do but see that it is done as he is the "high man" around here.

A new German decree has just come out. All farmland owners must declare their property and must plant only those products decreed by German authority.[34] England is doing the same at present in order to have enough of the lacking and essential products she needs.

....

July 22, 1940

The first sign of a haughty unpleasant German, an officer, stood out when he came to inspect the men at the Montmarin. Jean, who being from the Saar and speaking German fluently, told this officer that the men occupying the property had been very correct. At once he turned her statement into an affront replying in a sarcastic manner, "Germans are always correct. It is only the English and French who are not."

Certain staples are becoming very difficult to find. Laundry soap is unobtainable. Canned sardines etc., sugar, coffee, rice, all very difficult to

34. One reason the French suffered from food shortages throughout the war years was the German control and requisitioning of French produce.

find, even with ration cards.[35] Coal is no longer being delivered and we have almost none left.[36] What a life, and it rains all the time.

We hear that all unmarried people between 18 & 35, girls included, must register at the Town Hall, in order to be given work. For the Germans I presume.[37]

Germany has impressed its criminal law on Holland. Beware those who dare to oppose the Nazi regime.[38]

During that time, Nicole and I fished shrimps yesterday. We caught most of them in sea puddles left by the tide and only with our hands. The nets were impractical due to the stones under which the little rascals swam for safety.

....

Friday, July 26, 1940

Philippe has written "Come if you can" and I am going. Went to the Town Hall in Pleurtuit yesterday to see if I had the right to go. From there I was sent to the German Kommandantur where I was politely received by two officers. The interpreter observed my English accent and I told him I was American. He appeared surprised but pleased. He said he spoke English a little but continued speaking in French. I was told that he would have to get my authorization from Dinard and that he would let me know the result. They examined my passport and took my name and address.

Afterwards I went to the Railway station, found out I could go by train, changing eight times for a distance of roughly 350 miles! Had to change at Dinan, Dol, Rennes, Redon, Nantes, Saintes, Limoges, and one more place. The station master said it would require two full days (and nights incidentally). I plan to go to Rennes by bus however, thus saving three

35. Rationing began in the summer of 1940 and by September most essential goods were rationed. Julian Jackson notes that "the level of rations for the largest category of the population was 1,327 calories per day as opposed to an average of 3,000 per day before the war." Jackson, *France: The Dark Years*, pp. 249–250.

36. The French also suffered from fuel shortages, including a scarcity of coal, throughout the war years.

37. During World War II the Germans conscripted thousands of Frenchmen and -women to work in French and German factories.

38. Following the defeat of the Dutch on May 15 and the subsequent exile of Queen Wilhelmina to London, the Germans installed a civil administrator, Arthur Seyss-Inquart, to rule Holland.

hours. Will leave I hope, Tuesday morning and this whether the Germans give me a pass or not!

A German churchman (priest) came to the de Jesseys to ask for the use of their Chapel for a service. The priest invited the de Jesseys to attend. The service lasted two hours and was divided into both Catholic and Protestant. At the end they sang together a prayer for victory! of whom?

Some friends who have a large château near here came home one day to find their sitting-room and front lawn full of Germans listening to Hitler's speech by means of their radio!

Another family we know, with a large house have 25 men living there and a yard full of military equipment.

An acquaintance of Grandmère, who lives alone in her house except for an invalid son, had her house taken over by the Germans and was forced to move to a tiny room in the attic. They are also using her vegetable garden on which she ordinarily lived as she has little cash.

Probably the main reason for the fact that we have not been taken over yet, is that we are near Dinard where they find more convenient accommodation.

"Our Germans" put horse manure in our garden yesterday. They have also cleaned the eaves of the stables etc. and repaired the roof! Nothing like having one's victorious enemy do one's dirty work! These men are nice and I find it fun trying to communicate with them. The noncommissioned officer no longer impresses himself. Guess he understood or found someone else!

My request for a pass to join Philippe has been refused without explanation. As I said earlier, I have decided to go anyway! I am taking my bicycle, so when I cannot find a train or a bus, I will hop on my bicycle. This is going to be quite an adventure no doubt; even more of an adventure now that the Germans have stopped all intercommunications by rail between the occupied zone and the free zone where Philippe is of course.[39] So, off for an adventure! Will continue my journal later and am leaving it behind as I do not wish to be intimidated in any way by carrying it with me.

---

39. Travel between the Occupied and Unoccupied Zones was extremely difficult and by August the demarcation line had become a "virtual sealed frontier." Paxton, *Vichy France*, p. 53.

August 29, 1940[40]

Left Cancaval on Monday July 29th in the afternoon. Cycled in to Dinard and spent the night at Mlle Lavoquer's house.

Took bus for Rennes at 7: AM Tuesday July 30th. The bus was crowded. At Rennes, I bought a train ticket to Nantes and registered my bicycle. Went to the German Kommandantur to ask again for a permit to go to the non-occupied zone. This was refused but had my identity card stamped by the French police. Lunched at Restaurant held by a cousin of Mlle Lavoquer. Rennes overrun by Germans. My train left at 2: PM. Changed at Redon where I had to wait 30 minutes.

Beautiful hilly country from Rennes. Four Germans in my compartment, also old Frenchman and young woman in mourning. The Germans tried having fun with me. Reached Nantes at 9: PM. All large hotels requisitioned, but finally found a room 20 minutes from the station.

On train to Saintes five ordinary Frenchmen shared my compartment. They were very nice, three of them worked for a railroad company. Four of them had seen the last war and one this one. The latter was returning home without his left arm plus head and back wounds. He was awkward in the use of his available arm. We all helped him, cut his bread, poured his wine, opened his can of tuna fish. He was sweet, gracious, and brave. Only when his face was in repose did we discern the suffering. Wounded in Dunkerque in June, taken prisoner in Belgium frontier hospital and finally escaped from Paris Plage Hospital. All were concerned about my trying to enter the non-occupied zone without a permit. One even gave me his address in the vicinity of Saintes should I have difficulty. We passed by way of La Roche-sur-Yon and La Rochelle following the sea.

At Saintes, I was promised a ticket to Limoges on the following morning, was thrilled. Found nice room in station hotel, after having been to the Town Hall to have my identity card stamped again, I visited the town. Ancient Cathedral, main street lined with Plane trees, Roman ruins, all rather typical in sight and smell of a Mediterranean city. Had a drink at a sidewalk café and watched men playing bowls.[41]

40. This long entry, written from Nesles, follows Virginia's journey to Bussière-Galant in the Unoccupied Zone and her return with Philippe to Cancaval and then Nesles. She was away for almost a month; she and Philippe did not make their way back to Cancaval until August 23. Map 1 provides details of this journey.

41. Bowls, or *jeu de boules*, is a popular outdoor game in France that uses balls and is usually played by men. In Italy it is called *bocce*.

Left Saintes at 9:30 next morning. Arrived at Angoulême at 12:30. Told once again that it was forbidden to enter the non-occupied zone. No tickets being sold! I was surprised to find I had been sold one to Limoges. The ticket manager suggested I might take a chance in getting there. I felt hot and miserable at the thought of being turned back. I could not even eat lunch nor enjoy the picturesque old town built on a high cliff overlooking a river, hills, and wooded country.

Boarded my train at 3:PM in low spirits, very few people on the train, shared my compartment with two Germans, when we reached the frontier they got off, but another one got on and this one asked me for my permit! I showed him my ticket to Limoges and identity card. By means of an interpreter he asked me if I were going to stay in the non-occupied zone? My reply was affirmative and I pointed to my wedding ring and showed the direction of the free zone. "Mon mari là-bas," I said.[42] The German repeated the word in French, understood, smiled and let me pass. I was so thrilled that I almost went crazy, but did not dare to be too sure before the train really moved! After a little while that seemed ages to me, it did!

On entering the free zone I felt a heaviness fall away as there were no more grey-green uniforms in sight. Reached Limoges at 8:PM. Station jammed with refugees but all ticket windows closed! My ticket was marked through to Bussière-Galant which was to be the end of my journey, but there was no train until 5:30 AM. I was hungry following my extreme relief, so went to a Restaurant near the station. The city was over-crowded with refugees and French soldiers. No place to sleep but I enjoyed a good meal, told the waiter I had no place to spend the night and to my amazement he answered that I was welcome to spend it in the Restaurant! The place closed at 9: PM, lights out. They gave me a pillow and I stretched out on a "banquette." Slept well until the night watchman woke me at 4:30 AM. At the station, I found the whole floor covered with prostrate sleeping forms. They all had been unable to find accommodation for the night. I took my train and reached Bussière an hour and a half later. It seemed a dream when I saw the station appear. Could it be true that I had succeeded in my enterprise of crossing the new frontier that divides France without a permit and also without too much difficulty!!

42. My husband [is] there.

Map 1, France

Route of Virginia's exodus from Le Perray to
Cancaval, June 11–12, 1940

. . . .

Route of Virginia's journey, July 29–
August 23, 1940

1. Dinard (Cancaval)	*Creuse River*
2. Rennes	16. St. Aignan
3. Redon	*Loire River*
4. Nantes	17. Montrichard
5. La Roche-sur-Yon	18. Amboise
6. La Rochelle	19. Tours
7. Saintes	20. Luynes
8. Angoulême	21. Saumur
9. Limoges	22. Angers
10. Bussière-Galant	23. Candé
11. Chalus	24. Châteaubriant
12. Rochechouard	25. Rennes
13. Bussière-Poitevine	26. Dinan
Vienne River	27. Pleurtuit
14. Chauvigny	28. Dinard (Cancaval)
15. La Roche Posay	

Paris Area

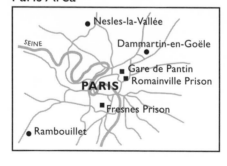

RANCE RIVER

(Cancaval) Dinard
Pleurtuit
Dinan

Nesles-la-Vallée

SEINE

Dammartin-en-Goële

Gare de Pantin
Romainville Prison

PARIS

Fresnes Prison

Rambouillet

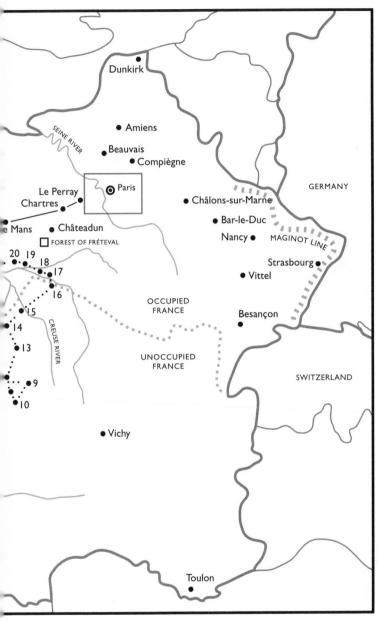

Dunkirk

Amiens

Beauvais
Compiègne

SEINE RIVER

GERMANY

Le Perray
Chartres
Paris

Châlons-sur-Marne

Bar-le-Duc

e Mans
Châteadun

Nancy

MAGINOT LINE

FOREST OF FRÉTEVAL

20 19
18
17

Strasbourg

Vittel

16

OCCUPIED
FRANCE

15

Besançon

14

CREUSE RIVER

13

UNOCCUPIED
FRANCE

SWITZERLAND

9
10

Vichy

Toulon

map by bill newkirk

After enquiring a bit around the station, I finally came across André whom I knew at Le Perray and who offered to take me to Philippe. After we had gone quite a distance, we arrived at a little three room house and there was my honey. Again we were reunited!!

The days spent at Bussière were very happy days for Philippe and me. The surroundings were lovely and peaceful, the weather perfect and we had nothing to do but take care of ourselves. We swam every day in a beautiful lake near by and sunbathed. I was allowed to join the noncommissioned officers mess and everyone was so nice and friendly. The mess, the French call it "Popote," was in our house and we had so many enjoyable meals there.

After a few days all the demobilized men were grouped according to the region into which they would be going. As Philippe is to go to Nesles, all the men belonging to the Seine & Oise were reunited at Chalus, 8 Kms. away. As the entire region is full of refugees as well as soldiers and the usual population, there is little food to be found, also very few lodgings. Philippe was therefore allowed to remain in Bussière. He only went to Chalus for the daily roll-call. Often we went together always on our bicycles as Philippe also had one now. Chalus is an interesting old place, two ancient towers, old houses and narrow streets. From one of the two towers came the shot that killed William of Orange![43]

After the men were regrouped thus breaking up the "Popote," I started cooking for us in our house, on a wood burning stove. I succeeded fairly well, but it did not last long as Philippe was to be demobilized very shortly.

My noncommissioned officer was demobilized on Monday, August 12th. However we were not anxious to leave right away so we remained a couple of days in order to settle certain things and enjoy another swim. We decided to cycle to Cancaval even though it was quite some distance, see the family, and then go to Nesles if possible by car if the Germans would let us do so. We knew there were plenty of "ifs" in all this, but we thought it was the best solution.[44]

43. Virginia probably confused William of Orange, who died in England from complications resulting from a fall off a horse on March 8, 1702, with Richard I, the Lion-Hearted, who died on April 6, 1199, from a wound he received in a skirmish at the castle of Chalus.

44. The distance from Bussière-Galant to Cancaval was approximately six hundred kilometers. With gasoline in very short supply, the French relied on the bicycle as a major means of transportation.

Besides our last swim, we cycled around a bit. The saddest sight was the horses. There were several hundred of them that had taken part in the battle of France and the retreat. They all had suffered, many were sick, the majority suffered from wounds and sores. At Bussière, they were neither fed nor cared for properly. No food for them, not even men to care for them and the men that still were there were disinterested. The poor things were always breaking away and wandering all over the country side. No one seemed to pay the least attention. All the men could think of was demobilization!

Speaking of demobilization, when one of our group left, all the remaining ones would go to the station in a gang to say goodbye. Often it was very touching, tears came easily. It is sometimes difficult to leave comrades found in time of war. Christian de Neucheze was also at Bussière. We were invited to join his "Popote" a few times. The cooking was done by the wife of one of the men who retreated with the army!

On Wednesday the 14th of August at 7: AM we mounted our bikes and were off! The first day, we did about 100 Kms. Not bad for novices! The first part was smooth and easy, but after Rochechouard, the town of the spiral Church tower, we started having hills. Parts of the route were beautiful. After a light lunch in a "Bistro" when we added slices of our own veal roast we had brought to the menu, we took a two hour sleep behind a hedge besides the road. At 8: PM we reached Bussière-Poitevine and were lucky to find a room with a charming view of old tile roofs.

We overslept and left late the next morning. Lunched besides the Vienne River at a modern Restaurant. In peace time we would have found a hundred cars on a Sunday. Today, August 15th, an important holiday in France, we were the only guests![45] That is what the lack of gasoline does and they of course have no means of supply. Nevertheless, they prepared us an omelet, cheese and a salad to which we added more of our veal roast! Beautiful trip along the river. At Chauvigny, an ancient fortified town, we attempted to cross into the occupied zone, but found the route barricaded and were told the Germans had closed the frontier at that point. This meant a detour of 34 Kms. to La Roche Posay. Disappointed, we took a lovely swim in the Vienne. Arrived at La Roche Posay at 7:PM

45. The Feast of the Assumption, commemorating the ascension of Mary's body into heaven, is observed by Roman Catholics on August 15. It is a pubic holiday in France and normally celebrated with religious parades and popular festivals.

and found the route to the other zone open but the next town was 20 Kms. further and being tired, we decided to spend the night there. We found a room in a hotel on the square, empty except for two old ladies.

The next morning, upon leaving we found the route barricaded and the square beginning to fill with refugees cars wanting to enter the occupied zone. Every room in the hotel was being snatched up in case of a delayed departure. Thank heavens we were able to retain our room and it is a good thing we did, as we were retained three days! The large shaded square was finally jammed with cars from the smartest American models to the poorest of little trucks. The stores were soon emptied of anything eatable and cooking was going on at every street corner over little wood fires. People with money ate at our hotel, the only Restaurant open in town. In peace time La Roche Posay was an active thriving watering place.

Philippe and I did not dare eat at the hotel as our cash was running low and we had no idea how long we would be there. We still had some veal roast left to which we would add fresh tomatoes, cheese and fruit. For the first time since ages we found butter and cream so had salads with cream salad dressing. (no oil to be found) We ate our little meals in our room. In the afternoons we walked up the river "La Creuse" to a bathing place where we swam and sunbathed. It was great.

This state of affairs continued from the Friday to Monday morning when we were told that the frontier would remain closed at La Roche Posay, but that we could cross it at St Aignan, 84 kms. away. This was bad news for us as it meant a detour of almost 200 kms. Also we were afraid that being on bicycles we might arrive after all the cars and find the frontier St Aignan closed also.

Having thought the matter over, we decided to push off at 4: AM (The designated time for departure was 7: AM). It was dark, but with a morning full moon, beautiful stars, fog in the valleys and over all a vast stillness. We felt alone in the world. It was exciting and a bit frightening.

We arrived at St Aignan at 11: AM. On approaching the town, at about four kms. from the center, we found refugees' cars parked one behind the other all the way in, waiting to get through! We just pedaled passed them all, passing all the cars we had seen in La Roche Posay. They did not even catch us up until we were there! It is probable they did not cross the line for hours. Were we thankful to be on our bicycles!

At the frontier barricade we had our papers examined, (my permit delivered at Bussière, Philippe's demobilization order) by a nice little German Corporal. All about were standing Prussian looking officers with expressions of stone. We crossed the bridge and were in the Occupied Zone, Philippe for the first time since it was taken over by the enemy; quite an experience for him. At once we saw sentries, traffic cops, cars, trucks, everything German. I felt the heaviness of it oppressing me again!!!

We followed the Loire in the direction of Tours. Lunched at Montrichard, all restaurants closed but one and even then we had to bring our meat. We had heard that a dear friend of ours, Claude Boell, was prisoner in Amboise, so we decided to find out whether we could see him or not. We inquired and found out where the camp was. In approaching it we suddenly saw Claude and others being marched in after having been some place. Claude's eyes popped when he saw us. He looked well, sun tanned, but a bit queer with his head shaved. We were able to have a few words with him by permission of the German guard.

Claude had been taken prisoner during the retreat. He did not know what was going to happen to him but hoped that he would be free fairly soon. In fact, he should never have been in the army as physically he was not fit for it, but when the war broke out he did everything he could in order to be mobilized and succeeded!

When we left Claude and Amboise, we did not feel too discouraged in respect to him, as we also felt that he would not be kept prisoner very long. We took the road leading to Tours and soon found the lovely border of the Loire again. We pedaled along until it was time to find a place for the night. Not far from Luynes, we saw a funny little café on the edge of the road that seemed attractive and found out they had a room which they could let us have. Just in front of the café, they had a couple of tables where one could have a drink so we sat down and had our evening snack under the best conditions. It was a lovely summer evening quiet and peaceful. From where we sat, we could watch the Loire gently following its course around many sand banks. The waters were low at this time of the year but it still was as lovely as ever. We seemed to be the only living souls around. Once again I had that feeling, is it possible that there is a war on, and that at this very moment people are suffering, losing their homes, getting killed?

The following day, after a good and warm bowl of something rather [words missing], we pushed off again towards Saumur this time. We wanted to follow the Loire as far as we could without adding any distance to our final destination. It was easy pedaling along the Loire and we made pretty good time. The scenery was so beautiful. I just love that road along the river. We had taken it many times before the war, and even Mother and Eleanora, my sister, had driven along here with us in our blue baby Fiat, when they came to visit us in 1938.

At lunch time we stopped, found a few things to eat and had a picnic on the river bank. We no longer would be close to the river towards the end of the day, as that evening, we should be nearing Angers and hence going towards Châteaubriant and Rennes with a less interesting land-scape. However our main objective was to reach Cancaval and we figured that all going well, we should be there the day after tomorrow in the afternoon. As a matter of fact we did reach Angers or at least its vicinity in the evening and spent the night in a farm where they gave us marvelous hot soup and a funny old squeaky but comfortable bed for just a few francs.

We were nearing our target, but the road appeared less easy. We were getting tired and our pedaling was no longer what it had been when we started out. We passed Candé in the morning and went on to Châteaubri-ant where we stopped in a café for a rest and something to eat and drink. We had hardly sat down than a German came in, said "bonjour" and sat next to us. He was not young and immediately started to make conversa-tion. He seemed a nice type of fellow, so we listened to what he had to say,—Where he lived in Germany, all about his family, his job in peace time etc. He was happy here in France and was also of the opinion that the war would soon be over and that the crossing of the Channel was an easy task for the German army. He insisted upon buying us a drink and we finally had to give in, before leaving the place for our next, and we hoped last night before reaching home.

We spent the night in Rennes, it was in an old street leading down to the Canal d'Ille & Rance where we found a small hotel. We were now in Brittany, seventy Kms. away from Cancaval. They had "craquelins"[46] here and good cider. We were feeling better, our depression of the last 48 hours was lifting and the thought that tomorrow we would be dining in

46. Hard biscuit.

Grandmère's house with Mum, Tante Germaine and Nicole was a most comforting thought.

The last part of our trip seemed fairly easy. We were pedaling over ground that we knew well and that we knew even better as we got closer. The last town we passed was the charming old city of Dinan that the English had adopted towards the end of the nineteenth century, a beautiful place, and a place that we just love. I do not think we even had any lunch on that day as we were thinking of the evening meal that would surely be plentiful, even though we were not expected!

We were in high spirits when we arrived at Pleurtuit at about 5: PM, and turned right for the last short lap on the lane to the Rance, Cancaval and Grandmère's property. This was down hill most of the time. Soon we arrived at the hamlet of Montmarin, then the Château, and just around the corner, the large wooden gate of the outbuildings and stables of Cancaval. We did not see anyone in the courtyard so we went towards the back of the house and entered the kitchen door. To our amazement it was full of Germans having their supper around the long wooden table. They stared at us and appeared just as astonished as we were!—Where is our family Philippe asked? The answer came as a bomb, "They all left a few days ago for Paris—the property is requisitioned—but who are you?" Philippe told them. We felt aghast. To think that we had come all this way on bicycles pedaling for over a week to find out that the family had gone and that the house was taken over by the enemy was a bit much for our morale!!

The Germans that were there, a completely new unit from the one I knew previously, were not unkind. When they found out who we were, one of the officers said, "We will give you a room to sleep in for a few days until you are prepared to leave—you may take your car, but you must find some gas, we have none." At that time, two more officers arrived on horse back. They asked Philippe in what army he had served? He answered that his unit was a cavalry unit. They seemed pleased and asked him if he would like to ride one of their horses! Philippe said: No thank you. They appeared to be disappointed but did not insist.

We were given Grandmère's room, the best in the house! and so we stayed with the Germans and started searching for gasoline. The blue baby was OK and had not been touched since I had last seen her.[47] Our

47. This is a reference to the Fiat automobile that they owned.

luck went on, after a day or two, and thanks to some friends, we were able to get enough gas to reach Nesles. We also needed a permit which we obtained from the Kommandantur in Dinard, then, we were all set to go.

In the meantime we had been able to talk about the war with some of the men in the house and were amazed to find out how naïve they were. One of them took us to a room overlooking the Rance estuary and said, "You see the estuary, well the English Channel is no wider than that, and we will cross it very easily when we decide to do so." Poor thing, if he had known that the Channel that was going to prevent them from ever laying a foot on English soil was perhaps a hundred times wider than the estuary where he was pointing out to us.

We left the Germans to their illusions and after a last look around our beautiful and dear Cancaval, drove off towards our own little home at Nesles-la-Vallée. As we left, we could not prevent ourselves from wondering how long it would be and even if we would ever see Cancaval again? Now that it was in the enemy's hands, anything could happen to it and anything could happen to us as well!

Our journey to Nesles did not take us more than a day, and everything went smoothly. Hardly any traffic, hardly any Germans to be seen besides one or two controls. When we reached the house, we were happy to find everything in order and also to hear that Nesles itself had no German troops staying there.

In a few days we will have reached September and we soon will have to face a winter. If the war does not stop and I do not see why it should, we are not going to have an easy time. However, we are together, we are in good shape, and we now have a home and land on which there is plenty to be done. We are therefore very privileged in comparison to so many others and we turn over this new page of our lives prepared for what has to come; thankful to God for all that we have received so far in our lives.

3 Life after the Fall of France

....

September 1940

We have remained at Nesles all month. These are peaceful days after the excitement of last month.

Bought 100 Lbs. flour—800 Lbs. potatoes.

In order to try and find something to eat, I am obliged to go to bi-weekly market in l'Isle-Adam; City badly damaged, several Germans buried at side of road. No more bridge across the Oise River! Have to cross on a small boat with a bicycle and all.

No more gasoline at all for the public. Only Public services on the road with their large "S.P.S." on windshield.[1] Our blue baby [Fiat] is under the shed at the "Faisan Doré," a used to be restaurant not very far from the house. The owners, Mr. & Mrs. Fleury were the ones that helped us to acquire our land, and they have become friendly and most helpful neighbors. Wonder how long it will be before we can use a car again?[2]

No buses or taxis in Paris (except bicycle trailer taxis—two seats, closed to inclement weather—cute as can be). As a result, the Métro is having record business—and everyone from "Mademoiselle Dupont" to the "Comte & Comtesse de la" whatever pedals around the city on their bicycles![3]

1. S.P.S. stands for Service Protection Sociale, a government program in France that deals with health, welfare, and social services.

2. Lack of gasoline led to the development of vehicles that were powered by a combustion engine, the gazogène, which burned wood, charcoal, or coal; the engines were mounted on buses, cabs, and cars.

3. Virginia is emphasizing that even very wealthy individuals, such as counts and countesses, were now required to take the Métro, the Paris underground. Jackson notes that "since the Germans issued permits for only 7,000 private cars in Paris, the streets of the city were eerily empty." Describing the wartime years as the "heyday of the bicycle," he comments on how the people of Paris turned to bicycle-rickshaws for taxis. Even bicycles, however, "were subject to German requisitioning and the

October 1940

Spent the month in Paris apropos the apartment of 1 bis rue Vaneau being sold. City depressing.[4]

Bought over 2,000 Frs. worth of canned goods and pasta to put on reserve at Nesles. (80 Lbs. of pasta—40 Lbs. of dried beans)

Collided into an elderly gentleman while crossing the Place Vendôme with my bike. Knocked him down, sprawled myself over the pavement. Result: Monsieur said not a word, either concerning myself or himself,—walked off rather disgruntled. I broke a bottle of wine and sustained a beautiful bruise on upper leg. A policeman nearby was most upset about the wine! (ordinary wine, practically impossible to find. I laid pieces of broken bottle at foot of Napoleon's statue!!)

Laughed as I saw myself pedaling across the Place De la Concorde towards a luncheon rendez-vous at "Pruniers,"—a stunning hat with veil ribboning out behind, coat of fur and velvet, our dog Pax taking in the view from his vegetable basket in the rear. I love cycling in Paris, it is real sport—and one makes time.

....

November 1940

—England suffering under heavy bombardments.[5]
—No milk.
—Very hard to get meat. Never enough for all even with ration tickets. I went to the butcher shop before it was even light early morning to find fifty women standing in line before me!
—City gas restricted.

Philippe had quite an experience on the day we left Paris again for Nesles. He was walking down the Rue Royale when he saw a German Shepherd dog on the loose, wandering amongst the traffic and risking to

---

scarcity of rubber made tyres difficult to replace. The price of bicycles rocketed, and there was a black market in stolen ones." Jackson, *France: The Dark Years*, pp. 251–252.

4. With Philippe no longer employed, the family had to sell the apartment at 1 bis, rue Vaneau, though they maintained use of it after it was sold.

5. This is a reference to the intensive German bombing of London from September 1940 until May 1941, known as the Blitz.

be run over any minute. It took him a long time to approach the scared animal, but finally managed to do so. The dog had a collar but nothing was marked on it. It was a female and very skinny indeed. Philippe stopped at a café and tried to get her to eat something, but no luck, he then decided to make a leash with some string and take her to the Gare du Nord where we were to meet in order to take our train back to Verville, the nearest station to Nesles. Everything worked fine until the train stopped and we got off, but in doing so, the poor scared dog jerked and broke off the leash thus disappearing into the night. Stations have no lights these days. We called and whistled, but nothing happened, so we went on our way feeling most frustrated. In order to reach our house, it meant a three mile walk on a country lane. When we had done roughly half the distance, we suddenly were conscious of something following us and there it was, our new friend had traced our scent and was joining us for a new chapter of her life. We were thrilled to death. We gave her a name, "Nan," and from then on Nan and Pax became great friends and we love them both.

....

December 1940

December 25th, first letter from home in six months!

Geneviève Jeanrenaud and her daughter Arlette spent ten days with us including Christmas. Mum out for the holidays also.

Claude Boell died after short illness.

Went to the Caserne in St. Denis to try and see interned Englishmen. Not allowed to enter at last minute.[6]

For New Year's midnight supper had octopus—the only fish available (No meat!)—Stood in line hours at market in the rain to have that! And a bit of cheese.

Bread in Paris dark grey in color and of disagreeable taste, but always white and good here at Nesles.

What will 1941 bring to us? All we can do is thank God that we are alive and together.

6. British Commonwealth civilians living in the Occupied Zone were interned as early as 1940.

January 1941

Another letter from Home, Eleanora's baby born Nov. 24.

Have had three weeks of snow and severe cold. Cry my eyes out trying to light our kitchen stove with wood that has not had time to dry. Once we were so cold that we remained in bed 48 hours![7]

No potatoes to be had in Paris—people eating rutabaga in their place. Food supplies in Paris are in the hands of the Germans and as they have not been able to maneuver the Vichy Government to give them all they want, they are retaliating by cutting down supplies for the population. Much unrest in the city. The Germans are spreading "National Revolution" propaganda lately.[8]

Found tracts dropped by English planes all around the house. They look like a baby newspaper which is called "Le Courrier de l'air"[9] and includes Roosevelt's speech![10]

Whoopee. We have a chicken! Managed the acquisition by giving 4 Lbs. of pasta and two of dried beans, in exchange.

No butter to be bought this month hardly.

7. The winter of 1940–1941 was exceptionally cold, with seventy days of frost in Paris.

8. After Pétain abolished the Third Republic, he used his full legislative and executive powers to launch a socially conservative program known as the National Revolution. Replacing the French slogan of "Liberty, Equality, Fraternity" with "Work, Family, Fatherland," the National Revolution aimed to construct a new France that would revive the country's former glories. In contrast to the democratic values of the Third Republic, Pétain preferred order, hierarchy, and discipline as a way to create a French national identity that focused on the importance of the countryside, the family, and Catholicism. The first two years of the Vichy regime are usually referred to as the era of the National Revolution. Given the shock of military defeat as well as the disarray and hardships experienced by many French, it appears that, at least initially, there was widespread support for the Vichy government and the National Revolution. Vichy propaganda was quick to exploit Pétain as France's savior; posters, advertisements, books, and songs with this message abounded. As the war wore on, however, the Vichy government became increasingly repressive and authoritarian, and public opinion turned against it. Much has been written about the National Revolution and the Vichy government. A good beginning point is Paxton, *Vichy France.*

9. Airmail.

10. The speech was probably a copy of President Roosevelt's January 6, 1941, address to Congress in which he stated that he looked forward to the creation of a world founded upon four essential freedoms: freedom of speech, freedom of worship, freedom from want, and freedom from fear.

English women put in camp at Besançon. This includes French women who became English by marriage. The women were picked up without warning in the country—with buses. In Paris, they were called to the "Mairie" (Town hall) and then given half an hour to return home and get a suitcase.[11]

Market in l'Isle-Adam: Stood in line half an hour for carrots—two hours for ¹/₅ Lb of butter!

....

February 1941
We now have strict rationing.
150 grammes butter for the month—90 grammes oil and 150 grammes cooking fat, also for one month.
Italian troops losing ground on all fronts—Albania, Abyssinia, North Africa. On February 16th, the English were two hundred miles from Tripoli![12]

11. The Besançon internment camp was located near the Swiss border with France. According to Severin Hochberg, a historian at the United States Holocaust Memorial Museum in Washington, D.C., British Commonwealth civilians were interned as early as l940 at various camps in the Occupied Zone, including Besançon and Vittel, a spa and resort in the Vosges Mountains about sixty kilometers south of Nancy. Besançon remained a camp primarily for British Commonwealth passport holders. Internment camps for enemy nationals, such as British and American citizens, were subject to the Geneva Conventions (see the Introduction on this point). Conditions at prison camps for enemy nationals, while often harsh, were far better than those at German labor and extermination camps for civilian prisoners, where the work of the International Committee of the Red Cross was very limited or even nonexistent. At Vittel, one of the better camps for enemy nationals, prisoners were lodged at the first-class hotels of this famous spa. E-mail communication with Severin Hochberg, January 22, 2004. For a memoir by a Canadian in Paris who was arrested and interned at Besançon and Vittel, see Claire Fauteux, *Fantastic Interlude* (New York: Vantage Press, 1961).

12. In April 1939 the Italians seized Albania and began building up their troops in preparation for an invasion of Greece that was launched in late October 1940. By February 1941, however, the Greek army had pushed back the Italians and had advanced into Albania. On April 6, 1941, Germany came to Italy's assistance and invaded Yugoslavia and Greece. By the end of the month, both these countries had fallen to the Nazis, and Germany had also driven the Greek forces out of Albania. Italian forces then reoccupied Albania. Ethiopia, originally called Abyssinia, had been captured by Italy in 1936. In February 1941 British General Andrew Cunningham led an attack on Italian forces in Ethiopia, forcing Italy to surrender on May 17. In Sep-

Germans not content with Vichy government.[13]

"Marché noir" (Black market) in full swing—Due to it, one eats well in the better restaurants, but at what price! Chickens are 44 Frs. the kilo in value, but Madame Bosc who owns a restaurant we go to, must pay 70 Frs. the kilo and obtain them through the black market. The Germans allow this racket and cash in on it heavily.[14]

Frontier between the two Zones being severely guarded. Dangerous to pass letters. Young men have been joining the Free French Forces via the free zone.[15]

Bought five laying hens in Paris for 190 Frs. each!!!

Will soon have ration tickets for clothing, already do for shoes. Until clothing and shoe ration tickets are distributed all sales are stopped—and I need a new coat!

Cooking is slow work in Paris. Gas is kept at such a low pressure.

Here is a list of the present rationing:

------

tember 1940 Italian forces in Libya began an offensive into Egypt. In early December the Western Desert Force, under the command of British General Richard O'Connor, launched a counteroffensive against Italian forces that sent them backward along the coast toward Tripoli. The retreat did not stop until February 7, when British forces were four hundred miles west of Tripoli. The British success, however, was to be short-lived for two reasons. First, Churchill decided to intervene in Greece, thereby depriving the Western Desert Force of the necessary strength to advance as far as Tripoli. Second, German General Edwin Rommel arrived in Tripoli on February 12, 1941, to command the Afrika Korps and launch a successful offensive against the British on March 24. By mid-April Rommel had gotten back all the British had taken except the port of Tobruk.

13. From 1940 to 1942 the Vichy government was somewhat successful in distinguishing itself from the German occupation government in northern France. Many countries, including the United States, granted diplomatic recognition to Vichy. Following the Allied invasion of North Africa in November 1942, Germany invaded the Unoccupied Zone and dismantled the Armistice Army, and Vichy became little more than a puppet state of Germany.

14. Black market prices were considerably higher than official market prices, but shortages forced many French citizens to resort to it.

15. The Free French forces consisted of volunteers who, upon making their way to England, joined up with the Free French Army led by General Charles de Gaulle. In September 1940 Free French troops unsuccessfully sought the capture of the French naval base at Dakar in French West Africa. They also fought against the Italians and Germans in North Africa and against French Vichy troops in Syria. In the fall of 1943 some 120,000 Free French troops joined the Allied forces in fighting Italy.

The ration tickets are for one month.

Bread—18½ Lbs.

Cheese—½ Lb.

Meat—3 Lbs. includes Ham etc

Butter—1 Lb. (includes all fats)

Pasta—1 Lb.

Rice—⅕ Lb.

Coffee—½ Lb. (Not real coffee)

Jam—½ Lb.

Sugar—1 Lb.

Coal—130 Lbs.[16]

Mrs. Mollet, a good friend of Mum's, interned since two months at Besançon camp has been freed, as well as women over 55. Mum is over 65 so we believe she will be OK. Mrs. Mollet was not too unhappy. She mentioned that the hospital contained 80 women in one room. Their day started at 6:30 A M.—Lights out at 7:30 in the evening. Those that wished so could have meals in bed. Beds in room in rows with a yard in between each. They were sufficiently heated and the food was not bad, many soups and even some meat at times. In the camp itself, conditions were different, it is like military barracks. Women do all the work, scrubbing floors, emptying refuse, peeling potatoes etc. Upon arrival Barracks were not ready, French prisoners just evacuated. Water standing—many women sick, some died. Children from a few months to twelve years included in total of 6,000 internes. Two thousand of them now freed due to age and sickness. Conditions in camp being improved.

French definition of German / French collaboration: "Give me your watch and I will tell you what time it is."

In a café a Frenchman and a German converse—the German is relating Hitler's victories, "We have taken Poland, Denmark, Norway, Holland, Belgium etc." The Frenchman: "Do you think you will also take a beating?" German replies: "Oh yes, we will take that too."

Philippe was approached by a German in a café.

16. Virginia's comments about wartime shortages and rationing confirm the findings of Julian Jackson that "in general, the Occupation was the time of the ersatz economy: wooden soles instead of leather, grilled acorns instead of coffee, sunflower leaves instead of tobacco." Jackson, *France: The Dark Years*, p. 252.

G: You have a nice face, you must speak German?

Ph: Thank you for the compliment but I do not speak German.

G: French and Germans are good comrades, but English are bad.

Ph: Have you been to England?

G: No

Ph: Have you any English friends?

G: No

Ph: Well in that case you are unable to judge

G: Germany socialist—England capitalist no good—(Then in English!)—Do you speak English?

He spoke English fairly well, had been taxi driver in Berlin.

....

March 1941

Practically impossible to find chicken feed. Farmers cannot find any fertilizer—Hard to find garden seeds.

Food in restaurants better now, due primarily to Black Market. Three months ago no choice. Some places are strict in ticket taking, others take very few, some none at all! It depends if you are a good client or not. It is forbidden to serve meat in the evening, on the menu it is erased, but the Headwaiter orally offers it if he knows you. Cheese, butter are more plentiful. No exciting desserts, only fruit. Pastries forbidden. It is also forbidden to serve sugar for coffee but it appears often all the same— otherwise it is a saccharine pill or the same thing in liquid form. It has a taste I dislike.

No more Glycerine—Tooth paste flows out of the tube! No Turpentine, kerosene, Alcohol, Kotex, Starch. Thread scarce, wool also (for knitting). Automobiles run on "Gazogène" wood burning. No delivery service whatsoever.

Germans always modest, polite, well behaved. Allow French women to pass before, give up their seats in Métro, step down from sidewalks to allow French to pass. Will it go on this way?

Saw Etienne G. His father well known circulates from one zone to another. Says that Maréchal Pétain as long as he is head of the State will neither collaborate or break with the Germans—and in the meantime only hold off to gain time.[17] The French hold two strong cards—North Africa and the fleet in Toulon harbor.[18]

....

June 1942

At our little bar the "Norland" in Montparnasse, where everyone speaks English and where even the Germans do, we had an interesting conversation with one of these.

He lived in America several years. Has a house on Miami beach, spent four years in Japan representing his father's revolver factory. Has an American wife, got married in the States in 1938. Returned to Germany for mobilization. Is on leave in Paris after two months of Russian front as machine gunner in Stuka bomber![19] Is to return this week. He keeps repeating how horrible war is, and how terrifying it is to be a rear machine gunner on a Stuka when it dives towards the ground. Said we could not imagine what it was like and seemed very depressed, hinted at not coming back. His face was grim, and one could see he had suffered, but he added, "We must win this war, if we do not, the Russians, English and Americans will wipe us out. We will do everything to win, will fight like the Japanese!"[20]

Everyone excited about the 1200 plane raid over Cologne.[21]

Terrific tank battle taking place in Libya. Germans trying to take Tobruk but not making headway.[22] One senses the new superiority of the Allies in the Air.

17. In striking contrast to this opinion, Robert Paxton has demonstrated that the Vichy regime was united behind some type of voluntary collaboration with the Germans from its very earliest days. Paxton, *Vichy France*, pp. 51–63.

18. The armistice with Germany included the provision that the Vichy government would be responsible for governing French colonies, including those in North Africa. Of the five ports to which the French fleet was to be sent, only Toulon was not in the Occupied Zone.

19. The Stuka was the standard dive-bomber for the Luftwaffe.

20. Although the Soviet Union and Germany had signed the Nonaggression Pact on August 23, 1939, that pact was nullified on June 22, 1941, when German troops invaded the Soviet Union. The Soviet Union then joined the Allies.

21. On May 30–31, 1942, British Air Operations Bomber Command sent more than one thousand bombers to raid Cologne. The raid was a considerable success: only forty bombers were lost and forty-five thousand people in Cologne were made homeless.

22. Virginia is referring to the fierce land and air battle in Libya between British and Germans forces that resulted in the German capture of Tobruk and its thirty

Starting from today June 9th, all Jews from six years up must wear a yellow star in order to indicate their race![23]

....

August 1942

Bought sugar—125 Frs. a pound!! black market.

Butter—220 Frs. a kilo

Veal—180 Frs. A kilo

Germans pressing on in Russia, attacking Stalingrad from the south; cutting the railroads in the Caucasus.[24]

Tomatoes, string beans, onions to be had only with ration cards.

Hitler's best troops, the S.S., have been withdrawn from Russian front, transferred to Paris! Staged large military revue.

---

thousand defenders on June 21, 1941. For this capture General Rommel won the baton of field marshal.

23. For centuries the Star of David was a symbol of Jewish pride. During World War II, the Nazis required Jews to wear a yellow star as a way to segregate them from the general population. Punishment for not wearing the yellow star included fines, imprisonment, and beatings that sometimes resulted in death. In June 1942 the Germans required that Jews in the Occupied Zone wear the yellow star. By this time the lives of these Jews had been severely restricted. They were not allowed to own radios and bicycles, were subject to a special curfew, could travel only in the last car on the Métro, and were banned from all public places except between 3:00 and 4:00 P.M., when they were allowed to shop. The Vichy government also imposed harsh restrictions on its Jews.

July 1942 marked the roundup of 13,000 Jews in Paris, followed by the roundup of Jews in the Unoccupied Zone in August. There were also roundups of Jews in the Occupied Zone outside Paris. Gildea, *Marianne in Chains*, pp. 272–273. Julian Jackson gives the total number of Jews deported from France as 75,721. He also states that "another 4,000 Jews died in French camps or were executed in France. This gives about 80,000 Jewish victims of the Holocaust in France—of whom 3.5 percent (2,500) returned alive." About 30 percent of those deported were French Jews and 70 percent were foreign-born, which "represented approximately 12 percent of French Jews and 41 percent of foreign Jews in France." Jackson, *France: The Dark Years*, p. 362.

24. Stalingrad, on the Volga River some fifteen hundred miles east of Berlin, was the scene of a decisive battle during the winter of 1942–1943 in which the German advance into the Soviet Union was halted. German forces launched their attack on August 21, 1942. Not until late January 1943 did the Germans finally surrender. Hitler had ordered the attack to help secure the German drive to the rich oil fields of the Caucasus.

St Malo bombarded recently.

The Allies attempted to land at Dieppe and along part of the coast nearby, but it was a disaster![25]

....

September 1942

For 200 gr. of brass you can get one litre of wine, free of charge and at once! Paid 40 Frs. for ¹/₂ Lb. of honey.

This morning, 24th September, the Germans interned American women. When is my turn coming?[26]

Frenchmen between the age of 18 & 50 without regular jobs of at least 30 hours a week must sign up within two days for obligatory work!!![27]

25. On August 19, 1942, British and Canadian forces launched a raid on German-held Dieppe in an effort to let the people of the occupied countries know that they were not forgotten. The Allied forces met with stiff German opposition, however, and by early afternoon what was left of the Dieppe raiders were on their way back to England.

26. Severin Hochberg states that there are no records of Americans being sent to internment camps in occupied France during 1942. Americans were sent to Liebenau on the German-Swiss border near Lake Constance in 1942, however. Hochberg also states that it is certainly possible that American women were arrested in 1942 and held in prisons around Paris. There are records that show that Americans were sent to Vittel in late January 1943. In November of that year, there were 467 U.S. nationals (women outnumbered men but there is no exact breakdown) among a camp population of 2,425 internees. By February 1944 the number of Americans rose to 819. Jews who held Latin American passports, mostly from Poland, were also interned at Vittel in 1943. In late April 1944, 137 of them were transported via Drancy to the furnaces of Auschwitz. E-mail communication with Severin Hochberg, January 22, 2004. For an account of the experiences of one Polish Jew at Vittel, see Yitzhak Katznelson, *Vittel Diary*, trans. Myer Cohen (Israel: Hakibbytz Hameuchad, 1972).

27. In June 1942 the unpopular *Relève* (relief) was initiated; it promised that 50,000 French prisoners of war would be repatriated for 150,000 skilled French workers. When recruitment efforts fell short of quotas, the Vichy government adopted a law on September 4 "requiring all male workers aged between eighteen and fifty, and unmarried women aged twenty-one to thirty-five to 'undertake all work that the government sees fit in the higher interests of the nation.' . . . Between 1 June and 31 December 1942 the *Relève* had furnished 240,000 workers for Germany." Gildea, *Marianne in Chains*, pp. 287, 291. On February 16, 1943, the Service du Travail Obligatoire (STO), which subjected Frenchmen to forced labor, was established. Paxton states that "total French labor figures in Germany, including prisoners of war who were sent to work, amount to about 3.3 percent of the total population." Paxton, *Vichy France*, p. 369.

....

February 1943

Paid Sugar   250 Frs.—Kilo
Butter   500 Frs.—Kilo
Coffee Nat   225 Frs.—Kilo
Can of milk   150 Frs.—Kilo

....

March 1943

The tension is growing. Men are being sent to Germany by the thousands. Philippe getting nervous. Everyone is waiting for the Allied offensive, when will it come?

Had dinner in a Restaurant—600 Frs. a piece . . . but so good!!

Huge colored posters up now in Paris with Churchill and Roosevelt tearing the African continent apart in their desire to have it each for themselves![28]

Since March 1st, the line of demarcation between the two zones no longer exists. The Germans have taken over the whole of France. However, before they reached Toulon, the French managed to scuttle the remaining fleet that was in the harbor.[29]

All flower and Antique dealers are obliged to show only lower qualities in their show windows. We hear that it is because German soldiers on leave from the Russian front find life in France too normal and luxury items too abundant!

....

April 1944

We were in Paris for the last bombardment; it was the worst I have witnessed. We were at Jessie-Ann's flat and had a perfect view of the sky

28. This is an example of German anti-Allies propaganda.
29. On November 11, 1942, three days after the Allied invasion of North Africa (Operation Torch), German forces marched into the Unoccupied Zone and disbanded the Armistice Army, effectively occupying all of France except for the small Italian zone in the southeast. With Italy out of the war in the summer of 1943, Germany occupied all of France. On November 27, 1942, Admiral Jean de Laborde, commander of the French fleet, ordered that the French ships at Toulon be scuttled rather than be captured by the advancing German army. Much to the despair of the Germans, some fifty-eight warships were either sunk or put to sea to join up with Allied forces. The total occupation of France by German troops in November 1942 made the demarcation line irrelevant, although it was not officially eliminated until February 1943.

and the dome of the Invalides. The brilliant yellow flares lighted the whole sky, as they floated over us and no bombs yet having been dropped we thought we might be in a dangerous area, so we took the children and went to the cellar. We were not the only ones. We stayed for an hour, and when a pause came, we went upstairs again. This was just the interval as the bombing started again more severely than ever and lasted for another hour. We watched it all from the window. The objective was the marshaling yards at the Gare du Nord. It all seemed very close however, and with the drone of the plane engines, the heavy flack, the shell splinters, the rattling of windows, and the powerful search lights painting the sky, not to speak of the explosion of bombs, the great fires and the clouds of smoke, I must say that henceforth any fireworks display will seem too tame to even watch. There were such powerful concussions caused by the explosions that my heavy skirt was wrapped about my legs! (Over 500 dead from this raid. Stray bombs fell around the Sacré Coeur.)[30]

Ten days ago, we watched from our terrace a Flying Fortress fall in flames. We saw five men bail out. All that happened some distance away, while we were at Nesles.[31]

No trains running from the Gare du Nord. In order to get to Nesles, we had to take a train from the Gare St. Lazare that took four hours! And what a crowd!

---

30. The central city of Paris was, for the most part, spared bombing, but industrial manufacturing in the suburbs drew British and U.S. air raids. This is probably a reference to the April 20, 1944, bombing of Paris, which resulted in 651 dead and 461 wounded. Jackson, *France: The Dark Years*, p. 535.

31. By this time Virginia was actively involved in work with the Comet escape line, and she may have actually aided the five men that she saw bail out. Of course, she was careful not to provide any references to her clandestine activities in her diary. The B-17 Flying Fortress was the most famous Allied bomber of World War II.

1. Virginia d'Albert-Lake, ca. 1940.

2. The d'Albert-Lake home at Nesles-la-Vallée, where downed Allied airman were hidden.

3. *Virginia and Louis, a radioman, at Nesles in December 1943.*

4. *Virginia at Nesles, 1944.*

5. *Virginia with downed Allied airmen at Nesles in 1944.*

6. *Downed Allied airmen at Nesles, 1944.*

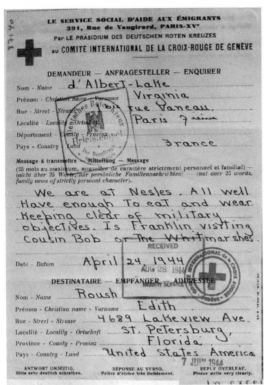

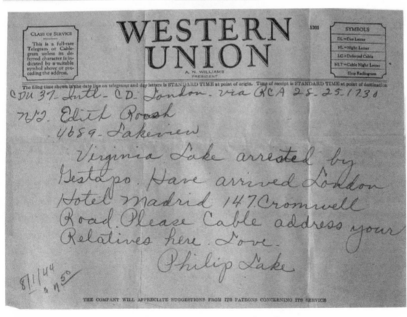

7.
Letter from Virginia to her mother in St. Petersburg, Florida, April 1944.

8. *Western Union cable from Philippe to Mrs. Roush, July 1944.*

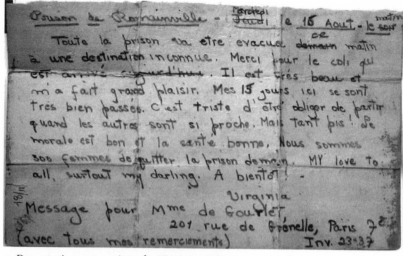

9. *Deportation note written by Virginia, August 15, 1944.*
Translation: "The entire prison is being evacuated this morning to an unknown
destination. Thank you for the parcel which arrived yesterday. It was a lovely
one and brought me much pleasure. My fifteen days have passed very agreeably.
It's very sad to be obliged to leave when the others are so near. But what can we
do? The morale is high and I'm in good health. We are three hundred women
leaving the prison. My love to all, especially to my darling. See you soon!
—Virginia"

10. *Jeanne Marie Boissard,*
Virginia's trusted friend Janette,
who died at Ravensbrück in
February 1945.

11. Virginia at the time of her release from Liebenau, May 1945.

12. Virginia and her son, Patrick, November 1946.

13. Virginia holding her Lègion d'Honneur medal, France's highest civilian honor, 1989. (Photo: David Hume Kennerly/ kennerly.com)

14. Virginia and Philippe d'Albert-Lake at Cancaval, 1989.
(Photo: David Hume Kennerly/kennerly.com)

The Memoir, "My Story"

4 Working for Comet Escape Line and Arrest

FALL 1943–JUNE 14, 1944

The hideout in the garden of our country cottage was practically finished.[1] All day long we had worked without stopping. A stranger would never have guessed that at a stone's throw from the house was a refuge large enough for two people. We had dragged a piano box to a hollow among the trees. We had camouflaged it with rocks and moss and a thin sprinkling of pine needles so that it looked like any of the other hillocks which surrounded it. Life was dangerous during these days of German occupation. Every day hundreds of arrests were made, hostages were shot and French citizens sent to forced labor in Germany. We did not feel secure; we wanted a hide-out for the day when they would come for us.

We were gazing with satisfaction on our day's efforts so successfully and secretly completed. Suddenly Philippe seized my arm. "Listen," he whispered.

There was the sound of a car straining to climb the hillside road which led through the woods to our secluded house. Who would be coming here at this hour and with a car? We ran quickly to the high terrace back of the house, from where we had the advantage of being able to see in all directions. Suddenly a small truck came into view and as it stopped a man climbed out. It was Mr. Renard, our baker. He appeared to hesitate a moment, then plunged resolutely toward the house. My husband called him; he turned to approach us.

"Excuse me" he said, speaking directly to me, "but I have something to say privately to Mr. D'Albert." I assented and turned toward the house. I had barley reached the door when I heard Philippe calling to me.

"I must leave for a few minutes; don't worry, I won't be long."

---

1. This is a reference to the d'Abert-Lake's country cottage located at Nesles-la-Vallée. This event took place in the fall of 1943. Virginia wrote this memoir in 1945–1946.

I wondered what was happening. It seemed strange that Mr. Renard whom we hardly knew should want to speak privately to Philippe and then wish to drive away with him in so abrupt a manner.

The time seemed long. I disliked staying alone in a place so isolated and at a period so fraught with uncertainty. Suddenly the silence was broken by the shrill ring of the telephone bell. I grabbed the receiver. Yes, it was Philippe!

"Come to the bakery, will you?" He sounded rather excited. I sensed that I should not ask "why," so I only replied, "Yes, of course."

I threw on a coat and ran as quickly as I could down the wooden path to the winding dirt road which stumbled its way across the rocky fields to the village. After ten minutes I arrived at the shop, breathless and intrigued.

It was closed to the public at this time of the afternoon, but the door was opened when I knocked and Mr. Renard led through the store-room to the dining quarters at the back. I was conscious of the delightful odor of freshly baked bread—bread, the precious article to which we had the right to only half a pound. On entering the family dining-room I found Philippe and, seated in chairs in a semi-circle, three young men, one of whom stood out particularly because of his black hair and slanting eyes.

"Bone joor," they said, almost in unison. At once I recognized the agreeable accent. "Oh, but you're Americans," I cried out. I was shaking with excitement. These were the first American men I had seen in three years.

One of them remarked: "You speak English just like an American. Are you American?"

"Yes, of course, but tell me what you are doing here!"

For the next three hours they told us their stories and how they were airmen of the same crew shot down over France and their experiences in the air, the fatal crash, where they were from in the States, all about their families, just as homesick men will do when they find sympathetic ears to listen. The dark-haired, slanting-eyed Willy was from Hawaii. He was an oculist; a graduate of Ohio State University. There was serious, love-lorn, just married Bob from California, and Harry, a jolly factory-worker from Detroit. They seemed so happy to be able to relax for a few hours and to talk with us who spoke and understood English. The Renards, unfortunately, were not familiar with the language, but Philippe and I translated all the important and interesting items for them. Mr. Renard insisted that we stay for supper—a supper that turned out to be a banquet. The host, in honor of the occasion, uncorked his best bottles of wine and his wife exploited her culinary art to the utmost. Willy could not bear anything alcoholic, but he wanted to be polite, so forced himself to drink and, after each swallow, he made such a sour face that we cried with laughter.

Gaily time went by and we almost forgot what we were risking. There, just on the other side of the door, men and women were passing in and out of the bakery, choosing their bread, counting out their bread tickets, laying down their "sous."[2] They were not always French. Sometimes they were German. If anything had happened to let them know what was going on in that room just beyond the shop, it would have meant arrest, probably torture and perhaps death. As the evening wore on we realized that it was time to become serious again. Already, it was 11 o'clock—the curfew hour. If we were stopped by a German Military patrol on the way home, that would mean trouble too. Bob, Harry and Willy were leaving on the next stage of their journey the following day. I promised to come down the next morning to see them off. We said good night, tiptoed out into the street, crept through the shadows and along unfrequented narrow paths until we could breathe again inside our own four walls.[3]

We did not sleep much that night. Instead, we talked over the whole evening, discussed the boys and made a big decision: we would work in the Underground. Dangerous, yes, but we would be careful. It would be worth every risk run just to meet more boys like those tonight and lead them from right under the German noses back home and the work yet to be accomplished.[4]

The next morning, I went back to the bakery; I had taken along some pre-war issues of the *Reader's Digest* to help the fellows pass the hours of waiting and relieve the nervous tension that was already back on them

2. A sou is an old French coin worth very little. It is a word that denotes small bits of money or hard-earned money.

3. A reference to this meeting appears in Philippe d'Albert-Lake, "Report from Philippe d'Albert-Lake." See Appendix 1.

4. As Julian Jackson has noted, "Until at least the end of 1942, the Resistance was too small to be a presence in the experience, even the consciousness, of most people." By contrast, 1943, the year that Virginia and Philippe joined the Resistance, represented the year of its "fastest expansion." Jackson, *France: The Dark Years*, pp. 240, 475.

with the thought of the next move. We lunched together at the bakery, after which Renard received a mysterious phone call. He slipped a Colt into his pocket and indicated to the boys that they were to follow him. We tearfully kissed them good-bye, then quickly packed them into the rear end of the bakery truck and let the canvas drop. It was the curtain falling on the prologue of a new play.

Busy days were before us. Philippe contacted the proper authority which resulted in Jean's first visit.[5] I shall never forget the morning when I opened the door of our Paris apartment to the tall, calm, distinguished looking young Belgian. Jean was to be our 'Chef.'[6] After having done valuable Underground work in Brussels, the Gestapo was on his heels and he had been obliged to cover up his traces and escape to England. Now, after weeks of training, he was back on the Continent, having been parachuted into France on a special mission. His mission was the evacuation of fallen allied aviators, by plane pick-up operations. He was to find fields for landing, contact London by radio to arrange for the date and hour of the plane's arrival, and assemble the men to be picked up. This was to be done not once but as fast and as often as possible. More and more men were falling in Western Europe as air activity increased. It would not be easy: there were so many things to be taken into consideration. First, it was difficult to find fields uncultivated and hard-surfaced enough to land a plane; when one was found, it could be used but once, or the Germans would soon know. There was always the question of radio contact with London to arrange for the date and approximate the hour of the pick-up. That in itself was very dangerous because the Germans had a method

5. This is a reference to Jean de Blommaert (also known as Jean Leduque and John Rutland), a Belgian who had been an important agent for the Comet escape line until a series of arrests caused that line to be broken, and he had been forced to escape to England. Philippe's cousin Michel de Gourlet had arranged the meeting between the d'Albert-Lakes and de Blommaert, which took place in December 1943. See "Report from Philippe d'Albert-Lake," p. 1. The Comet escape line, extending from Brussels to Paris, southward to San Sebastian in Spain, and finally to Gibraltar, had been founded in 1940 by a twenty-five-year-old Belgian woman, Andrée (Dédé) de Jongh. The Comet line also had many French members, including Virginia and Philippe d'Albert-Lake. See the Introduction for a discussion of the importance of these escape lines.

6. Chief. Chiefs, who were often trained by military intelligence organizations, acted as overseers of escape lines. They identified agents and other volunteers while also aiding downed airmen.

for detecting and discovering transmissions. There must be a moon and favorable weather conditions. Sudden changes in weather would oblige sudden changes in plans, often complicated and detailed. No, it would not be easy.

There was much work to do and things had gotten off to a bad start. When Jean had landed in France, he had Louis, his radio operator with him. The radio transmitter, along with food, guns, and ammunition, had been parachuted at the same time; a very few days later, all the supplies were discovered in the temporary hiding place, by the Germans. Of course, everything was seized and arrests were made. Fortunately, Jean and Louis were in Paris at the time. Now the work could not advance until more supplies arrived including the most important of all, the radio transmitter. This meant contacting London; it was not easy to find another Underground operator to send the S.O.S. and, even after we succeeded, London misunderstood and, being naturally cautious, would do nothing until the whole story had been verified.[7] They were afraid that there had been arrests and that the messages were a German frame-up to capture more men and material. So Jean was obliged to return to England. All this delay made us miserable. In the meantime, Louis had been staying with us as nervous as an old wet hen, with time being heavy on his hands and he not the type to sit still and wait patiently. Louis contended that his mission had failed; he was a radio operator without a transmitter so he went with Jean.

Philippe and I were anxious to start to work but there was little we could do at first. Jean had left Philippe in Paris as his "second" and he was to handle all contacts that might turn up. One day, a little Belgian girl, Michou, came to see us.[8] She had been evacuating airmen for the "Comete" line by the Spanish border but, recently, extensive arrests had been made and the line was broken. Michou was trying to re-establish it and came to Philippe for help. At first, things moved very slowly but, by Jean's return, we were evacuating men as fast as we could by the Southern route.[9]

7. Virginia is referring to MI9, the British intelligence organization, which gave valuable assistance to escape lines such as Comet. See, for example, Foot and Langley, *MI 9: Escape and Evasion.*

8. This is a reference to Lilly Du Chaila, also known as Micheline Dumon but best known as Michou. She had worked for the Comet line since its earliest days.

9. "Report from Philippe d'Albert-Lake" states that "few evacuations" through southern France were made during this period. See pp. 1–2.

Living in our apartment had become too dangerous. Instead, we had moved into a studio, in the same building, which had been rented for Jean under an assumed name.[10] We spent a good part of our time at Nesles too, where hiding men was less dangerous than Paris. This little house, as I have already indicated, is off the main road and hidden away in the trees on a hill side, forty kilometers from Paris. Very often, we picked up airmen at the Gare du Nord, led them around Paris streets until time to board the train for Nesles. Once at Nesles they would stay perhaps one, or two or three days—the length of time necessary to arrange for the train tickets and Underground guides to take them down to the Spanish border where native mountain-guides led them over the Pyrenees and into Spain.

Convoying men was thrilling. I never walked in the streets with an aviator without pretending to know him well, in order to avoid suspicion. We usually walked arm in arm, engrossed in friendly conversation, being very careful to lower our voices when people were within hearing distance. I remember one day, in the Trocadero Gardens, while passing time this way, we ran into an old friend of Philippe's; he pretended not to see me and I ignored him; on that occasion I felt that my reputation as a faithful wife was badly compromised. Of course, we never told the secret of our Underground activities except to those who were very close to us and who wished to cooperate.

Sometimes, we took the men sightseeing in Paris, which meant rubbing elbows with Germans, doing the same thing. This was dangerous sport, but sometimes we sensed their vital need of getting out of the house and stretching their legs. Every now and then an incident occurred which called for quick thinking. A guide never took care of more than three men at a time and, in the street, one would walk alongside, while two followed as strangers. If there were two men, both would walk with the guide, but, in the subway or on trains, the guide ignored them completely. Even the boys among themselves had to be careful. They could not speak French and they dared not speak English. We always gave them pro-German magazines and newspapers in which they kept their noses buried. This warded off friendly attempts at conversation by other travelers. The one thing necessary was that we keep within their range of vision; this gave them confidence and eased their nervousness. Before going into a subway or boarding a train we always gave the men their tickets

10. This studio apartment was located a 1 bis, rue Vaneau.

beforehand and, as sometimes, it meant going directly from one to the other, they were given tickets for both. One day, in a train, an aviator passed his subway ticket to the conductor instead of his train ticket; when it was refused he did not seem to understand and things were becoming complicated; Philippe came to the rescue just in time by explaining that the boy was not in his right mind and extracting the proper ticket from the fellow's breast pocket. One can imagine the outcome if a Gestapo official had by chance been sitting alongside! Another time, a friendly French woman insisted on trying to make conversation with one of our airmen; it finally got to the point where the guide had to explain that he was deaf and dumb. It was not uncommon for an airman under similar circumstances to put on the deaf and dumb act.

One afternoon at Nesles, Philippe took one of the boys for a walk in a very solitary part of the country where, suddenly they encountered a German officer out hunting with his gun and dog. He looked most suspiciously at Philippe and Nelson, wondering no doubt what two city-dressed men were doing in that part of the country at that time of the day. He stopped and was just on the verge of addressing them, which no doubt would have resulted in him asking to see their identity papers, when Philippe superseded him in his perfect French to comment on his beautiful dog and ask about his luck. This visibly threw the German off and he talked hunting. They parted after a diplomatic handshake! But Philippe and Nelson admitted later that they had been really scared.

I am amazed that our airmen did not attract more attention. To me they stood out like sore thumbs, being so self-conscious and dressed in such ill-fitting clothes. I will never forget the day I waited for a new convoy at a sidewalk café just outside the Gare du Nord. Suddenly I saw a girl guide emerge from the crowd with five men straggling at her heels. They were trying to be nonchalant. One was a tall, dark, round-shouldered and heavy-lipped boy, with a felt hat perched on the back of his head. His black overcoat was unbuttoned and so long that it nearly dragged on the street. Out of each pocket stuck a bottle of wine. He looked a real boozer! One of the others, a short, stockily-built fellow, wearing an unbecoming grey overcoat and a dark felt hat pulled low over his right eye, appeared to be an authentic Chicago gangster—though in reality he was off a Wyoming ranch. Two others were slight, nervous looking fellows who tried to express self-confidence by sticking their hands deep into their pockets. All of the men were walking too slowly, but it was not their fault as the guide was setting the pace; this added to their awkwardness however, and made them stand out in a crowd of people hurrying back and forth. There was only one who looked the part of a real pedestrian, though too fair-haired and blue-eyed to appear French; he was well dressed in a raincoat and grey felt hat and, unconcernedly, crossed and re-crossed the street stopping to glance into shop windows as he would have done in his own hometown. I came to the rescue of the others by catching up with the guide and, after slipping some tickets into their hands and whispering a few words of English into their ears, we divided up and plunged down into the subway.

About the time Jean returned, a very serious incident occurred which stopped our evacuations for three weeks. Just after a train for Bordeaux had pulled out of the Gare d'Austerlitz, Gestapo agents arrested two of our boys riding in one of the coaches. There had been no prologue to the arrest and no demanding of identity papers. The Gestapo walked directly up to the airmen, snapped on handcuffs and led them off. By a miracle the guide escaped. It was not uncommon for a man, with all the necessary credentials for work in the Underground movement, to turn out to be a German spy.[11] This had obviously happened to us! It might not be easy to detect and track the person down, but it had to be done before our work could continue. The final effort fell to Daniel, one the most courageous men on our line. He followed our rat into a hole; in this case it was a small "bistro" somewhere in Paris and where they both ordered dinner; the spy evidently sensed danger for he showed signs of nervousness and, after ordering a drink, went into the back of the place to make a phone call; during this interval, Daniel dropped a poisoned tablet in the drink, and disappeared. However, he stayed in the vicinity long enough to see the arrival of a German ambulance and to ascertain the death of a man by poisoning. What a relief! Now we could start work again!

During those weeks, Marshall, Jerry and Max had been living with us at Nesles. They had been jolly company and a real help in all the domestic duties. They made their own beds, helped to wash the dishes and to prepare the vegetables. Marshall taught me how to jitterbug! Sometimes we would go to the baker's to enjoy a good meal and a gay evening. The

11. The sheer size of escape lines meant that they were vulnerable to infiltration and lines were broken many times. This incident occurred in the spring of 1944 and is described in "Report of Philippe d'Albert-Lake," p. 2.

baker was host to some other airmen who had come through our hands, as were also a woman and her daughter who lived in the same vicinity. While the break in our line existed, men were beginning to multiply in the Paris area and we were hard pressed to find people who would take them in. The two women whom I just mentioned had a German officer in their house at the same time that our men were there! Fortunately the house was large so that they were able to keep out of each other's way. The Nazi who was on leave and had requisitioned a room for himself, took the habit of going hunting every morning at an early hour, only to return late in the afternoon. During this time the Americans had the run of the house and garden. The hunter always returned with pheasants, rabbits and partridges and, sometimes, a deer. The airmen raved about the good meals they had—and no wonder. As luck would have it, the only person in evidence to the country people round about was the Nazi officer. At the moment of the liberation in August 1944, they shaved both the girl's and the mother's head for having "collaborated with a German"![12]

Jean was back in Paris now and, with his return, the future looked brighter.[13] He had a new mission which consisted of organizing a hidden camp, or "maquis," as it is called in France, for fallen aviators. With the increased air activity prior to the invasion, rail communications were bombed constantly and it was becoming more and more difficult and dangerous to evacuate men by the Spanish frontier. Eventually it would be impossible. The solution was the "maquis."[14] Here the aviators would

12. Following the liberation of France, women accused of collaborating with the Germans often had their heads shaved. On this topic, see Jackson, *France: The Dark Years*, pp. 580–583. This particular incident is an example of the complexity of the challenges faced by resisters. In this case, two women necessarily collaborated with the Germans in order to provide a safe haven for downed airmen. On this topic, see Gildea, *Marianne in Chains*, pp. 65–88.

13. Jean de Blommaert returned to France in April 1944 with orders from MI9 to establish a clandestine camp for downed aviators in the densely wooded Forest of Fréteval, about eleven kilometers south of Châteaudun. See the Introduction for more information about this camp. See Map 1 for the location of the clandestine encampment.

14. *Maquis* originally referred to the thick underbrush on the island of Corsica where anyone fleeing from justice could safely hide. During World War II the term was used to designate places where Resistance fighters and downed airmen could hide as well as to refer to the paramilitary resistance groups that formed in the winter of 1943.

in due course, and praying God, be released by the advancing allied forces.

Jean was accompanied by a new radio operator and the transmitter was to come over by way of the Spanish border. Someone must go down to pick it up at the frontier. This was a job for Pierre who wanted to earn a place of responsibility on our line. He decided to act as a guide on the trip South and take Marshall along with him. His destination reached, he would contact the necessary person, in this case a clergyman, who would see that he obtained the transmitter, and take care of Marshall. But all did not work out as we had planned; the clergyman had never seen Pierre before and the first thing he noticed was that Pierre had a missing finger. This alarmed him because he knew that there was a member of the Gestapo who had a finger missing—a man who already was supposed to be on our trail. Nothing that Pierre could do, show or say was convincing enough to make him admit that he was a member of the Underground and a link in the evacuation chain of our line. Pierre became nervous and discouraged. He abandoned Marshall to his fate and came straight back to Paris without the radio. This meant complete failure. The camp was growing rapidly and yet it had no means of contact with the allied authorities in London. We were having no luck with transmitters.

Jean had moved down to the "maquis" and left Philippe in charge of the Paris area. It was the month of May. Events were moving fast now and we sensed that the Invasion was not far off. There was more and more air activity. The Germans advertised daily in the newspapers the long-awaited disembarkment. We had more and more men to shelter and were very busy; more and more to feed and to sleep and to cheer up. There was no longer time to take them out to Nesles. Instead, we crowded them into our Paris studio, five or six at a time. We were obliged to rely on the black market and false ration tickets for most of our food in order to have enough to give them.[15]

One afternoon I was hurrying back to the studio on my bicycle, with my basket strapped on behind, full of canned food, coffee and ginger bread, far more than anyone had a right to have at one time. It had been raining and just at the rear of the Madeleine Church I skidded on a car track and went sprawling. The basket broke off and the cans, coffee and

15. On meeting the challenges of shortages, rationing, and the black market, see Diamond, *Women and the Second World War in France*, pp. 49–70.

gingerbread rolled in all directions. I didn't dare look up to see what kind of an audience I had. I was afraid of the police. I was embarrassed too and was miserable due to a banged up knee and a heel off my shoe. But a little old gutter cleaner came to my rescue. He must have sensed my discomfiture, because he very quickly and politely stuffed everything back into the basket and fastened it on. I rewarded him with a ginger bread, and started off again. But the basket hadn't been well attached, it tipped and everything went flying again. But the old man was there again, as if by miracle, and this time he earned a sack of coffee. This was my first accident and it hadn't been very serious. I had always been lucky, especially when I recall the number of times I pedaled up and down Paris streets, laden with butter, meat and other articles. I had been stopped a number of times by the police because of that suspicious-looking basket; they glanced inside but always when it was empty!

At this period, it was very difficult for me to get the meals on time as the gas was on for only an hour at noon and a half hour at night. To cook a meal for from six to ten persons on the two-burner stove in that length of time was real sport, especially if I were late in starting. Sometimes the potatoes were not thoroughly cooked and the hamburgers underdone, but we ate them all the same.

This was an exciting but enervating period. Because of bombed communications it was impossible to send all the men through to Spain, so about half of them were being taken to the "maquis" in the region south of Chartres. I regretted one thing about this period—there were too many men and they were with us so short a time that we couldn't get to know them half well enough. But a few stand out in my memory due to striking circumstances. There were the two black South-Africans; there was the tall young man from my birthplace, Dayton, Ohio; he had bailed out of a Fortress on his first mission over the Continent; he must have misunderstood the order that came over the Inter-Communication phone, as no one else bailed out, and while he drifted towards the earth, his plane went on unconcernedly without him. There followed a very young New Zealand boy whose clothes bulged. He was wearing his uniform under his civilian suit and all his pockets were stuffed with souvenirs and flying equipment. He would have attracted attention any place. Philippe made him give everything up and he wept. He reminded me of another young aviator 19 years old, an American from the Middle West. David came to us in a very nervous state, upset because he and the rest of his crew had bailed out over the same area, but he had been unable to find any of his companions. He and a group of other men were to start South early the next morning. That evening, however, David smoked excessively in the hot stuffy studio and was so ill during the night that he was unable to leave with the others. But his illness turned into a blessing because all the members of his old crew turned up the next day. I found blood stains all over the pillow of another aviator who had been severely burned around the face and ears when leaving his plane. Then there was a Texan, a tall good-looking fellow with a charming drawl. He loved horses and a beautiful girl whom he had recently married and left back in Texas and about whose marital fidelity he was always worrying; we wanted to send him back by the Spanish border, but he refused; he was afraid that he would never arrive and that he would be responsible for the arrest of the others; so we took him to the "maquis." Another very polite and chivalrous airman always made a point of being next to the curb as we turned corners and crossed streets in Paris. It was enough to betray him as this rule is not in a Frenchman's book of etiquette! He thought that women should have nothing to do with the Underground front: "They risk too much" he said, "too dangerous." There was a fighter pilot who was very much in love with a Belgian girl to whom he was engaged; she was a member of the family who had sheltered him after his crash in Belgium. He would have risked another crash just to be reunited with her again. Among the last to come was a handsome, charming, devil-may-care Scotsman who liked nothing better than to wander about Paris streets—alone!

Thus, they came and went. Philippe and I had been personally responsible for sixty-six airmen up to the day of invasion and the last trip we made—the trip that for me was a fatal one. Very early in the morning of the 6th of June, a friend 'phoned us to say, "It's happened!"[16]

"What's happened?"

"Well, turn on the radio."

Philippe banged down the receiver and I leaped to the wireless. It was the debarkation! We went crazy, dug out the maps, peered out into the streets. Now, what were we to expect? Many people were of the opinion that on the day of the invasion, the Germans would declare martial law

---

16. This, of course, was the long-anticipated D-Day invasion of Normandy.

and no Frenchman would be allowed out in the streets. We were worried because there were six aviators at the studio, while we were sleeping in a new hideout nearly a mile away. Philippe and I had always planned to go to the "maquis" ourselves after this event, although we did not know just how we would do it. But now, as we leaned out of the window, we saw men walking in the street and, as far as we could see, things looked normal. We had to make a decision. We dressed quickly, jumped on our bikes and pedaled madly over to the studio. We explained to the men the situation and gave them the choice of being sent back to the Paris homes where they had recently been staying, or to make a dash for the "maquis" before it was too late. Already communications close in on Paris were being bombed; there was only one train which could take us out of the city and that only 30 of the 120 kms. to the region of the "maquis." This meant walking the last 90 kms., which would be dangerous because the Germans would probably be checking the identity of everyone on the roads. In the meantime, five more men arrived. It was evident that people wanted to be rid of the responsibility of sheltering allied airmen at this crucial moment. Ten of the eleven voted for the "maquis," and the eleventh changed his mind the following morning. We could not get train tickets before three days. We thought about bicycles, but it would be impossible to get eleven of them in so short a time without stealing them. We could not do that. We managed to get one besides our own and that's all. We made final plans; we filled out false identity cards; we bought train tickets for ten men and three girl guides for as far as the train would go which was Dourdan. We prepared box lunches; we sought out shoes for the boys whose own were in bad shape. I recall rushing to the dentist with an airman's false tooth, half of which had broken off, but the dentist could do nothing without the owner of the tooth, and I did not dare bring him around. I packed a small case with essentials. The day before leaving, we all went to bed early as the train left at seven o'clock the following morning. The ten boys with the three guides left at close intervals for the station, taking the subway.[17] I went to the station on my bicycle to make sure that the train was still leaving and at the appointed hour. Everything went smoothly. I returned to the studio and from there, Philippe, the last

17. "Report from Philippe d'Albert-Lake" (p. 3) gives the names of the three guides as Anne-Marie, Michèle, and Any.

man, and I started off on our bicycles. We had made arrangements to meet the others in a wood just beyond Dourdan. They had arrived fifteen minutes before us, and we found them stretched out on the ground, resting. After a bite of lunch, we began dividing up and setting out by groups of two and three, at intervals of ten to fifteen minutes. Late in the afternoon, the sky clouded over. This was unfortunate as we were crossing a grain belt and there was no cover; only field upon field of ripening wheat and oats bending before the stiff breeze. It was not long before a torrential rain drenched us. Philippe and I kept bicycling back and forth, contacting the men and the guides in order to cheer them up and to say it would not be long now before we would be stopping for the night. But, of course, we did not know where! They were a wary, wet and stragglylooking lot, but they were good sports. They were suffering from their feet too for they had been inactive for too long, hiding away in homes from which they dare not go out; big blisters were forming on the soles of their feet. Philippe and I were beginning to wonder how they could support walking the next day. In the near distance, through the mist of rain, we saw a little village, on the outskirts of which was a large shed. We sought shelter there and pulled off our wet shoes and socks, hanging them up to steam out a bit. Once we were no longer moving, we began to feel chilly. Philippe went into the village to inquire for a place to spend the night, having in mind a barn as the perfect solution. But he met only a cold reception. No one wanted to risk taking us in. Philippe thought that he would find more cooperation if he said that the men were French fleeing from the threat of forced labor in Germany, but it appeared that only recently several people had been arrested in the vicinity for taking in and hiding just such individuals, and they were afraid.

One thing was certain: we could not go on shivering under that open drafty shed, so, after painfully pulling on our wet socks and shoes, we started forth again onto the open road. We purposely stayed off the main highways following only secondary routes. Since leaving Dourdan, we had not seen a German, but at this stage, we were all so tired, wet and hungry that our sole desire was to find shelter for the night. It had stopped raining but the low running clouds indicated only a short respite. In the distance we could see another village on which laid all our hopes as villages were so few and far between. Philippe had gone ahead in order to investigate, but when we arrived at the main intersection of the town, he had not yet reappeared and, within a few minutes, our entire group had gathered in one spot, thus ignoring all elementary precautions. I was getting very nervous and was without inspiration as to what step to take when Philippe reappeared and told all the guides, including myself, to follow him. He had found a farm where the people were willing to shelter five of us. He hadn't dared admit that we were more than that for fear of arousing suspicion, but planned for us to distract the farmers while he maneuvered all the boys into one of the barns. Everything worked out all right but, later, when the farmer unexpectedly entered the barn, he was faced by four talkative girls doing their best to cover up suspicious silence of eleven strange men. The moment was a tense one, but the farmer was a patriot and he made no remarks. On the contrary, he and his wife, later, brought us great bowls of warm milk, fresh bread and a huge kettle of steaming soup. Nothing had ever tasted so good. We soon buried ourselves in the friendly hay and fell sound asleep. The next morning, we reconsidered our original plans. It was evident that we risked wholesale arrest in staying so close together and trying to keep in contact. We would be forced to spend another night on the road and that entailed again the difficult problem of finding a safe place for hiding. Besides, some of the men were suffering more from their feet than others; this obliged the more capable men to drag along in order not to get too far in advance. We made drastic decisions. One of the girl guides was to start ahead with two men. They would spend the night at a farm, the owners of which were her personal friends, and the following day would go direct to the "maquis." The second girl guide was to take one man; they would trust to chance for finding a place to sleep and continue on to the same destination the following morning. The last eight men had very sore feet. They probably could bear up for half the distance which remained, but that was all. We decided that I should go on ahead to Châteaudun on my bicycle to contact the Underground and get hold of a vehicle of some sort with which I would come back to pick up the boys at a pre-determined place. We studied the road map and decided on a small wood about 30 kms. from Châteaudun. Philippe drew separate maps for the three groups, each of which was to set forth on its own responsibility to meet once again in the small wood the following morning at approximately 11 o'clock. Philippe thought that he should bring up the rear along with one of the boys who would ride the third bicycle. I said good-bye to the farmer and his wife. They had soon realized that they were harboring allied airmen and not fleeing Frenchmen, but this made no difference except that they seemed all the more pleased. I was only about a kilometer out of the village when a tire went flat; I tried to repair it but it kept losing air and I could not find water any place to help discover the leak. The only solution was to return to the farm. All the hikers had caught up and passed me, but Philippe and Sam had not yet come along. I found them still at the barn, working on a tire too and, in the end, we three set out together. We passed all our marching men and, as they seemed confident and in good spirits, we continued on our way. There were few cars on the road. The British Broadcasting had warned the French to stay off the highways as allied planes were bombing and strafing every moving object they observed. At one place we watched a long convoy of German military vehicles and supplies pushing along toward the Western front, on the main route which crossed our small road. This sort of thing was meant for observation planes.

A man on a bicycle, passing us but going in the opposite direction, cried out, "Be careful up ahead." He was pedaling so rapidly that he was at once too far away for us to ask him what he meant. We were afraid that he had warned us of a German "barrage"[18] but we soon found out that he was referring to the machine-gunning by allied planes. We discovered a battered French truck reclining at a crazy angle, blocking half the road and badly pot marked by machine gun bullets. It was completely deserted, and we couldn't resist the tempting piece of coffee cake we found abandoned on the driver's seat.

Our first night out, we had witnessed the attack on the munitions train. It was frightful to watch; the exploding munitions shooting out in all directions in a perfectly insane manner, but it was thrilling and beautiful too, seeing those bird-like planes, black silhouettes against the brilliant orange sky of an after-rain sunset, circling dipping and rising, screaming and spitting fire as they went into the attack.

We reached Châteaudun about 5 o'clock. Coming into the city, we saw the results of the bombing of the station and railroad yard. The destruction was great and we had constantly to pick our way around giant bomb craters. The town was crowded with Germans. We went directly to the address of a little grocery shop where we found a long line of people waiting to be served. It would not be diplomatic to push in there, so we

18. Roadblock.

went around the corner to the side entrance beside which hung a swinging rabbit's foot of which we had already heard. I gave it a tug and the
door was soon opened by a tall, fair young man with a baby boy toddling
at his heels. I repeated our pass-word and told him my name. Having
been warned of our arrival, he hospitably welcomed us in and, after a
short conversation, we arranged to meet him 15 minutes later at the town
square. From there, we followed him on his wobbly bicycle out into the
country. Everyone we passed called a friendly greeting to him. About a
mile out, we stopped beside the road where we waited while he returned
to the city to find another member of our Underground line, who was to
put us up for the night. After half an hour there arrived this new stranger,
a young man who greeted us warmly and energetically. He took us to his
flat where we enjoyed a copious and delicious dinner—the last I was to
have for nearly a year! His charming wife was there, as well as their baby
boy, and his parents. Everyone was so friendly and generous that we
could not help but relax and feel at home. We learned, however, that it
would be unsafe to spend the night there. Henri himself had been sleeping elsewhere for the last several nights as the Gestapo was trying to clean
up the Resistance at Châteaudun and several arrests had already been
made. We must be very careful. With the early dusk, we left the house
and cycled once more out into the country, this time to a farm. Here we
again were warmly greeted and spent that night in the hay-loft of the
barn with the other members of the Châteaudun Underground who were
armed to the teeth. The next morning we arranged for a horse and covered wagon to go back to pick up the boys. It was decided that Philippe
should go to the "maquis" only a few kilometers away, to contact Jean
and arrange to receive our boys while Henri and I, on our bicycles, along
with the wagon driven by the farmer's son, would go back to pick them
up. It was a beautiful morning. Philippe had already left and it was while
waiting for Henri in the courtyard that I heard the wail of air-raid sirens
in Châteaudun. After five minutes, German Army trucks arrived full of
soldiers, to park and hide under the trees beside the farmyard gate. I
watched the formation after formation of Fortresses go over, but their
objective was not Châteaudun.

With the aid of maps, we followed a winding and complicated itinerary
which led us finally to our destination—the rendezvous in the wood.[19] As

19. These events took place on June 12, 1944.

we approached the spot, I began to feel shaky. It was 11 o'clock and I kept asking myself over and over, "Will all the boys be there?" By what seemed to me a miracle, they were! Yes, all seven of them, along with our third guide girl. We greeted each other like long lost friends and with tears in our eyes. One of the boys cried out with spontaneous enthusiasm: "Virginia, may I kiss you?" Luck had followed the two South Africans; they had not been intimidated in the least by walking unguided through enemy occupied territory; when hungry or thirsty, they would stop at a farm house and ask for food and drink; they had passed a good night in a comfortable bed! The other boys, more nervous, had not dared to approach people so often; they had managed to get something to eat, but had slept either in haystacks or under sheds.

Relief and relaxation made us hungry. I had brought along sandwiches and hard-boiled eggs. There was cold chicken too and beer. We enjoyed the real picnic. In the meantime, the little covered wagon arrived. The boys were happy to know that their walking days were over. The farmer's boy had brought along another bicycle as there was so little room in the wagon. Al offered to ride it.[20] The rest of the men made a dash for the cart. We soon were on our way with six airmen, one guide and the driver in the wagon, while Al, Henri and I led the way on our bicycles. The route was so complicated, so many turnings and cross-roads, that we had to study the map carefully in order not to lose our way. About 8 kms. out of Châteaudun, Henri, having an important rendezvous, left us. I was beginning to breathe easier as the end of this hazardous journey was in sight. We were now on our last stretch of road, with which I was already familiar, so I put away the map. We had ridden too far in advance of the cart, so we stopped to wait. Al was too warm. He took off his coat and put it in my bicycle basket; then, with a happy smile he said, "Isn't it wonderful that we're nearly there! To think that we hesitated about making the trip and nothing has happened at all! I do admire your courage!"

"Thanks a lot, Al, but don't say such things yet. It's still too early. We're not there yet." I couldn't account for my answer—just then.

The cart came into sight around the bend. We mounted our bikes and rode on. A stranger joined us, pedaling in from a side road and we continued this way for about a kilometer, the three of us in single file, the wagon about fifty yards behind. We would soon be coming out into the main

20. This airman was Alfred Hickman.

highway. I could already see it in the distance, as well as the formidable mass of buildings on the hill beyond, which was Châteaudun.

A large black car turned abruptly from the highway into our narrow side road. I suddenly felt nervous. What would such a car be doing on such a desolate road? I went off the side to let it pass, but instead of passing, it stopped. There were three men in it—and they were German police! One of them ordered us to get off our bicycles. They left the car and came over to ask for our identity papers. As I write this, I start trembling again. The entire scene comes back in all its frightening vividness. I was the first victim; I handed over my identity card which stated that I was born an American citizen. I had never pretended otherwise, as it would have been impossible considering the strong accent with which I spoke French. The Nazi glanced at my card.

"What are you doing in the region when your identity card states that you live in Paris?" he asked gruffly but in perfect French.

"We have been searching the farms for fruit and eggs," I lied.

"Ah," his voice rose with interest, "you have an English accent. I see now your card states that you were born in the United States."

"Yes, but I am French by marriage." I lied. "I took my husband's nationality when I married. I have the right to circulate."[21]

"Perhaps." Then, he quickly added, glancing back to Al and the stranger, "Are you with these two men?"

"No, we're riding together quite by accident; they joined me from a side road further back." This was my only chance of escape, but all the time I was conscious of Al's coat that was very much in evidence in my basket, and it was a coat which very obviously matched the trousers he was wearing. I wondered if they had noticed it.

I tried to appear unconcerned and prepared to mount my bicycle, but I was tense and trembling. I knew that this moment was a climax in my life. These few seconds would prove the success or failure of my effort to escape. I hopefully pushed down on the pedal.

"Stop," he roared out. "Not so fast."

Something broke inside me. I knew somehow that it was all over. There was no more reason to hope. The sun that only a few minutes ago was so bright and warm, now seemed eclipsed by a grey fog. Disappointment and fear clothed me in a hot vapor. Sweat started in my armpits;

21. After Virginia married Philippe, she retained her U.S. citizenship.

my scalp tingled; I had no choice but to stand there in the center of the dusty road, grip my handle bars, and wait.

Now they questioned the man in black. His papers were in order and it was evident that he was French. He said that we were strangers to him and so they let him leave. Then, it was Al's turn. He looked tense and wretched, but he handed over his identity card with perfect dignity. They started questioning him. His card stated that he was French, but he could not speak the language. He tried bluffing at first with a "oui" or a "non," but it did not make sense.

The Police Officer pointed at him and said in forceful English: "You are American. Aren't you?"

Al declined to answer and from then on, he said nothing.

During this time I glanced back for the cart. It had stopped beside a farm-house, about 30 yards away, and I saw the boys stealthily climbing out and disappearing into the underbrush at the side of the road. I was so grateful. Once the game was up, I know that I appeared very calm and in perfect command of myself, but, inside, I felt a throbbing excitement and a kind of deep heavy misery, clutching and dragging me down.

Now that these Feldgendarmes had guessed what we were, they began searching us.[22] They acted very pleased with themselves! The Officer tore open my handbag and, with his gesture, I suddenly recalled something which made terror clutch at my heart. Before leaving Paris I had disposed of every incriminating evidence, but I still had the list of addresses of the Underground at Châteaudun that Philippe had given me only yesterday, prior to my leaving alone to make the necessary contacts. The feeling of guilt which came over me was worse than anything I had yet suffered. All the people I had met the day before: the grocery man and his toddling son; Henri, his wife and baby boy; the farmer and his family—visions of them all rose up before my eyes. I was miserable. The German, in the meantime, was carefully examining everything. He saw the map, food, tickets, an envelope with paper money, my fountain pen, compact, nail file, and the piece of note-book paper on which were written the addresses. He hesitated over this and, then, to my amazement, he put everything back into my bag, addresses and all, and handed it back to me! Then he discovered Al's coat. He made but a simple comment: "It was not right for you to have said that you were not together."

22. The Feldgendarme were the German Field Police in Occupied France.

He went over to Al and left me standing in the middle of the road, with a Sergeant to guard me. I had taken off my jacket and was holding it over my arm while my hand clutched the bag hidden underneath. Now was my only chance. Unconcernedly, I slipped my right hand under my jacket, slowly opened the bag and managed to get hold of what I thought and prayed was the right paper. I tore it into tiny bits, found one of the pockets of my jacket and slipped them in. It was impossible to dispose of them in any other way for the moment as I was too closely guarded. Nothing of interest was found on Al though, fortunately, he had his "dog tag" to help prove that he was not a spy. After having searched Al, the Officer ordered one of his men to wheel our bicycles back to the nearest farm-house and to leave them there. Now they ordered us into their car. I sat in front between two of the police, and Al was in the back with the third. They were very jolly and kept making gay remarks, none of which I understood. After ten minutes, we stopped before the Feldgendarmerie of Châteaudun. We got out and walked through a door and down a narrow hall, turning at last into a big room which proved to be the main office. Before the windows, which looked out on the main street, were two desks and, behind one of them was a German Officer. The man responsible for our arrest went directly over to his superior and began proudly to relate his story. There was considerable activity in the big room. Uniformed police were constantly walking in and out. No one appeared to be watching me with any special attention, so I wandered aimlessly around the room, grasping the bits of paper in my hand and, at the first opportunity, popped them into my mouth. I had great difficulty in swallowing them. They simply would not be chewed and I had no more saliva. Minutes passed before I was successful. The relief I felt was indescribable. Almost immediately afterward, the German seized my hand-bag; he emptied the contents onto the desk and I could tell that he was interested in finding the list of addresses. He searched once, turning everything over and over and, then, repeated his search. He became nervous and agitated. "Where is the paper?" he exploded at me. "What paper?"— "You know, the one with the addresses."—"How should I know? I thought you put it back in my bag with the other things. Perhaps you let it drop out on the road."—"No, I didn't. It was there." He began searching again, and looked on the floor, in the hall, even in the car. In the meantime I was seated in a comfortable arm-chair, but Al had been led away. The German came back again. He had started a more careful search of the room, when suddenly he made a grab for something on the floor. It was one of the tiny bits of paper I had unknowingly let fall. He looked at me with a deep disconcerting stare. *"You ate it,"* he said finally. "Yes," I answered simply. Never again did I hear mention that list of addresses. He had committed such an unforgivable fault in giving me back my bag that it was deemed inadvisable to admit it to the Gestapo![23]

Since arriving at the Police headquarters, I discovered in my pocket one of the penny-size compasses that the airmen carried as part of their equipment. I didn't know who had put it there. It was more evidence against me, not that it mattered now, but I suddenly felt sentimental and desired to keep it. I was wearing a scarf around my head, draped and tied in turban style, and I slipped the compass into one of the folds. Shortly afterwards I was ordered into another room where there were two German girls in uniform, waiting to search me. I was obliged to undress, but they did their job very lackadaisically and never thought of examining my turban. I had been led again into the first room where, without warning, the little compass slipped out of my head dress and rolled slowly across the floor, in front of all the Germans. They stared at it and then at me in amazement. The girls were severely admonished and were ordered to take me back and search again. This time they did a thorough job. They undressed me completely, searched my clothing and ruffled my hair, but there was nothing more to find.

It was 6:30 now. Some of the men drifted off to their Mess, but two stayed as guards. One of them talked to me seriously; I did not like him. He had a superior conceited manner and I knew that he could be cruel. "You better tell everything you know," he warned, "and don't do any lying. That's the only thing that might save you. As it is, you will probably be shot tomorrow morning. We haven't time to judge people since the Invasion."

He was sitting on a desk, his legs dangling. I was standing in front of him and I remember feeling quite weak in the knees, but I thought "if they shoot me—they shoot me, but I won't talk." No matter how frightened I might be, I would not give him the satisfaction of showing it. So I remained erect, confidently smiling. I must have succeeded in my purpose because the other man gruffly bloated out, "How can you smile all the

---

23. Virginia evidently confused the Gestapo with the *Feldgendarmerie*. An account of Virginia's arrest is included in "Report of Philippe-d'Albert Lake," p. 4.

time? Aren't you frightened? Don't you realize that you'll soon be in the hands of the Gestapo?" I did not answer. I only caressed his beautiful dog. This appeared to soften his heart, and he began telling me about his wife and children!

I was given a Bologna sandwich and a cup of ersatz coffee. I could not eat, but drank the coffee and stuffed the sandwich into my pocket. Shortly afterwards Al was brought in. He was handcuffed and, as we were forbidden to converse and were constantly guarded, I could not find out where he had been. They led us shortly out to the same black car. I was ordered to get in front, with the driver. Al was in the back with the guard who held his cocked rifle very much in evidence. I kept searching the streets as we drove along, waiting for a miracle to happen. I thought that Philippe and the others might be at most any corner, waiting to attack the car. I could tell by the road signs that we were going in the direction of Chartres. About 60 kilometers to the North, on the way, we had some trouble with the car and twice, while going up inclines, we had to stop. The driver left his gun stacked against the dash board while he got out to do something to the engine. If only Al had not been handcuffed! I found out from him later that all sorts of ideas had passed through his head too at that moment; without handcuffs, he would have attacked his man and I, with the abandoned gun, could have taken care of mine.

It was dark when we arrived in Chartres, but I glimpsed at the beautiful spires of the cathedral, silhouetted against the starlit sky. We stopped before the high stone wall and great heavy door of the City prison. We got out and one of the men yanked a chain hanging beside the entrance. There were footsteps and the door opened. We followed a path, fenced high on both sides with barbed wire and which led to the main building. We entered a small dimly lighted room where a German in uniform was sitting behind a desk; other soldiers came in. Al disappeared with one of them and then I was obliged to follow another who led the way with a flashlight, along shadowy corridors and down lengthy stone stairways. The slightest sound echoed and re-echoed. It was lugubrious. We were soon underground. My guide stopped in front of one of the endless cells, fitted a key into the lock and pulled open the heavy door. He shoved me in, indicated a straw mattress on the dirt floor, and threw me a smelly blanket. I heard him close the door, turn the key in the lock and slide a heavy bolt into place. Then his footsteps died away. There was complete silence and utter darkness. The cell was cold and damp. It smelled like the blanket. I sensed a lack of air. "This is like I used to read about in the story books; it must be a dungeon," I thought, and I fell exhausted onto the mattress. I slept very badly, waking several times out of terrifying nightmares, and suffered nervous chills.

After many hours, a dull light fused into my cell down a long narrow shaft. I had no idea of the time, but felt it must be early morning. After what seemed hours of hopeless waiting, I heard footsteps; the bolt slipped back, the key turned and the door opened. What was going to happen now? Was I to be taken out and shot? I was shaking from head to foot. The guard ordered me to follow. Once more I saw the long corridors and the steps which led up into the light of day; then more steps and always up. There were charwomen—evidently prisoners—scrubbing the stairway and corridors; men—prisoners down carrying large lidded cans. "On their way to empty their chamber pots," I guessed. I heard people talking, orders being called out and the familiar hustle and bustle of house-cleaning. It was wonderful after the lonely black silence of my miserable cell. We passed through a wrought iron gate and into a short hall, into one side of which opened four doors. Women stared at me as I came in. There must have been eight or ten of them, of all ages. They were preparing to go down and empty their pots too. This was life! I guessed I was not to be shot just yet. I was directed into one of the rooms, a fairly large one, where I thought I might find company, but as the door locked and bolted behind me, I found that I was alone. There was a long barred window through which brilliant sunshine was pouring in. What a tonic! After the nightmares and the chills, I became alive with hope again. I wandered about my white-washed room. There were four iron cots, a bare table and a low stool, a cracked mirror hanging from a rusty nail. I peeped in, convinced that I would find myself changed, but I was hard to recognize from the dirt. Someone, as though in answer to my wish, opened the door to hand in a basin of cold water and a towel.

A period of quiet in the hall gave way to renewed activity. Doors were opened and shut with definite rhythm—bolt, key, key and bolt. I can hear them yet. And now it was my turn. Bolt and key; bread, soup and cheese were shoved at me across the threshold then, key and bolt. I tried eating the watery soup. I forced half of it down, but I couldn't eat the cheese; it was grey and wormy and soon my cell was stinking with it. The bread was black and soggy. I felt tired again, so I laid down and slept for some hours. I was awakened by the same haunting sound of the bolt and key. I recognized one of the Germans who came in, but the other, a young, attractive-looking Officer, was a stranger. He was making his visit simply to satisfy his curiosity; he had to see "the American." He spoke perfect English and was friendly in a haughty self-conscious way. He talked to me as one might interview a new servant to whom he felt decidedly superior.

That night I was awakened by the screaming and wailing of someone in delirium. The sounds came from the adjoining cell where a woman had lost her mind. I could hear others trying to quiet her. But the cries and the tears and the mad talk went on and on, in the dark of the night. It was horrifying. I could not lie still and listen. Suddenly there was activity in the hall, and I heard the sound of the bolt and the key. Then all became very quiet again. They had taken her away.

The following morning I woke to the rattle of buckets and brooms. It was soon time to empty the chamber-pots. We went off single file, each with his can, down the stairs, along a hall and out into a courtyard, the German prison matron leading the way. There we saw a number of men, some lounging around, others sawing wood. I felt embarrassed as I emptied my can down the open lavatory but the others seemed already habituated to this regime. Everyone was staring at me because I was the newcomer. I followed the example of the others and rinsed out my can with water and lime. We were forbidden to communicate, but a bent, shriveled old lady managed to whisper that she didn't know why she was there; the Germans had just come and taken her one morning, and that was six months ago.

It was time to go in again. We were climbing the stairs when the air raid sirens began howling. The panicky guard pushed us into our cells, locked and bolted the doors and the iron gate, and rushed off some place to apparent security. I soon heard the vibrant hum of Fortress motors. I ran to my window and climbed up on the table so that I could see out. There they were, a whole formation of them! I was trembling with excitement. There followed the whine of the bombs as they fell to the earth and the mighty explosions that shook the thick prison walls as if they had been made of cardboard. It must be for the airport. There came another formation; yet another. Smoke began to cloud the sunlight. I was frightened but I was thrilled. I cried out, "I may be a prisoner, but here come my liberators!"

After a while all was quiet again—too quiet. Time began to drag. I wondered if there was any way to get out of here. I climbed upon my table and grasped the bars. They were all solid. But even if they had not been it wouldn't have helped. From the window there was a sheer drop of about thirty feet into a small court enclosed on the three sides by the prison, the fourth by a high stone wall. I lay down on my cot. Suddenly a girl's voice called out from somewhere on my left, and was answered by man's voice somewhere on my right:

"Hello, hello, Claude, are you there?"

"Yes, what do you want?"

"Nothing. What are you doing?"

"Playing rummy."

"Are you winning?"

"Don't know yet."

"Were you frightened a while ago?"

"No, of course not. Were you?"

"Yes, a little."

A short silence—then: "Claude, do you still love me?"

"Yes" he sounded a bit indifferent, I thought.

"I love you too."

"That's good."

"Good by now. Don't forget to say good night, will you?"

"No, I won't."

A prison romance.

I felt so sorry for those two. Then I thought of Philippe, but slowly, almost reluctantly, like one testing the thickness of ice on a frozen lake. No, I couldn't go on, my emotions were not hardening, tears were just below the surface, and I drew back.

The following morning, about 9:30, I was led out of the prison to a waiting car. We drove through the streets of Chartres, soon coming to a stop in front of an attractive-looking house. My heart sank when I read the sign in the gate "Gestapo Headquarters."[24] I was rushed into a pleasantly furnished office, the windows of which looked out on flowers, grass and trees. Behind the desk was a distinguished-looking officer of the Gestapo, at his side, a trim attractive secretary, ready with her typewriter, while, nervously pacing the room, were two magnificent police dogs.

The Officer politely indicated that I was to sit down. He hardly looked at me. His whole attitude was very impersonal. I was of the impression

24. Whether this was actually the Gestapo or another branch of the Reich Security Police in France is unknown.

that he didn't like his job. The secretary was to act as interpreter; she was modest and treated me kindly. I soon lost my nervousness. The man began posing his questions after admonishing me to speak the truth. The woman typed my answers, my name, age, and birthplace and, from then on, the whole history of my life, where I had lived, dates, schools I had attended, details concerning my parents, my occupations, travels; then questions regarding my work in the Underground. He didn't seem particularly interested; it was easy to answer just as I pleased. He desired all the details of my trip from Paris to the moment of my arrest. I didn't dare admit having spent the night at Châteaudun, so I pretended that I had stayed with the boys all the way. This was a formal questioning. I had the feeling that the worst was yet to come. It lasted from 10:00 A.M. to 4:00 P.M., except for the half hour at noon during which the two went out to lunch. While they were gone, I waited in the front office, behind the desk of which was a very stout, common-looking, unsympathetic individual in uniform who kept gulping coffee and munching sandwiches. I wasn't hungry but was dying of thirst, and asked for something to drink. A glass and a bottle of beer were brought in. He flirted disgustingly with the French maid who brought him more coffee. I only drank my beer and caressed the dogs who kept coming to lay their big heads on my lap. After a while, he deigned to speak to me:

"To think that you dare to save the men who cause so much death and destruction." He was no doubt nervously recalling the bombardment of the previous morning. "You have been helping murderers!"

I didn't reply. He disgusted me.

After returning to the prison, I was exhausted. The questioning had been more a strain than I thought, but I felt contented. At least it was over.

The next morning we were given a real treat: a fifteen minutes' walk in the courtyard below our windows! We walked around and around, always in the same direction—an endless circle. Only those living in the same cell were allowed to communicate, so, of course, I had a very solitary walk, but enjoyed watching and studying the women. I soon decided that a few had probably done Resistance work, but the majority were common law criminals. They all smiled at me, in sympathetic interest. My nationality was responsible for that. It hadn't taken them long to learn that I was an American.

Later, the same morning, the Germans came to get me again. We went down the stairs and into the small office which I had entered the first night of my arrival at Chartres. Al was there. I was so happy to see him again. We were forbidden to talk but we could smile at each other. He was unshaven and looked so tired and unhappy. As I smiled I knew that I should never forget him. This experience was binding us together.

After a few minutes, we were led to the black car again. This time Al and I were together in the back. There was one guard behind with us and two in front. Al was handcuffed again behind his back, I could see how tight the cuffs had been locked and, as he was forced to lean forward, I realized how uncomfortable he was. I managed to slip my arm back and found his hand which I pressed to express my sympathy. We were going in the direction of Paris. I knew the route well, having covered part of it only a few days before.

5 Imprisonment at Fresnes and Romainville

JUNE 15, 1944–AUGUST 15, 1944

It was mid-afternoon when we came into Paris, along the Avenue du Maine, down the Boulevard du Montparnasse, up the Boulevard des Invalides and across the Pont Alexandre. This was my "quartier." The sight of those familiar streets made my heart beat faster and I felt almost certain that I would see one of my friends or neighbors but was disappointed. None of the Germans were familiar with Paris so I was obliged to direct them to the well-known Gestapo Headquarters, rue des Saussaies.[1] It was like directing my own funeral! We got down at the arcade entrance, crossed the court and went up the stairs. There was a great deal of activity: men, women, German and French, in civilian clothes and in uniform. We were led into the office of a Gestapo official, evidently the one who was to handle our case. This seemed to be the first he had heard of us—a fact that both surprised and heartened me. He was a man of distinguished bearing, 35 to 40 years of age, dressed in civilian clothes, tall, slender, blond, blue-eyed and wore a small mustache. I know now his name to be Geinser.[2] His attitude was one of polite active interest, like that of a life-insurance salesman. He spoke good French and could express himself in English but with difficulty. After having asked us to sit down, he started going through the contents of my handbag which had again reappeared. He asked me several informal questions regarding the objects he came across, but that was all. The interview was a short one, and we were dismissed.

We had to wait a few minutes downstairs, herded into a kind of waiting-room beside the main entrance, where there were fifty or sixty other prisoners, men and women, some who had just been arrested, others who

1. The Reich Security Police had a number of offices in Paris, including this one at 11, rue des Saussaies.

2. Later in her memoir Virginia refers to Geinser as Genser. No record of a Geinser or Genser at rue des Saussaies has been located.

had spent the greater part of the day being questioned. A "voiture cellu-laire," or prison car, backed up to the door.

"Prison du Cherche-Midi" shouted the Italian guard.

One by one, as names were called, men began to file out the door, and to disappear into the car without windows. After it had driven off, another backed into its place.

"Prison de Fresnes," he shouted again; more names, and this time, Al's was called, and mine.[3] We climbed in. There was a narrow passage down the center of the car, onto which opened the doors of tiny cells. There was just room for one person in each cell, but they forced us in by two's. Even then, there weren't enough cells and those left were allowed to stand in the passage. I was one of these. A guard with a machine-gun seated himself next to the driver, while another blocked the rear entrance. As we pulled out, I could see, over the shoulder of the rear end guard, a large open car following us. It contained four armed police, ready to oppose any attempt by members of the Underground to liberate us. How people stared in at us as we drove along! It was with an intense feeling of frustration and envy that I stared back.

I had never seen the prison of Fresnes, but I knew that it was somewhere in the southern outskirts of Paris. After riding for approximately twenty minutes, we passed through the prison gates and into a large courtyard. Here the car stopped and we were ordered to get out and to line up. The prisoners were of all ages. I recall one particularly: a very elderly white-haired, bearded gentleman dressed in black; he was wobbly on his slender legs and only kept standing by the aid of his cane which he grasped on one hand, his old carpet bag in the other; he looked neither to the right nor to the left, but held his proud head high and steady; in his buttonhole glowed the Rosette of the Légion d'Honneur.[4]

3. Fresnes Prison, the largest prison in France, was constructed between 1895 and 1898. During World War II it was used by the Germans to house captured Special Operations Executive (SOE) agents and members of the French Resistance. These prisoners, held in horribly dark and dank holes, were often tortured and sometimes executed. This was the last time that Virginia would see Alfred Wickman. Al, like Virginia, revealed nothing to the Germans. He was sent to Stalag Luft I at Barth in Germany and survived. Mrs. Alfred Wickman to Virginia d'Albert-Lake, March 17, 1993, d'Albert-Lake Family Papers. See Appendix 14.

4. The Légion d'Honneur is the highest civilian honor of France. In 1989 Virginia was awarded this honor for her work with the Resistance.

After a few minutes we crossed the courtyard and went up a short flight of steps into the entrance hall of the main prison building. After an identity check up, we followed a wide, empty corridor in which our footsteps made thunderous echoes. Passing through a door at the far end we entered a long, narrow, high-ceilinged room onto which opened numberless doors. While the men disappeared, the women were placed in cells by a prison matron wearing a light blue uniform. I found myself alone. Against the wall was a cot on which were piled four straw mattresses. I was exhausted, and climbing up on top of the pile, fell at once into deep sleep. Night had already fallen when I was awakened by a light on and my door being opened. I was suddenly aware of the fact that I had a cell mate. We silently pulled two of the four mattresses onto the floor and, when the door was shut again and the light flashed off, my companion began to groan and weep as though in great pain. In reply to my words of sympathy, she told me haltingly of her day at the rue des Saussaies where she had been called for interrogation. When she told me that she had been tortured, I shivered with apprehension. They had suspended her for hours from the ceiling by an arm and a leg! As she spoke French with a marked Germanic accent, I wondered if she was not an Austrian. She was trembling now and had a burning fever. It was terrible to see her suffer like that.

At early dawn our door was abruptly opened by a German Officer who called her name. I still can hear her apprehensive query, "Oh, have they come for me, already?" I never saw her again.

An hour or so later I was handed in a piece of soggy bread and a bowl of tinted tepid water erroneously called "coffee." Later I was ordered to follow the matron, along with the other women with whom I had arrived at the prison. We went down another broad corridor like the one of the evening before, and through a narrow door which opened into it. Here was a part of the prison which reminded me, with its rows of individual cabins, of the dressing room of the beach house or swimming pool. We were each locked into one of these metal cells. I sat down and began reading the names and inscriptions scratched on the sides. I quickly realized that I was in here preparatory to another search, and that what money and jewels I might have, would be taken away from me. I gazed sentimentally at my lovely engagement ring and at my wrist watch. An inscription had warned "Don't let them get your jewels; hide them!" Hide them, but where? I took off the jacket of the tailored suit I was wearing in order to examine it. The shoulder paddings were very thick and I was able to tear open a seam of the lining wide enough to slip in my watch. My ring, I tucked in the hem of my skirt which was made of heavy worsted wool. I sat in the hot airless compartment for over an hour before my turn came. I was led into a small room and ordered to undress; the search was a very casual one; my handbag was on the table and I was told to count out what loose change it contained—sixty francs it came to, and to go through the other contents with the matron who allowed me to keep only my comb; anything sharp like a mirror, pointed like a nail file, or frivolous like a lip stick, was forbidden. All the paper money, identity card and maps had already disappeared. When I was redressed I was taken into an adjoining room, a kind of office, where uniformed men were seated behind a long counter. One of them sealed my bag and its contents in an envelope, while I signed a receipt for my sixty francs. The search over, we were led once more down the broad hallway, which brought us into a section of the prison which impressed me as nothing else had up to now. I felt as if I were playing a part in a Hollywood prison drama, for this was the real thing; just as I had seen it pictured in films. We entered an immensely long room like a giant corridor, high-ceilinged and sky-lighted, with four balconied floors running around it, attained at each end by wide stairways climbing upward before great barred windows. Everything was iron and cement; every sound was amplified and echoed without end; armed guards and prison matrons were everywhere, shouting orders, and opening and closing the numberless doors which gave out onto the main floor and all the balconies. Here we were made to line up and a German sergeant pompously began to read names from the list which he held in his hand. One by one the women disappeared behind locked doors. Now it was my turn. I followed a plump, blond, uniformed guide down the corridor and up the stairs—one flight, two, three. I was to be on the top floor. I glanced over the railing to the deep well below. I wondered if anyone had ever committed suicide by jumping over. We stopped abruptly in front of cell 431. The matron shoved the key into the lock, pulled open the door and motioned me in. Now I saw for the first time the ugly cell that was to imprison me for many weeks to come. It was white-washed, high-ceilinged, about three yards long and two wide, with a beveled glass window opposite the entrance. On the left was an iron cot fastened to the wall and a shelf with some hooks. On the right was an open toilet with a brass faucet over it, and a small table and chair, both attached to the wall. Under the window, on the floor, there were what appeared to be two or three mattresses stacked one on the other, with a blanket draped over them. On this sofa of fortune lounged a girl. With a welcoming smile, she urged me to sit down beside her.

And so, I made the acquaintance of Marguerite. She was a young, attractive Rumanian jewess, arrested as the accomplice of a man unknown to her, from whom she had rented an apartment and who worked in the Underground. No evidence had been found against her but she had been detained—just the kind of person to have for a cell mate. She acquainted me with the rules and regulations of the prison and we discussed plans and possibilities to help pass our aimless existence.

Just before noon I heard, for the first time, the soup cart rolled along the rails which were imbedded in the passage floor. It was time to get out the mess bowls and to stand ready at the door. One could easily hear the cart advancing, stopping for a few seconds at each door—just long enough to fill the bowls. When our door opened, I saw a low flat car with an immense kettle on it out of which a girl prisoner, carefully watched all the time by a matron who accompanied her, rapidly filled our bowls with the aid of a long handled dipper. The soup was hot and thick. It tasted good to me, but Marguerite, who had already been on this regime three weeks, left most of hers. I wondered if I, eventually, would be inclined to do the same. I decided at once that no matter what my inclination, I would always eat my soup. I must keep my strength. Toward the end of the afternoon, the cart came by again, this time with bread. We were each given 400 grs. Every day the distributions were the same: coffee in the morning, soup at noon and bread at night, with an extra ration of cheese or meat twice a week. But the Red Cross food parcels helped break the monotony of this diet. We were given one a week and, at each distribution, my throat became tight with the emotion engendered by this proof that we had not been forsaken by the world outside. There was always sugar, jam, cheese, crackers, a "paté de fruit" and chocolate-covered candy bars; there was a little butter too and, with these elements, we made up our evening supper. It meant careful planning and even abstinence to make the parcel last the week, because whether we were two, or whether we were five, the parcel was the same; so someone must be in charge and this person's judgment never questioned. It was because I love the cooking and planning of meals that the job fell to me—I was the "économe"![5]

Up to the morning of the invasion, private clothing and food parcels could be sent in, but now that privilege had been stopped. We had no contact whatsoever with our families. As a result I was without soap, tooth brush and extra clothing, but Marguerite came to my rescue. She had arrived at Fresnes before private parcels were forbidden, and was able to lend me a nightgown, as well as an extra blouse and a skirt. She shared her soap too, and we both used her toothbrush, always giving it a good washing in between. She had some yarn and knitting needles, so I made myself a wash cloth, some booties and a pair of shorts. The weather was so warm that we wore as little as possible. It was absolutely forbidden to open the window, already bolted shut, so the only air came through the transom at the top. Nearly every day, however, the door into the passage was left open for about half an hour, which let a draught through, and it was during these precious minutes that I did my exercises. Twice a week we were allowed a "promenade." We would file down to the ground floor and along a narrow corridor onto which opened a row of little rectangular courtyards. As occupants of the same cell, we were allowed the "liberty" of a courtyard for twenty minutes; the "liberty" of looking at the sky while walking round and round the narrow cement walk which bordered the little grass plot in the center. Hemming us in on each side was a high brick wall in common with the adjoining courtyards; in front were iron bars and, in the back, the locked door and wall of the corridor. Overhead was another corridor, an open one, on which strolled our matrons attentively watching us. Communication with anyone outside of our own cell mates was strictly forbidden. We had to keep moving, so we did gymnastics on the grass plot, walked, ran and skipped around the walk, or played "follow the leader." Sometimes I pressed my face between the bars which gave me a strange illusion of freedom as I looked out onto the grass and trees beyond. But I could never stay long. Tears soon blinded me.

At Fresnes I suffered greatly from my loss of liberty. It was very hard to go suddenly from the stimulating worthwhile life I loved, fraught with danger and excitement, to this stagnant one.

5. Bursar or steward.

I detested the knobless door with its little peek hole through which the tiptoeing guards, unknown to us, spied on our activities. I abhorred the open toilet so immodest and humiliating to use. I hated the beveled-glass window through whose translucent surface, iron bars showed darkly.

But there was another side to our prison existence. We found it good sport and amusing to "put one over" on our enemies. For example, we also had a peek hole! A prisoner of the past had smuggled in a scout knife and with it had carved a narrow hole in the window casing, through which we could see across a wide open space to another wing of the prison occupied by the men. We could see over the prison walls too and watch the guard as he made his rounds. The knife was now in our possession and, with it, we cut our bread in appetizing slices; how much better than using a corset stay, or tearing it apart! One day we used it to take out the screws of the bolt which held our window shut and from then on (that is until we were discovered), we opened the window a half hour every evening to let in some of the delicious cool air. At that hour all was quiet in the corridors and there was not enough daylight for the guard outside to see us. We went to bed with the sunset, because there wasn't electric light by which to read or play cards. Lights could be turned on, but only by means of a switch outside the door. However once, just by accident, we discovered that our bulb was loose in its socket and, by screwing it in, the light would come on! After that for several evenings by careful shading of the lamp, we were able to enjoy some night life. But then, one evening, very late, we suddenly heard rapid steps in the corridor. We quickly unscrewed the bulb and pounced onto mattresses. The door opened and we were deafened by a volley of explosive German, but we "played possum" and nothing came of it, except that when we screwed the bulb back in, the light no longer came on!

Sometime during the day, while one of us listened attentively at the door, another would climb up from the end of the bed onto the window sill in order to have a really good view of the surroundings by the transom, or to call greetings and messages to the prisoners across the way. Our neighbors once were caught while doing the same thing and were relegated to spending twenty-four hours in the dungeon.

We had several methods of contacting our neighbors. One was by means of the faucet which, in some way, communicated with the faucet next door. Before starting a conversation we would tap the wall, then, cupping our hands, would telephone through. Another method was to press the metal mess bowl against the wall and to speak through it. To receive the message it helped immeasurably if one pressed one's ear against the bowl. In order to contact the prisoners underneath us, we used the hot air shaft which was about a foot square. Using strips of cloth tied together, we used to "elevator" messages, books and food, up and down! But the keenest satisfaction came each day at sundown when one of the prisoners possessing a lovely voice would sing out to us as we confidently waited for Evening Song and Taps. Every night a deep emotion born of common suffering welled up within us. As the last notes drifted away, they were replaced by the victory knocks systematically relayed from wall to wall and from cell to cell. We picked up the rhythmic message on our left wall and sent it on by our right. Gradually the sounds faded into silence, and the silence brought sleep.

I rarely slept well because of the fleas, but as the weeks wore on I seemed to become immune to them. They were difficult to catch in the dark, but to kill them was nearly impossible. Every evening I placed a bowl of water beside my straw mattress and, whenever I caught a flea, I plunged it into the water; every morning I enjoyed counting my quarry!

I always awakened about 6:00. That was the hour when prisoners were warned if they were to leave at 7:00 for the Gestapo Headquarters. A visit to the Gestapo signified questioning and possibly torture—so, at that early hour, I was always wide awake, listening tensely to the opening and closing of doors, and wondering if my turn would come today. If someone in our cell were called, we became nervous and excited; our nervousness was born of apprehension for our comrade and excitement over the prospect of fresh news from the outside, which she would bring us at the end of the day. But, otherwise, once the opening and closing of doors had ceased, we would lie quietly on until the sound of the "chariot"[6] on the rails announced the morning coffee. After breakfast, we washed, dressed, made up the beds and took turns at the housecleaning. There was always so much loose straw and dust from the mattresses. Before piling them up and arranging the blankets, we always searched the seams for fleas. We engaged in a daily contest to see who could catch the most. Every week we Lysoled the floor, but it didn't frighten the fleas though we used to

6. Wagon or cart.

sprinkle the solution all over the mattresses, and the cell would smell strongly of it for days. When the room was clean and neat, we would settle down to one of our various occupations: knitting or mending, playing rummy or "belote," washing or ironing.[7] To iron, we folded in place an article of clothing which had been washed and was still slightly damp, and, then sat on it until it was dry. Now and then we would have a lice scare and would search each other's heads daily until the danger seemed passed. We had still other distractions: we used to sing together. Marguerite could speak very little English but she knew by memory both the words and music of all the American and English popular songs of the past quarter of a century. Every two weeks we were allowed a hot shower and there was a Catholic mass once a month before dawn. The prisoners went to the Service, not only for the purpose of seeking comfort, but to see if there was anyone there they might know. Once every eight or ten days, the cart stopped by with books. We were never allowed to choose but given a stack which allowed one a piece in exchange for the old ones. Once I was lucky enough to get hold of an English book. I simply devoured it! I was so happy to contact, even in such an indirect way, the world I had known.

One early afternoon, our door abruptly opened and two of the matrons came in. They ordered us to leave the cell. It was a raid. They were going to search our cell! As I got up off the mattress I tried to shove my watch under it, but without success, as one of the women observed my gesture.

"What is that?" she demanded.

I realized that the "game was up," so I handed it over. We were all going to miss it; a watch is a friendly thing.

We waited for more than half an hour in a store-room at the end of the corridor. There wasn't anything we could take away, except some small pieces of soap which we hid in our hair. The previous day we had asked for soap and had been told that there wasn't any. When we were ordered back to our cell we found it looking as if a bomb had hit it. We were really angry! Everything was turned upside down and thrown all over the floor. There was straw and dust every place. Our precious knife was gone! And the unbolted window had been discovered, for the screws had been replaced properly! Even our wash line had disappeared. They

7. Belote is one of the most popular card games in France.

had been mean, but we felt fortunate not having been more severely punished.

Nearly every day there were air raid warnings. When a day passed without any, we felt discouraged and neglected. But one evening we had an experience which made us feel differently. A warning had sounded and this time the raid was for the Paris area because we soon heard the hum of motors and shortly afterward, we could see the planes! We were terribly excited! We climbed up on the window sill, not caring who saw us. We had nothing to fear from the German guards however; they all disappeared when a raid was on and, to help preserve the race, they took the German prisoners along with them. We used to see them through our peek hole, running like scared rabbits to the underground shelter outside the prison walls.

I had never seen Fortresses fly so low. I had the impression that they were too low considering the importance of the anti-air craft.

Suddenly we saw one of the planes in obvious difficulty. It swerved and appeared unable to right itself. We counted four chutes as they opened. What was happening to the rest of the crew? In any case, it was too late now; the plane was diving completely out of control. Almost immediately there was another one hit. It made a bee line for the earth and there were no chutes. We were shocked to see still another one in trouble! It exploded in midair and was followed by a fourth one which burst into flames. Again there were no chutes! The planes and pieces of planes fell over in the hills and we could see smoke rising against the horizon. Were there only four boys alive, out of how many—forty? We trembled with emotion and wept over the tragedy of the missing men. We prayed that the four who came down in chutes would fall in French hands, but the next day rumor said that they had been captured by the Germans and brought to Fresnes.

Twice during my seven weeks at Fresnes I was questioned by the Gestapo, rue des Saussaies. The hours I passed there were long and strenuous, but I tried to adopt the same attitude as that at Châteaudun, trying to appear dignified, but not proud, confident, but not aggressive. I was brought to the Headquarters in another compartmental car and, after my arrival, was placed in a cell with men prisoners who had just come from the torture chamber. They were hand-cuffed, swollen and bleeding. My heart ached when I saw them. They were in such misery they could not even speak. I recall one young fellow who had blood streaming down his face from a wound in his head; he had been beaten and his whole body was throbbing with pain; he had let his head fall forward on his chest in utter despair, and groans were escaping his swollen lips; he had not eaten for 48 hours, so I fed him the sugar and crackers I had brought with me to eat at lunch time.

I knew that exposure to these suffering men was meant to serve as a warning and to frighten me into telling the truth, but the method only revolted and angered me. I was determined that I would not be responsible for the arrest of young men such as these and for the tortures they would be forced to endure. At the same time I realized that it is easy to make resolutions, but not nearly so easy to stand up to them under physical torture. Officially we had always been warned that it is sometimes impossible to bear up under torture and that those who "talked" could not always be blamed; the traitors were those who talked before they were touched, usually through apprehensive fear. Personally I was never put to the test of torture. Herr Genser, the only one with whom I had any dealings at rue des Saussaies, treated me the whole time with perfect respect, nor did he even threaten me. Almost at the beginning of our interview he said:

"You are a belligerent and you will be treated by me as a woman and patriot."

Can you imagine my relief? I was dubious at the time and I still can't understand his attitude, especially as I have since heard that Herr Genser was one of the most feared men at the Headquarters. It is unlike a Nazi, especially an officer of the Gestapo to be so chivalrous and high-principled! Did he like my attitude? I had always been told that to show weakness or to crawl before a German was very poor policy, and this I had tried to avoid. Perhaps it was something personal on his part. Perhaps it was because I was an American. I shall never know. But the point that really matters is that I escaped torture with its uncertain results. I told the truth whenever I considered it would be of no importance, but I lied about everything else. I didn't have the privilege of asking Genser any questions, but I found out what I really wanted to know.

First, that Philippe had not been captured, and secondly, that my mother-in-law was not at the apartment when they went to search it and to arrest her. Herr Genser remarked, "Your mother-in-law had gone but we'll find her. We intend to hold her as hostage until we get your husband." Then, as if in afterthought, "You have a very attractive apartment, but there isn't anything of value in it."[8]

This amused me. The Germans only went to the flat the Friday following my arrest on the previous Monday. What did they think Philippe and Mum had been doing during the five days' interval?

Can you realize what it is like to be confined night and day in a tiny cell and to spend week after week with women few of whom you ordinarily would choose as friends? Personally I was fortunate as most of the women in cell 431 were easy to know, agreeable and diverting. I have already mentioned Marguerite who stayed on during five weeks after my arrival. Mme. Rousseau was a woman of 65 years of age, with a young face and luxuriant hair; she had amazing energy, was quick-tempered, possessed a keen but crude sense of humor, was extremely cultured and had an infallible memory for facts.

I remember her saying, "Memory is intelligence. One can't be intelligent without it."

She was keenly interested in politics and believed that all women should be, but, in spite of her feminism, she was an adoring wife and in great anxiety for her 85 year old husband who had been arrested with her. She insisted that her husband was entirely innocent and that it was only she who had supplied false identity papers for those needing them in order to escape Nazi tyranny. She was very proud of her husband who, many years before, had been a Deputy and now, though officially retired, was continuing to teach his Greek and Latin courses at the Sorbonne. He had nearly completed a work of several volumes on early Greek and Roman culture. Mme. Rousseau was very worried about the fate of his manuscript which had been seized by the Gestapo.

"And to think," she said, "there were three huge armed SS that came to arrest us, and they put handcuffs on my husband! I told them I thought it disgusting that big fellows such as they had to handcuff a poor old fellow 85 years old, so they took them off."

8. Following Virginia's arrest, Philippe briefly returned to Paris and Nesles to warn friends of what had happened and to destroy incriminating documents. He made his way to London in July 1944 and was never captured. This information is related in "Report from Philippe d'Albert-Lake," p. 4. It would be several weeks before Virginia would learn that Philippe had made his way safely to London. Virginia's mother-in-law remained in France and also escaped arrest.

Though Marguerite and I could not meet this remarkable gentleman, we at least were able to see him one day through our peek hole. The promenade cells on the men's side were just opposite our windows. When the men were out walking, we enjoyed the diverting occupation of watching them and calling out words of cheer and encouragement.

We took turns at the peek hole.

"Look, Mme. Rousseau, is that your husband? That short elderly bent man with the long beard? He's in the second cell from the left."

She jumped to the window. After a moment's search: "Yes, that's he! Quick help me to climb up so I can call out to him over the transom. Maybe he'll be able to *see* me!"

Marguerite and I made a chair with our arms and Mme. Rousseau mounted on it from the bed, but in trying to grasp the window frame lost her balance and fell back. She was so heavy we couldn't hold her. We were terribly frightened when we saw that she had fallen backward with all her weight onto the horizontal iron bar at the foot of the cot!

She was weeping and groaning, "My back is broken, my back is broken!"

This was serious, not only for Mme. Rousseau but for all of us. People don't break their backs in prison cells unless they're doing something they shouldn't.

We quickly lay Mme. Rousseau on the cot and proceeded to examine her before deciding to call for help. Her hip and small of the back had taken the fall. We could see that there would be a bruise, but were practically positive that no bones were broken. During the days that followed, Mme. Rousseau felt very sorry for herself as a huge bruise developed, gradually fading into all colors of the rainbow. She was sure that she would develop kidney trouble or have a blood clot. So we massaged her daily and, in the end, her bruise was advantageous as it served as an excuse to keep the cot for herself.

When the bruise was in its most startling stage, we were given an additional cell mate, a very sweet Polish woman. We called her "Madame Caroline" because none of us could pronounce her family name. Mme. Caroline had successfully wiped away several of her seventy years with becoming hair dye, and it was only when she admitted her age that Mme. Rousseau, several years her junior, realized that the priority for the bed belonged to the other woman. Ah, but, there was the bruise!

Abruptly and deftly she pulled up her skirt and gloatingly displayed her purple posterior. "Look, Mme. Caroline, just look what the Gestapo did to me."

Mme. Caroline was a gentle religious woman, even-tempered and modest but she was very superstitious and, with cards, told her fortune and ours, all day long. We taught her to play "belote." Mme. Rousseau wouldn't touch the cards. She took a very superior attitude toward Mme. Caroline who appeared so indifferent about culture, memory and politics! Nothing appeared to upset her and diplomatically she warded off Mme. Rousseau's pointed parries. It was easy to see, however, that she was deeply concerned over the fate of her two daughters arrested with her and from whom she had been separated upon arrival at Fresnes. One morning, while returning from our "promenade," she suddenly spied one of her daughters with her group of cell mates, some twenty-five feet behind us. We were forbidden all communication with other groups, but here was a mother who, after days of worried uncertainty, suddenly saw her daughter, a daughter whose face had received such heavy blows that it was swollen beyond recognition. She stopped and cried out to her, but in doing so lost pace with us and received a volley of blows and a brutal shove from the prison matron. Mme. Caroline couldn't get over the shock of seeing her daughter in such a state, but several days later, in the shower room, she had another glimpse of her, which revealed her condition to be definitely improved. She saw her second daughter but this one showed no signs of torture. These sisters were young attractive women. I believe that they had been doing patriotic work and that Mme. Caroline had been ignorant of it. While at Fresnes, she was never called to the Gestapo Headquarters for questioning. She had yet another daughter, married, and living in Warsaw, and from whom she had no news for many long months.

About this time, Yvonne Lemarchand came to stay with us. Yvonne was a frail, dark-haired, dark-eyed young woman from Normandy who, along with her husband, owned and managed a stock farm near Rouen. She was one of the most sincere and kind women I have ever met. Deeply religious, she repeated her rosary and read her prayer book daily. Being a great talker, we soon became acquainted with her whole family, including her four children—the youngest of whom was five, and the oldest fifteen. We soon knew all the occasions when her husband had left the "straight and narrow path" for the temptations of a sinful world! We learned of all the maladies that had been survived by each member of the family since his birth. We understood the trials of running a stock farm and, of course, we learned why Yvonne had been sent to Fresnes. Before and following the invasion, the Germans sent reinforcements to the Channel Coast. From one of these reinforcement divisions a Polish soldier turned deserter and struck back in the direction of home. He sought shelter at the Lemarchand farm, and the following morning, after leaving, was picked up by the German police. Upon being questioned, he told where he had spent the night and, as a result, M. Lemarchand was arrested and taken to the prison at Forges, from which he escaped almost immediately. This followed in the arrest of his wife as a hostage. I am able to relate the rest of the story because, since leaving Yvonne behind me at Fresnes, I have received a letter from her in which she tells me what happened afterward.

I will quote from her letter: "My husband, after escaping from the prison at Forges, hid at the home of some splendid people who took him in like a son. My children continued to work on the farm and their grandmother Jouanne came to help them. The work was done without their father who sent them advice and told them just what to do, not daring to leave his hideout. My family, however, encouraged him to give himself up in order that I might be released and allowed to go home to my children. This he did, but only stayed five days. Being afraid that his family would be the victims of a bombardment, he broke again the bars of the prison and escaped." She continues: "I left Fresnes the 12th of August. The prison matron said to me: 'If you are not a political prisoner you will be liberated.' Crazy with joy, I went down the stairway nearly singing, but my joy was very short, because a half hour after having been returned my money and identity papers, I was taken from Fresnes only to be sent to the prison of Loos at Lille. I arrived the 12th of August to be liberated the 1st of September. That day was one to cry with joy at the thought of shortly being able to embrace my children and my husband. I say 'shortly' because though liberated the first, my money and papers were to be returned but the 11th. Having found a new cell mate at Loos, I went to live with her. I returned to our farm the 22nd of September. You can imagine the happiness of the whole family to see me again safe and well."[9]

One day about noon, the matron came to get Marguerite. We had no idea where she was going, but evidently she was to leave the prison. We

9. This letter has not been located and is not part of the d'Albert-Lake Family Papers.

helped her to get her things together and, in five minutes, she was off. Her leaving left a vacuum in our cell. Nearly always gay, courageously overcoming her fits of depression, giving a peculiar intensity to every minute she lived, we couldn't help but miss her. We discussed probabilities as to her future. We were practically certain that she was being transferred to the camp for Jews at Drancy.[10] Already two of her three sisters had been arrested, as well as her brother. We were very anxious about her, knowing how the Jews were made to suffer. Marguerite was deported to Germany and she went through hell, but she is back now. I saw her recently; very thin, her prison number tattooed on her left arm, an expression of defiance on her face and vengeance in her eyes, I could see that she had suffered and was still suffering. I had always remarked her profound attachment to her family, and now she is distressed without news of her brother and two sisters. The third sister, the youngest one, had been arrested too while Marguerite was at Fresnes, having been denounced by deceitful friends after they had offered to hide her in their apartment. She too was deported and has returned, but she had returned a physical wreck and is now in a tubercular hospital, in a critical condition.

Anna Kavellac came to replace Marguerite. We loved this attractive, dark-haired, blue-eyed young Bretonne from Brest.[11] She possessed a quiet deep calm which comforted us and helped sustain our courage. She arrived like a Santa Claus, laden with butter and bacon, canned meat and fish, sugar and jam! Before being transferred from the prison at Brest, she had been permitted to have all the food parcels that her family and friends were able to send her. What feasts we enjoyed, thanks to her generous insistence! For once the "économe" was able to offer a little variety in her menus. Anna and her husband and been very active in the French Resistance Movement. They had been doing sabotage and it had led to their arrest and to that of their sixteen year old daughter whom Anna had been forced to leave behind in the prison at Brest. Her constant hope was that her daughter would be liberated, in which case she would go immediately to her grandmother by whom she would be well taken care of. Anna had undergone a long, strenuous eight day trip from Brest,

10. The internment camp at Drancy, not far from Paris, was a transit camp for Jews who were then transferred to extermination camps such as Auschwitz.

11. Brest is in Brittany on the Atlantic coast and is 605 kilometers from Paris.

in a box car crowded with other prisoners.[12] They had been bombed and strafed along the way, but this was cause for rejoicing! On arriving at Fresnes, Anna had been separated from her Brest companions. There was one about whom she was deeply concerned: a poor woman who had received a very severe wound in the hip by her Gestapo torturer. Almost immediately afterward followed the long rail trip on a hard box car floor, and complications had set in, and then gangrene; she had arrived in Paris in an alarming state and had no medical care except what the prisoners themselves were able to give her, and now all we could learn was that she had been taken to the Fresnes infirmary. This tragic story appeared to make a particularly deep impression upon Mme. Rousseau!

It was shortly after Anna's arrival that Mme. Rousseau left us. She believed that she had successfully maneuvered her interrogation the day of her questioning at rue des Saussaies and, when she was called one day in late July, we were practically certain that it meant liberation for her and her husband. I have had no news of her since, but if she had been deported, I would probably have known it.

It wasn't long afterward that Yvonne Willems came. She was in reality a sweet, simple, honest, good-natured young woman, with a very diverting sense of humor, but, the first time we saw her she was in tears. She made a pitiful figure with her badly permanented thick blond hair uncombed, and her copious figure rudely dressed in a coarse black working smock. She was a "concierge" who had been abruptly snatched away from the husband and children she adored and who were her only interest in life.

She sobbed out her story to us: "The Germans came when I was scrubbing the hallway. They said I was a 'boite à lettres.' What is a 'boite à lettres'?[13] They searched everything; turned my little place upside down. My husband and the boys had left; only Marie was there; she cried when they took me away; she didn't understand."

There followed another fit of weeping. I believed every word she said. Some Underground Group had evidently taken advantage of the simple uncomplicated mind of this young woman, and she had been serving as

12. With rail lines cut off, the trip from Brest to Paris took much longer than it would have under normal conditions.

13. Letter box. This concierge had unknowingly accepted letters from members of the Resistance.

liaison between members of the organization, without realizing it. As is the duty of a concierge, she had accepted letters from and for her tenants, and she had done it without discernment. She should have been released. One of her questioners at the Gestapo Headquarters assured her that he believed her innocent, but she was deported all the same. We were together until the middle of October and since then I have had no news of her.

Now I have introduced my companions of Fresnes. There were three others, but they played minor parts and stayed only a short time. One was a distraught young woman, several months along in pregnancy, who never stopped weeping during the five or six hours she was in our cell. At the end of that time she was transferred to the section for pregnant women. Another was a young girl of about twenty years of age, and most cheerful companion, who was released after ten days. She had been arrested as a suspect. Her name and address had been found in the address book of a woman arrested for Resistance work. The third was an unattractive girl condemned to fifteen days' imprisonment for having been mixed up in the purchase of a stolen German truck. I remember her for three reasons; first, for her complicated and detailed ablutions; she washed herself from head to foot at least twice a day; second, for her forgetfulness, foreseen or otherwise, in taking her piece of soap with her when she left; third, for the first words she spoke at the dawn of each day: "I only have ten more days," "nine more days," "eight more," and so on until "I'm leaving today," as if we, who had neither trial nor judgment and for whom the days stretched endlessly ahead, didn't know it!

But the majority of these women were likable, even lovable and I am grateful for all they meant to me, for their affection and for their courage. It was on the first of August that I left them. The matron told me at noon that I was to leave at one o'clock but that she didn't know my destination. I didn't anticipate my departure in the least. It meant a step nearer deportation and, until that day, the two Yvonnes, Anna and I had constantly confirmed our faith in a common liberation at Fresnes by the Allies who we knew were rapidly advancing in our direction. The girls helped me to gather my rather pitiful effects together, and I was miserable when I had to say good bye.

Yvonne Lemarchand wrote in her recent letter: "I see you again today embracing us like a tender mamma leaving her children in anguish, and in spite of your great chagrin, having the force to smile and to say that we would soon see each other again 'à bientôt, courage, je vous aime toutes bien,'[14] these were your last words, and the door closed heavily, leaving us sad as to the uncertainty of your fate."

I was led downstairs and made to line up with a number of other prisoners, after which we were taken to the room where we had been searched upon our arrival at Fresnes. Here our handbags were returned to us. There was a mirror on the wall and I saw my image for the first time in seven weeks. I didn't appear to have lost much weight but I had become very pale. All my healthy tan and color had disappeared. The rendering of my handbag renewed my confidence and I was ready for the next move. We were locked into the cellular car again and I had no idea in which direction we were heading. However we made good time, and as there was little traffic, I presumed that we were skirting Paris. After what seemed to me half an hour's ride the car stopped and we climbed down. We found ourselves in an immense courtyard; I saw high stone walls, a few trees, an air raid shelter and some German workmen putting down a well. There was a building like a "caserne," into which we were told to enter. This was Romainville prison.[15] I knew now; the jumping off place for Germany! One by one our names were called. We passed into an office where there was a counter behind which were several Germans in uniform. One of them went through the few remaining contents of my handbag. He allowed me to keep some personal things, including a nail file and cosmetics. The German who dealt with me appeared to be a Camp Commander. He was young and not unkind in his attitude. He glanced at an identity paper he held in his hand and said:

"You're American, I see." I was startled. He was speaking to me in good English.

"Yes" I answered. Then, because I was curious: "Where did you learn to speak English?"

"In the United States. I lived in New York before the war. Was over there four years."

"Really! Why did you leave?"

"I was forced to. When war broke out I was obliged to return to Germany for mobilization." Then, after a second's hesitation, "But I'm going

14. See you soon, take heart, I love you all.

15. The large prison at Romainville, on the eastern outskirts of Paris within the Fort of Romainville, served as a holding area for prisoners before they were deported to Germany.

back as soon as I can. The United States is a great place to live, and will be the *only* place once the war is over."

The interview was over, but I must admit that it amused and pleased me. Those words from a Nazi—or was he? As soon as all the women had been interviewed, the English-speaking German led us out across the courtyard and down a path. Suddenly below us, Paris expanded its roof tops and church towers. I was delighted and home seemed no longer so far away! Our path curved around and down, and now I could see a rectangular, three-storied building, in front of which was a pebbled yard, the whole fenced in with barbed wire. I saw women at the windows and others walking about the outside, or stretched out in the sun. I became excited. To see the sky again, to breathe this fresh air—it was heavenly! Our prison was in a fortress, part of which was barbed wired off for us, and the rest occupied by the Germans. There were armed guards pacing up and down outside the enclosure. Now, as the gate opened and we were released into the guarded enclosure, I felt a freedom that I had not known since that fateful twelfth day of June.

I was shown into a fairly large room on the ground floor, to be shared with nine other prisoners. There was a smaller room giving off of the first one, in which six girls had their quarters. Each room had a large normal window *without bars* looking out on to the enclosure. The room had two-story wooden bunks with straw mattresses. I had a second story one, next to the window, in the large room, but after a sleepless night, due to bed bugs who had their living quarters in the wooden bed frame, I pulled my mattress on to the floor in front of the window. From that time on I slept perfectly well. I'll never forget those first nights. They were lighted by the moon and the fresh pure air was exhilarating. A small sturdy maple was silhouetted against the sky. But it was impossible to forget I was a prisoner; a huge detection spotlight kept flashing on at regular intervals to send its brilliant beam sweeping across the courtyard and into our room. A German guard came each evening at curfew to count us and lock us in. Then, after visiting all the other rooms for the same purpose, he went out the front door and double-locked it. Yet our windows were allowed to stay open and were only sixty inches from the ground! Life at Romainville was a pleasure resort after Fresnes. It was not surprising that everyone had a good word for the camp director. We had a very short roll call in the morning at 8:00, and another late in the afternoon. The rest of the time we did almost as we pleased. There were certain chores to be done, but sharing the work left little for each individual to do. A librarian came by with books every week; there were two cold showers in the washrooms to be used as often as one wished (they did one good during those hot August days); we were allowed to play bridge, hold religious services and give concerts. Once a week we were offered the facility for washing linen and even boiling clothes; there was the privilege of a weekly hot shower, medical examination and douche; sunbaths were allowed, which some girls managed with a minimum of clothing; the reception of Red Cross and private food parcels was permitted which, added to the camp's good soups, let no one to go hungry. There was an energetic Danish prisoner who held gymnastic classes twice a day, while other internees taught classes. Women bore their babies there too; there were four or five tiny ones who enjoyed the sun and air every day in cribs placed in another courtyard adjoining ours. Only at roll call were we conscious of close supervision. It sounds wonderful, doesn't it? But there were two phases of our camp life which I haven't mentioned, that marred prison perfection! One was that letters and visits were forbidden: no news from home can be hard to bear. The second was the 4:00 roll call which, every day, culminated for thirty or forty women the constant fear and threat of deportation to Germany. At this time the strain was particularly great because it was just after the first week of August, and we could already hear the allied cannons as they approached Paris. And all night long we listened to the rumble of retreating German trucks and tanks on the distant highways. There were constant air raid warnings, during which we were obliged to go into our rooms and close the windows. But we could see the planes all the same, and they never failed to bring us the thrilling stimulating sense of liberation. Can you understand the strain of the 4:00 roll call, as all of us breathlessly awaited the reading out of the names of those who were to leave the camp within the next hour? As each name was called, the woman to whom it belonged left the ranks to go to her room and get her things together. *Any* communication with those not leaving the camp was absolutely prohibited. This was to avoid their taking messages away with them. But we solved that problem easily; every afternoon, before the "appel,"[16] we wrote out little notes addressed to our families, on small pieces of paper and hid them in a place known to everyone in the room; then, if any of our group was called, she would take the

16. Roll call.

messages away with her. There was always the chance that the French-man who drove the bus would be a sympathizer and would accept to mail or deliver them; otherwise the only alternative was to drop them out of the window as the bus drove along, trusting to passersby to find and forward them to their destination. I know now that all the messages I sent that way arrived eventually! At Fresnes, we had used much the same system, sewing notes into the shoulder pads, and slipping them into the dress hems or under the shoe linings of prisoners whom we expected to be liberated. It was impossible to throw messages from the cellular cars because, during the short trips to the rue des Saussaies, we were too closely guarded and there weren't any cracks in the cubicles.

I admired the women as they were called from the ranks. They rarely showed what they were really feeling. They walked straight, their heads held proudly erect. Sometimes, they smiled or turned to wave good-bye. Others would call out "Au revoir, à bientôt! Vive la France!"[17] I always felt clutched by a deep emotion at those moments. Afterward we spent an hour in the enclosure, waiting to hear the roar of the big bus as it backed out of the garage. The girls boarded it from an exit unknown to us, but as they drove off up the winding road which circled around back of the caserne, we waved and wept and called out to them and sang the Marseillaise![18] I tremble again as I think of it! Each one of us who stayed behind was breathing the prayer, "Thank God, I'm not in that bus." After this daily strain of mixed emotions, we felt ready to collapse from nervous fatigue. Following a night's rest, the cloud would lift a bit, only to settle slowly down again as the hands of the clock moved toward the zero hour.

Day and night our ears were turned to the sound of the advancing cannon, and every day there was departure. It became unbearable!

One morning, I was notified of the arrival of a food parcel. The distribution was made by the camp Commander who recognized me at once. He must have sensed the strain I was under for he said:

"Don't worry too much, I don't believe Romainville will be evacuated to Germany. You will be liberated here by your compatriots."

I went back to my room, walking on air! I had been at Romainville for about ten days and as most of the women left after about fifteen, I still had a few ahead of me. However, the next day, at the "appel," the names

17. Good-bye, see you soon! Long live France!
18. The *Marseillaise* is the French national anthem.

of all but two of the girls in our double-room were called. I was one of the two, but I couldn't understand why because all of us had left Fresnes for Romainville on the same day. I was so upset that I was ill all that night—the most violent reaction to anything I had experienced up-to-date.

The next morning, the rooms filled up again with strangers, among whom was Janette, the girl who was to be my most faithful and affectionate companion for months to come.[19] I haven't spoken in detail of the acquaintances and friendships I made at Romainville. Some were short-lived because of the endless departures; a few still exist and have become deeply rooted after the months of suffering endured together; but the majority, which would have endured like these others, were cut short by death. As I go on with my drama, the names of those I knew and loved best will play their part.

Twice before the fifteenth of August, we were told officially that the camp was to be evacuated the following morning but both times counter-orders were given at the last minute. This encouraged us to no end. We adopted the opinion that the Germans wanted to evacuate us but that they couldn't for the reason that bridges were down, rail communications cut, and that all remaining transport facilities were needed for their own retreating troops. But we felt discouraged again one early morning as we saw the fortress being examined in detail by several important-looking officers of the Wehrmacht who appeared to be making decisions regarding gun emplacements and dispositions for the camp.[20] We wondered if this meant that Romainville was to be used as a strategic point of defense of Paris and if we were to become a military objective!

19. Janette, imprisoned for her work with the Resistance, was Jeanne Marie Boissard.

20. The Wehrmacht was the name of the German armed forces between 1935 and 1945.

6 Deportation to Ravensbrück

The fifteenth of August dawned into a brilliant, hot day. It was the Assumption, and permission had been given for a mass to be held at 10:00 in the courtyard by a priest from outside the fort. But about 8:00, there was another official announcement: immediate evacuation of the camp! We were ordered to pack at once and prepare to gather in the courtyard! Would the departure actually take place this time, or would there be another counter-order? The cannons seemed closer than ever. We were nearly crazy with despair! At the signal of the gong we dragged our heavy luggage outside. It was heavy due to the extra winter clothing sent to us at Romainville by our foresighted families; besides, there was the residue of our food parcels, plus the Red Cross food packages, and generous bread and sausage rations of a last minute distribution. It looked like a long voyage ahead! We were divided into alphabetical groups. The whole procedure dragged out; the Germans were evidently waiting for something. They were waiting for the buses which were to come and pick us up. Suddenly there was an air raid warning, but instead of being ordered back into the caserne, we were herded out through the gate and locked into underground caves dug in the sides of the high earth surrounding the fortress. We stayed on for hours, long after the end of the raid. At noon, soup was passed. Still the buses didn't come! Our hopes mounted again as the day wore on. Perhaps they wouldn't come; perhaps they *couldn't* come! But at four o'clock we heard the familiar grind of requisitioned city buses as they came down the incline and into the camp. They stopped in front of the barred entrances of our caves and, out of them, swarmed armed SS—the kind with hard cruel faces and rapid brutal movements. We were ordered by them into the buses, and soon were so crowded and hot that we could hardly breathe. I arranged to be among the last to get in our bus, so that I would be able to stand near the driver, who was a Frenchman. I had a fist full of messages that I wanted to give him. These were very important messages, notifying our anxious families of our actual departure. The driver was seated at my left, while, on my right, an SS with gun in hand guarded the open door. I had to be very cautious. Finally I was able to attract the attention of the driver and with a gesture indicated what I wanted. He nodded his assent but indicated that I wait a moment. The buses in our rear were still filling up. In the meantime, more messages and some franc notes were hurriedly passed along to me. The SS disappeared for a moment, giving me the opportunity or slip the money and messages into the hand of the driver. In a low whisper he said:

"This job makes me sick. All day long since early morning I've been driving prisoners from Fresnes and Cherche-Midi to the station at Pantin."[1]

"Then all the prisoners in Paris are being evacuated?"

"Yes."

"And the Allies—where are they? Are they advancing?"

"Sure, they're doing fine. They're at Rambouillet!"

Rambouillet!! Only 60 kilometers from Paris. We were being evacuated just at the eve of liberation![2] How cruel and ironic it seemed! (I have learned since that the bus driver went all over Paris to personally deliver the messages we gave him. Philippe has saved mine, which reads: "The entire prison is being evacuated this morning to an unknown destination. Thank you for the parcel which arrived yesterday. It was a lovely one and brought me much pleasure. My fifteen days here passed very agreeably. It's very sad to be obliged to leave when the others are so near. But what can we do? The morale is high and I'm in good health. We are three hundred women leaving the prison. My love to all, especially to my darling. See you soon! Virginia."[3]

The signal for departure was soon given. Our guard was back in his place. The bus gearshift ground into first and we lunged forward. But not for long as the overcrowded bus couldn't get up the incline. The driver went into reverse, and then made another attempt—but still without success. If aggravations like this would only continue! Anything at all to delay

1. At the Gare de Pantin the prisoners would begin their long journey to Germany.

2. Allied troops triumphantly entered Paris ten days later, on August 25, 1944.

3. See Illustration 9 for a reproduction of the note that Virginia sent to Philippe in care of his aunt Mme. de Gourlet.

Map 2, Germany

Virginia's deportation route from Paris to
Ravensbrück, August 15–22, 1944

Route Virginia traveled from Ravensbrück
to Torgau and back, September 11 –
October 6, 1944

Route Virginia traveled from Ravensbrück
to Königsberg and back, October 16, 1944
– February 4, 1945

Route of Virgina's trip from Ravensbrück to
Liebenau, February 28 – March 6, 1945

Paris

Châlons-sur-Marne

Bar-le-Duc

Nancy

Str

Vittel

OCCUPIED
FRANCE

Besançon

UNOCCUPIED
FRANCE

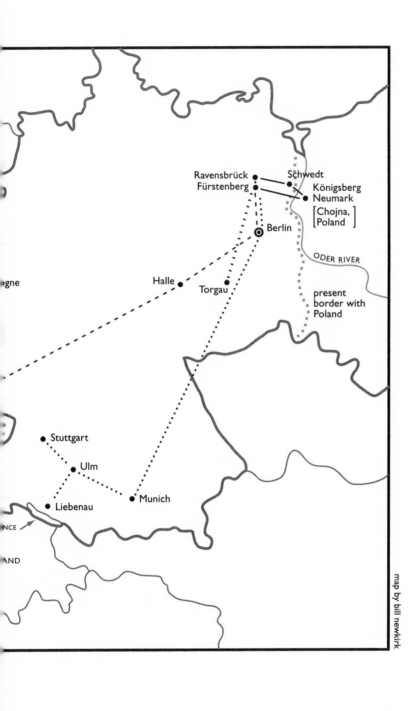

Ravensbrück
Fürstenberg
Schwedt
Königsberg
Neumark
[Chojna,
Poland]
Berlin
ODER RIVER
gne
Halle
Torgau
present
border with
Poland
Stuttgart
Ulm
Munich
Liebenau
NCE
AND

map by bill newkirk

our departure! The SS ordered us to get out, after which the bus success-fully mounted the hill, while we followed behind on foot. At the top of the incline, we again crowded in, and then slowly the long green buses in single file, loaded with their three hundred miserable passengers, lunged out through the prison entrance into the crowded quarters of Paris. This was a holiday, so the streets and parks were crowded with people who stared at us. They realized what was happening. One could read on their faces what they were thinking. They pitied us. As I looked at them, the same thought went round and round in my consciousness: "These people will soon see the liberation of Paris. I'm going to miss the day of which I have dreamed for nearly five years and which was to be the greatest in my life." Philippe and I had talked of it so often. We had painstakingly made a small reserve of canned delicacies and good wines too that we were saving preciously to celebrate that great day. Instead, the delicacies and the wine had gone into the mouths of the Gestapo, and my day of liberation seemed farther away and more uncertain than ever.

I shall never forget my impression when we drove into the rail yards of the Gare de Pantin. Most of the Paris stations had been destroyed by bombing, but this smaller suburban one was still untouched. How fright-ful if it should be attacked now! The yards were simply jammed with rolling stock, as this station served as one of the few remaining outlets from Paris for the Germans and everything they wanted to take with them. We stopped parallel with a track on which was waiting a line of box cars, so long that it appeared endless. From every car, as far as I could see, were anxious faces peering out of narrow rectangular ventilation openings and through the cracks in the half closed doors. So this is the way we were to travel! I was so stunned I unconsciously hesitated to leave the bus, but suddenly received such a brutal shove from a female SS that I staggered unwittingly toward the gaping door of the nearest empty box car.[4] I remember reading as I climbed in, "30 horses—40 men." They had forgotten to add "60." Yes, we were sixty women with all our baggage! We stacked the baggage against the walls and then sat down on the thin layer of straw with which the floor was carpeted, our backs supported by our valises. We squeezed tightly together one against the other, but there still wasn't enough wall space for everyone. The extra eight or ten had to

4. The "female SS" to whom Virginia refers were technically not members of the SS. They belonged to the SS Women's Auxiliary.

find a sitting place among the numberless legs and feet that met in the center of the car. The prospects of the trip certainly weren't very bright. If there was barely sitting space, how ever could we manage to find space for lying down? And of course we couldn't. Some efficient leaders tried to arrange a system whereby half our number would stretch out for the first part of the night, and the remaining, the last part. But some intended to lie down the whole night, while the majority preferred to sleep the second half of the night to the first half, and so no decision ever was reached. The best places in the car were near the doors or under the ventilation slits. Those in the corners were the most uncomfortable. But of course those near the doors objected to the placing of the "tinette"— our ten-lb. jam tin toilet—at their feet; however, it was the only place because that was the center of the car and the most convenient spot for everyone. Women at the ends of the car, rather than fall and stumble over bodies in order to reach the "tinette" for only a minor duty, took the habit of urinating in small tin cans and emptying them out the ventilation windows; this of course annoyed the women who were sitting under-neath. There was always something to cause trouble. Some wanted to talk just when others preferred to be quiet. Some wished to repeat daily an oral mass, to which still more objected. It is true that there were women who were disagreeable and unwilling to cooperate, but they were lonely and frightened and forced to leave all they really cared for—country, home, and family. Though some of us were there because we had been willing to risk our liberty for an ideal, there were others, far more unfor-tunate, who were still ignorant of the reason for their arrest. If you can imagine what it is like to be tired and sick and nervous, and to live under such trying conditions of overcrowding with lack of ventilation, night and day, in the stifling heat of a smelly box car, in the month of August, you will realize that, under such strain as that, women can't be at their best. I played as little part as possible in the discussions and feuds of the 144-hr trip. I observed that foreigners were quickly resented if they started "but-ting in" in the affairs of the French, so I tried to keep cheerful, cooperate when it was possible and let it go at that.[5]

5. This was one of the last convoys of deportees to leave France. See the Introduc-tion for a discussion of the significance of Virginia's refusal to reveal the true nature of her work with the Resistance to the German authorities during her two-month imprisonment in France.

Bombing had damaged rail communications so seriously that our itinerary became too complicated for me to trace.[6] As long as we remained in France we believed that a miracle could happen. Before leaving the station at Pantin, a young Red Cross worker, passing us drinking water across the threshold of our sliding door, remarked: "Don't worry, you'll never get to Germany. It's impossible; you'll be liberated before then." Of course, words like these were nourishment to our famished hopes. We believed them, forcing back any doubts that would try to edge to the surface.

The first night out, as I settled down to the most comfortable position I could manage that was fairly permitted, I recalled the last time I had spent the night on a train. It was just a year and a half before, when I left to spend several days with a friend at the quaint old town of Luxeuil-les-Bains, south of Nancy. Being an American citizen and living in Paris, the Germans had decreed that I had not the right to leave the city, but I left any way, using false identity papers. I had spent the night in one of these comfortable compartments of the Wagons-lits,[7] with a soft pillow, clean sheets and a warm blanket. This business of sitting on tickly straw, with valises jabbing into my sides and no place to rest my head, while all the time being jolted along over squeaking wheels a few inches under my cramped back, couldn't quite be compared to the other mode of traveling!

The next morning, after passing through Châlons-sur-Marne, we entered a tunnel. I never have liked tunnels; when I was a little girl, before air-conditioned trains existed, I was nearly stifled by soot and smoke while going through a long one at night, and I have never forgotten. This was a long tunnel, but I didn't mind it too much, not until our train suddenly stopped while in its blackest depths. Someone who had a watch and matches kept track of the time. Five minutes, ten minutes, one hour passed, and still we hadn't moved. What was happening? Now and again we heard heavy footsteps on the gravel beside the car, and hoarse German voices roaring out incomprehensible phrases. I began to feel nervous. Süni Sandoe was on my left. Süni was a husky Danish woman who had directed the gymnasium classes at Romainville. I could tell that she too was feeling the strain. We clutched each other's hand for mutual encouragement. One can imagine anything under circumstances such as these.

6. See Map 2 for the deportation route.
7. Sleeping car.

Were we going to be deserted to suffer a slow death in that black cauldron? Already the heat and thirst were becoming almost unbearable. All was strangely quiet in our car, but down the line we could hear cries of "Water, water!" and "Give us air, give us air!"

Were we going to be asphyxiated? Certainly it was possible—sixty women in a car ventilated by four narrow windows through which stale tunnel gases were seeping in! Two hours had passed and still there were no signs of our moving. One sensed that the breaking point was near. Suddenly a woman across from me burst out in a racking voice:

"We can't go on like this. I'll tell you some jokes!"

Then followed a number of such dirty stories as I never knew existed; just plain filthy with not a spark of humor to temper the licentiousness. Yet we had to be grateful. They did break the strain.

After three and a half hours, the train abruptly began to back out of the tunnel. I can't express the amazing relief that followed. How relative happiness is! I was being deported to Germany, under impossible living conditions, and yet, just backing out of that tunnel, into the light and air filled me with joy and courage.

As soon as we left the tunnel, the train stopped. Our doors rolled back and we were ordered to climb down. We were on a high steep embankment, below which stretched empty fields, a small wood and a tiny village. All the box cars were being emptied simultaneously and it was a dramatic sight to witness 3 thousand women and men slide down an embankment and swarm onto a great flat field that, five minutes before, had been devoid of any visible human life.[8] I suppose most of us thought of escape. But there was nothing to hide in or behind, and there were armed guards everywhere. The occupants of each car were ordered to group together. Once there was a semblance of order, we were marched off two by two. Janette and I were together. We hastily made a hammock of a blanket someone had given me before leaving Romainville, and tossed all our boxes and bundles into it. We struggled under the weight, and if we had only known what lay ahead, we would have dumped everything into the ditch immediately! We stumbled across the fields, skirted the wood and turned to the left to cross a bridge just before entering the town. It was while skirting the wood that someone ran up to me to say:

8. Men made up about twenty-four hundred of this number. The other six hundred were women.

"Virginia, your mother-in-law had been arrested. She is in one of the other groups!"

I nearly dropped everything, I was so shocked. Of course it was possible! Mum could have been arrested since my last questioning by the Gestapo and brought direct from Fresnes to the Gare de Pantin! I was literally ill! I visualized Mum as I had last seen her, so thin and tired! She was sixty-nine years old. How could she bear up under a trip such as this? I couldn't go to look for her then as it was forbidden to leave one's group. I must wait until we arrived at our destination.

About the same time, Nicole de Vitasse attempted to escape. Poor Nicole, if only she had succeeded she would probably be alive today instead of dead of starvation in Germany! After leaving the woods, we passed a small farm house beside which was a walled courtyard. Nicole suddenly disappeared into the enclosure and dived into a pile of straw under a hay wagon. But the Germans saw her and dragged her out. She was pale with fright; nor shall I ever forget the horrible blows in the face she received from one of the female SS. This attempt at evasion angered the Germans and they became unfortunately more attentive. After crossing the bridge near the wood, we followed a highway into another village. Here many of us abandoned our heaviest baggage beside the road for we couldn't go on any longer under such weight. Fortunately, the Germans requisitioned a farm wagon to pick it up and bring it along. All this time we were skirting the hill pierced by the tunnel. We eventually came around opposite its mouth, which gave onto a high railroad bridge partially destroyed during a bombing raid, which we were told had occurred but a few hours previous to our arrival.

We had passed through a third village. All the inhabitants were either at their windows, or out in the streets, watching us go by. Some smiled— tender, sympathetic smiles; others stood immobile with tears in their eyes. We called out to them: "Bon courage, à bientôt! Vive la France!"[9] I too was blinded with tears. At one place an earnest-looking young fellow suddenly broke from a group of people to take a heavy suitcase from the hand of weary woman who had not wished to abandon the few things she possessed. The Germans permitted him to stride along beside us.

After walking about eight kilometers we reached our destination. Here, opposite the bridgeless tunnel, was an empty freight train waiting to receive us. The Red Cross was there too, with boiled potatoes and milk,

9. Take good heart, see you soon! Long live France!

reminding us that we hadn't been abandoned or forgotten. I kept looking for Mum, but without success. Time proved that there had been a mistake. She had never been arrested.

The train didn't leave for two or three hours. In the meantime, some of us dared get out and sit on the side of the embankment beside the train, which was permitted until too many exploited the privilege at the same time. As I was climbing back in, I turned to see a familiar figure go by. It was a man, whose face I recognized but I was so stunned I couldn't remember his name. I only stuttered in trying to call out, and though I attempted to get down and run after his fleeting figure, the German guard stopped me. As he threatened to strike me, I could only turn back, disappointed. Can you guess who it was? It was Marshall, the American airman whom Pierre had abandoned down by the Spanish border!

Our human freight train pulled off again in the early evening. We were feeling more fit I believe, having gotten rid of our box car cramps, drunk to our thirst and eaten without jogging. We were still in France too and were buoyed by our hope of liberation. Later in the evening we came into Bar-le-Duc. The weather was stifling hot. Judging by the sound and conversation outside, we believed that the women who were seriously ill were being left at Bar-le-Duc. An ordinary box car attached to ours, just ahead, had been converted into a hospital car, which was already overcrowded. The advantages were a thicker bed of straw and more air, as the doors were left open during transit. The medical staff consisted of two women prisoners, one a doctor from St. Quentin, the other, a nurse.

The following day, our third one out, we were still in France. Our guards were becoming more and more agitated. There was one in charge of each car. They opened and closed the doors, answering our questions and guarded us in the early morning and late evening when we were allowed to get out to do certain duties and to empty the "tinettes." After the doors were closed and the train was starting, these men climbed in a box car of their own, farther along. We were fortunate in having a girl with us, born of German parents and who spoke the language perfectly. Annie was not timid and talked in a friendly manner to our guard. As a result, he became more lenient with us, answered our questions more frankly and allowed an aperture in one of the doors, about six or eight inches wide. This gave us considerably more air. After each "sortie,"[10]

10. Outing.

morning and evening, he recounted us. It was never very accurately done though he tried several different systems. The total number was chalk-marked on the outside of the car and varied slightly each day as prisoners who fell ill were transported to the hospital car, or, upon recovery, were brought back.

It was early afternoon of the third day. We had been passing through a forest and, as we came out of it, the train stopped abruptly. We looked for a reason, but there wasn't a station, nor a hamlet, or even a farm house—only fields stretching away on both sides of the track. Every time the train stopped we considered it an opportunity to ask the guard to let us out, but this time he promptly and gruffly refused. Instead, he ordered us to stay seated and to keep quiet. We felt that something extraordinary was taking place. A girl under one of the ventilators dared to stand up and look out.

She described what she saw: "There are several Germans in uniform, with guns in their hands, ordering out into a field three men, two appear to be prisoners, and a fourth, who is completely naked. Now this last one is being placed apart from the others."

It wasn't necessary for her to tell us what followed. Several guns were fired simultaneously. The shock of the explosion as it burst through the silence was terrific. We grew pale. Not another sound was heard for a moment; then our announcer feebly carried on: "Yes, the man without clothes had been shot. The other prisoners are carrying him back."

Suddenly our door was roughly rolled back. The girl at the window dropped to the floor. Our guard was in a dangerous mood. He climbed in our car along with another. They counted us and recounted us. Then one of them announced:

"If there are any other attempts at evasion, ten hostages will be shot from each car where it occurs."

They climbed down, pulled the door so that it was completely shut, and locked it. We were nervous, frightened and very subdued, and I'm certain that dreams and plans of evasion left the minds of most of us. (I have since learned from Marshall who was in the very car where the incident occurred, that there was to be an attempt at wholesale evasion; they had been working upon the floor boards of the car, but a traitor had denounced their activities.)

There was a girl with us, an attractive, dark-eyed native of Tahiti, who was constantly threatening to escape. We wondered how she would dare risk the lives of ten girls, but with all her charm she had a very emotional, moody, firebrand disposition, and some of us believed that there would be more peace in our car if she were not there. Early in the morning following the tragic shooting, our train stopped just outside of Nancy. When the door was rolled back, I observed that we were on an embankment, below which was a wide prairie. The guard allowed a few of us to get out, but the stop was a very short one and he didn't have time to count us. I presume that the "sortie" had been unofficial. It was only some minutes later, in the rail yards of Nancy, after we had been allowed to leave the car by turns of two and three, that we were counted. In the meantime, some of us observed that Morea was missing and, when the guard climbed in to check up on the number of "59" marked outside, I must admit that we didn't feel very happy. He counted once, and then he counted again. Yes, that was correct—fifty-nine! I couldn't believe it! Fifty-nine of us, and yet one had just escaped—still there were only fifty-nine! We thanked God that an error had been made in the count of the night before. One of the girls who had seen Morea's escape explained how it happened:

"Do you remember the fairly high weeds growing along the embankment at the stop outside of Nancy? Well, Morea hid among them pretending to be modest, and when the guard's head was turned, she disappeared down the incline."

Nancy is so near the French-German frontier that, as we pulled out of the yards, we realized that if we were to be saved from deportation, something would have to happen quickly. But nothing happened and, hardly before we knew it, we were reading German signs instead of French ones. No longer could we hope for liberation. We were in the dreaded Nazi nation, actually deported, and the mounting kilometers were taking us farther and farther away from home and country. The women became silent and depressed. Some were quietly weeping. But just the contrary was true of the Germans. They became more and more gay. They were happy to be home again, away from the uncooperative French, those bomb-throwing, sabotaging, resentful people whom they couldn't influence to "collaborate" with them. They felt much safer now and very proud of themselves for having emptied all the Paris prisons and successfully deported all the inmates to the Fatherland! Even the locomotive relaxed. It slowed down to an eventual stop and, for the first time, all the doors of all the cars were opened wide, allowing all the prisoners to get down all at the same time. Parallel with the track was a road, and parallel with the road was a row of ordinary small town houses. We were hot and thirsty and very dirty. All the Germans came out of all the houses to stare at us, and then, with the consent of our guards, brought us drinking water and filled up some buckets and washtubs with water, in which to wash. One of my friends, who had gone to help carry the water, came back, proudly announcing that she had been offered a real bath in a real bath-tub! When we had finished, we were ordered to sit down on the grass that bordered the road. We were cool and comfortable, and decided that perhaps Germany wasn't going to be so bad after all! A few of us had managed to slip into a small apple orchard overgrown with weeds, which was on the other side of the track. Our guard discovered us and, after ordering us back, remarked, "Someone must have escaped in those weeds."

We said "no," but he went off to look anyway. He was quite good-natured about it. He came back shortly to add:

"But someone *must* be hiding in those weeds! Are you sure there isn't anyone?"

"Of course we're sure!"

He went to look again. We had been sure, but we weren't sure any longer. We began to laugh. We munched our green apples. It was all very silly, and we decided that our German was not very clever!

The next day we were separated from our men prisoners. While we were in the rail yards at Weimar, they left us. We knew that there was a large camp for political prisoners in that vicinity, but had no idea that it was the now famous Buchenwald![11] The women whose husbands were in the convoy were allowed to see them for a few minutes to say good bye. During these formalities, the rest of us were allowed to get down from our cars and walk up and down beside the tracks. We questioned the guards. They wouldn't tell us our destination, but answered our other questions after their own fashion.

"Will we be able to keep our own clothes, or will we have to wear uniforms?"

"You'll keep your own clothes."

11. Buchenwald was one of the largest concentration camps in Germany. Of the almost 240,000 prisoners from thirty countries who passed through Buchenwald, some 43,000 died.

"Do they shave women's heads in that camp?"

"Of course not. That's only for severe punishment."

"Will we have to work?"

"No, only minor chores."

"What will we live in?"

"You'll be in big barracks with comfortable bunks. There are showers too with hot and cold running water."

All this sounded ideal for a prison camp. Our hearts looked up! I felt very cheerful and independent and left my box car to walk down past the others, to see if I could find anyone I knew. Suddenly I saw Vera! What a surprise! I didn't even know that she had been arrested. Vera was a charming woman of Russian birth who had done splendid work in the Underground. Her activities had been numerous, but we first made her acquaintance at the time she started convoying for us in the Paris area. She had good news for me—she had been arrested several weeks after I, some time during the month of July, just before her arrest she had seen Philippe!

"Yes, I saw him several days after you were arrested, after he had come back to Paris from Châteaudun. He came back to finish up some evasion work, take precautions for your property, and settle his personal affairs before leaving for England."

This was the first news I have had, and it was wonderful news!

"*England*! He's gone to England—London! Oh, Vera, how *wonderful*! There he's *safe*! Even though he'll probably be coming back later to the Continent on a mission, for the moment he's safe! Oh, what a relief! Did you have any news of him after he left?"

"Yes, from Spain. I know that he crossed the frontier successfully."

I can't describe my happiness! I nearly danced back to my box car. As long as Philippe was safe, it was all right. I could take care of myself. I was grateful that I didn't have my husband to kiss good bye at Weimer. I had always heard that women supported prison hardships better than men, and I had more faith in my future than ever, now that I knew that Philippe was out of danger.

The following afternoon when we arrived in Halle, we were dirty again and hotter than ever. Beside the spidery steel girder station of Halle was a large rectangular cement reservoir full of water, meant no doubt for emergency use during air raids, but our guard allowed us to go swimming in it. It was delightful! The water was neither clean nor fresh, and the sides of the pool were coated with sticky black tar, but we were careful to keep our heads above the surface and our limbs away from the tar. We caused a great deal of attraction and amusement for the Germans of Halle who suddenly saw a strange array of foreigners, washing and swimming in a water tank, after doing strip-tease acts down to the brassiere and panties!

7 Internment at Ravensbrück and Torgau

AUGUST 22, 1944–OCTOBER 16, 1944

The next day, the seventh,[1] saw us in Berlin. We only skirted the city and so couldn't see much of the bomb damage. About forty kilometers north of the city we pulled into a station called Fürstenberg. It was nearly midday and a pitiless sun was beating down. A rumor was passing around: "This was our destination, the camp of Ravensbrück!" As our doors were pushed back, we saw extra guards, new ones, very severe-looking, with the famous SS on their collars. Our old guards suddenly adopted the same swift brutal gestures, the same loud, raucous voices as the new ones. Those who had been lolling around in shorts, now were in immaculate tenue.[2] The atmosphere had suddenly changed. I began to feel tense and unhappy. We were ordered down from our cars, lined up five by five in one long column, and marched along a dusty hot sandy road which bordered a small wood of massive pine trees. We crossed a highway and followed a cobble stone road, flanked on both sides by small comfortable looking homes, out of those windows hung children and adults watching our procession. We were so tortured by heat and thirst we could hardly walk. We were still heavily laden, though less so than before because we had eaten most of our food. We had deliberately saved some things, however, which we felt might be lacking at the camp, such as jam and sugar. We went up an incline, passed first in front of a small camp enclosed with barbed wire, then before some large, attractive, substantial-looking houses with broad cement terraces and green lawns, on which little children were running about. On making a right turn, we could see in the near distance, a lovely lake and great tall pines silhouetted against the sky. Our road descended now. We turned left, passing some large, rectangular buildings facing the lake, which could be compared to

1. The "seventh" refers to the seventh day of Virginia's boxcar journey.
2. *Tenue* is French for dress or outfit.

college dormitories and which I presumed must be rest homes for German workers. They were new and surrounded by grass plots, charmingly landscaped with bushes and flower beds; neat little walks wandered here and there. It was all so clean and progressive-looking. I was impressed by this atmosphere of healthy modern efficiency, side by side with the natural joys of home and children, and believed that we would find a camp that in its own way could be compared.[3]

Suddenly, there loomed up before us a broad green gate and we passed beneath its high portals. On our right were several SS on guard, who surveyed us intensely as we passed by. As we entered the camp, we saw long, narrow, bottle-green barracks, with window facings painted white; narrow plots of grass surrounding the buildings with, here and there, a few bushes or straggly trees; alleys between the "blocs,"[4] of black coal dust. Then we saw some of the inmates, strange, gnome-like looking women, with shaved heads, dressed in blue and grey-striped skirts and jackets, with heavy wooden-soled galoshes on their feet. Some were struggling under the weight of huge soup kettles; others went by pushing a cart piled high with long, narrow wooden boxes, followed by eight or ten others pulling and pushing an immense wagon full to overflowing with garbage. Then, a detachment of others dragged by, horrible-looking creatures, thin and haggard, with huge, open, festering sores on their stockingless legs. Prisoners were giving orders to prisoners. We were made to stand in the broad main street, awaiting we didn't know what. I was horrified by what I saw. It was sinister, unreal, unbelievable! What contrast with what we had just seen. We were so exhausted after a week of sleepless nights. We stared at each other in dull incomprehension. A woman SS kept parading back and forth.[5] We cried out to her for water. I had never known real thirst until now. But no water was brought. We were told that the water was dangerous; that there was typhoid in the camp. After an hour or so, we were given a keg of coffee, but there was so little to go around, and only a few of us had cups or glasses. Women,

3. Ravensbrück was ninety kilometers north of Berlin, just outside the village of Fürstenberg, a resort area situated along a beautiful chain of lakes.
4. Blocks. This is a reference to the blocks of buildings, or barracks, where the inmates lived.
5. Although SS officials were responsible for the management of Ravensbrück, female overseers, often incorrectly referred to as SS women by the inmates, supervised what went on inside the camp.

frantically, began emptying jam onto the coal dust in order to have an empty can to use as a recipient; then they fought for the liquid, spilling the precious stuff. Other prisoners, who saw that we had just arrived and still possessed sugar, jam and canned food, pitifully implored us to share with them. They acted and looked starved. A few weeks later, we too would have given anything just for a spoonful of what was dumped onto the ground that day.

All afternoon we stood waiting in the glaring sun, while our names were checked with the files. We had been moved to a narrow alley where we stood in lines of five. Here, on our left, against a high fence, was a line of open, rapidly filling "tinettes." On our right, was a long narrow, underground cellar from which stole a nauseating stench. It was the morgue. Higher up, back of the morgue, was a fence of electrified barbed wire. We were warned of the danger by a prominent skull and crossbones.

After my name had been checked, I left the horrible alley to cross the main street to a large building, which contained kitchens, offices and shower rooms. I sat out in front with my baggage, with the others, while awaiting my turn to go in, and as the hours rolled by I realized that I must pass the night there. As evening fell, great lights flashed on, and proceedings continued. We lined up before the finance office for a final check on money and jewelry. I lost my sixty francs, but my engagement ring was still hidden away in the shoulder pad of the jacket I was wearing. Once during the night we were served barley soup. Then at 3:30 in the morning, we heard the wail of the camp siren and lights flashed on in the buildings. At 4:15 we heard them again, and immediately, women started swarming out of the "blocs," hundreds, thousands of them. They lined up for an "appel" in front of the "blocs," where they stood erect and still until the sirens wailed again at 6:00. Soon they began marching past us, out of the front gate, some with picks, others with shovels, others empty-handed, but all were on their way to work. While passing, some dared call out to us, "What nationality are you?" They called out in all languages, and we soon realized that nearly every country in the world was represented in this camp, though it was the Russians and the Poles that predominated.

About 10:00 A.M. a group of ten of us was ordered inside and told to undress. The room was small and crowded. On the floor was an immense pile of soiled clothes, to which we added our own. Behind numerous tables stood women prisoners whose work consisted of going through our baggage, under German supervision. They took everything away from us—everything, except comb and tooth brush. The suit and blouse I was wearing were put in a box, for which I signed an itemized slip which they attached to it. I wondered then if I should ever see my ring again. Still completely nude I was shoved along into a still smaller room, which was brilliantly lighted, where I was obliged to lie down on a table to be examined between the legs, to make certain that I had hidden nothing there. Next I sat down in a chair while a prisoner combed through my hair. Many of the women were having their head shaved, and I was so afraid that I would lose my hair too. I thought it a propitious moment to announce my nationality, and it had its effect, as all the head shavers stopped to smile and stare at me. Evidently Americans were rare at Ravensbrück. After this tense moment, which culminated happily for me, we passed into a huge room where there were at least fifty showers running around the sides and across the center of it. After being handed a tiny piece of ersatz soap and a blue and white-checked cotton towel, the size of a luncheon napkin, I enjoyed a good shower. At one end of the room there were tables covered with clothes. Here someone handed me a pair of cotton panties, a cotton underslip and a thin voile dress with a big X sewed into the back of it and another into the front.[6]

After dressing, our group was taken to one of the "blocs" where we joined the others and where we were to live under uncomfortable, crowded conditions. We occupied half of the "bloc," which consisted of a common room, a dormitory, a washroom and three toilets. The bunks, sixty inches wide, were in three tiers and we were obliged to sleep three to a bunk. The mattresses were of straw and covered with blue and white-checkered cotton sheets. They gave a very fresh, neat and clean appearance to the room, but the mattresses were full of fleas. I was already beginning to realize that the Germans can give a very beautiful, impressive finish to the ugliest and rottenest of foundations. At Ravensbrück there were well appointed infirmaries, but they lacked medicine, and medical supplies. There were huge kitchens furnished with the most modern equipment, but the prisoners were starving; the well painted "blocs"

6. By 1944 formal prison uniforms were no longer available at Ravensbrück. Therefore, a large X was sewn or painted on the front and back of the clothing worn by prisoners as a method of identification.

were attractive and the blue-checkered sheets glimpsed through the windows were charming, but, inside, women lived in overcrowded, unsanitary conditions. Everything seemed calculated that the prisoners die without actually being killed. How long could I resist these daily roll calls in the early morning. Already, in late August I suffered from the cold. To me, the most terrifying of sounds will always remain that of the Ravensbrück sirens. It was dreadful to be awakened at 3:30 in the morning by that weird, penetrating wail. There wasn't time to stretch or to lie quietly a moment. I must start to dress at once, groping about in the dark for my limited personal affairs, always unavoidably mixed up with the affairs of others, there being no hooks or shelves, no closets or drawers. I was lucky if nothing had been lost or stolen. Once more or less dressed, having bumped my head several times on the slates of the superior bunk, having received sprays of loose dust and straw from the movements of those up above, having been kicked or stepped on, or shoved by others crossing the bunks to the center aisle, I was ready to climb down. There was very little time left to fight for a place in the washroom and to take my place in the line of those waiting for a toilet—three toilets for six hundred women. Of course, there were some mornings when I went outside on the grass plot or in the alley, thus risking a good beating. If I had any time left before the next siren at 4:15, I would find someone to put my towel on my back, under my dress, as an extra precaution against the cold. If I managed to get hold of any kind of paper, I put that too, but neither towel nor paper must show, otherwise, I risked another beating. When the sirens howled, I hung back, trying to be one of the last to leave the "bloc." It was dark and cold outside and we had to stand still for two hours. Everyone tried to hang back; finally, however, we were beaten out of the "bloc." No matter what the weather, no matter what our state of health, we had to go. Once out there, lined up with thousands of others and shivering in my sleeveless summer dress, I would beat my arms together or jump up and down, to try to keep warm. Two endless hours during which I thought of the joys of home, while attempting to forget the early morning glow from the chimneys of the crematories.[7] "Achtung!

7. In 1943, as deaths began to mount at Ravensbrück, a crematorium was built at the camp. A second crematorium was built in Fürstenberg the following year. By the time Virginia arrived at Ravensbrück in August 1944, both crematoriums were operating full-time. By the end of 1944 they could not keep up with the corpses and many bodies were buried in mass graves. Morrison, *Ravensbrück*, pp. 282–286.

Achtung!" Quickly we would check up on our alignment, and stand at perfect attention, but our eyes followed the SS as she walked slowly past us, counting. After another fifteen minutes or so came the wail of the siren, which released us. We ran back to the "bloc" to drink our half pint of warm ersatz coffee and get ready for work—twelve hours of it. We might be obliged to do one of many things, but the best jobs were already held by those who had come to the camp long before we; jobs in the kitchens, the offices, the "blocs," the infirmaries, the sewing rooms, etc.[8] Besides, there were approximately two thousand women sent daily to the Siemens factory nearby.[9] But the great majority did manual labor, such as: wood cutting, the leveling of sand dunes, the filling in of swamps, gardening, masonry, painting, or loading and unloading of merchandise. However, it was not the work which caused the pitiful mental and physical deterioration of the inmates of Ravensbrück; it was the lack of food. The daily rations were ridiculously insufficient; they consisted of half a pint of coffee, one and a half pint of rutabaga or beet soup and just under a half pound of bread; there was a weekly distribution of one slice of sausage, one ounce of cheese, one or two ounces of margarine and one soup spoon of jam. It was never possible to satisfy one's hunger.

Upon arriving at Ravensbrück we were not obliged to work before the end of a ten day period of quarantine, but during this time we were forbidden to circulate in the camp. All morning we were crowded into the common room; crushed one against the other; six hundred of us in a space suitable for one hundred. There was only standing room and we were almost asphyxiated by the lack of air. We tried to forget our misery and boredom in conversation, but six hundred women conversing in such a limited space caused a din, which the prisoners directing the "blocs"

8. By the time French prisoners began arriving at Ravensbrück in significant numbers in late 1943 and early 1944, Polish and Russian women had already established themselves as prison leaders. Consequently, "French women were assigned to some of the worst jobs . . . [and] subjected to continued oppression, not only by the SS, but also by their fellow prisoners." Morrison, *Ravensbrück*, pp. 94–98. Although Virginia had retained her U.S. citizenship after she married Philippe, she was usually grouped with French prisoners and ordinarily did not receive preferential treatment because of her nationality.

9. As labor needs changed, prisoners were often moved from camp to camp or rented out to private companies for factory work.

couldn't support. They were constantly demanding silence under threat of depriving us of our soup.

The directing of prisoners by prisoners was successful psychological sadism on the part of the SS. Servile German and political women, anxious to conserve their privileges, were often more cruel than the SS themselves. The work columns also were directed by prisoners, not political prisoners, but common law criminals and prostitutes. They were haughty and tyrannical. We hated them.

During the period of the ten day quarantine, we underwent a physical examination. I have never experienced anything so humiliating. We marched across the camp to the open courtyard of one of the infirmaries, where we were ordered to undress completely. After leaving our clothes on the damp ground, we went into another courtyard where a number of German men and women doctors stood waiting to examine our hands, teeth and throats! I felt particularly sorry for the older women who seemed extraordinarily embarrassed by their nakedness. Another examination a few days later was even more distressing. It was a test made from the vagina presumably for the detection of sexual disease, all of which was accomplished under the most public conditions. A young a girl of fifteen, whose turn came just before mine, was trembling so with fright and embarrassment that it was pitiful.

At the end of the ten days, we started to work. We were identified by the prison number sewn on the left sleeve. I was number 57,631. We lined up five by five in a long column, marched across the camp, down the Lagerstrasse, and on, out of the front gate. Again we saw the lovely homes and the lake. We skirted the prison walls and passed before the truck gardens, poultry pens and pig stalls which supplied the SS personnel. Our group was divided. Half went off to level sand dunes, while the rest spent the day filling a huge wooden farm wagon with manure, pushing it to the gardens, dumping it, spreading the manure and hoeing it in. In the afternoon, it rained. We worked without any kind of protection, and by that time I had become so tired that I felt I must drop. It disturbed me to feel this unnatural fatigue.

The atmosphere at Ravensbrück was so distressing that we prayed constantly for one thing—to be allowed to leave. We realized that the camp was reaching the point where it couldn't accommodate any more women. Already there were approximately forty thousand prisoners in a camp built for fifteen thousand. There were daily arrivals, as the evacuation of prisons in the East and the West continued.[10] A huge tent was being put up in a vacant place next to our "bloc." I pitied the poor women I saw being herded in, even before the construction was completed. As many as seven thousand were crammed into the tent which covered the same area as two "blocs." Distinguished-looking Polish women, in beautiful fur coats which they were vainly hoping to keep, sat or crouched in the dusty coal dirt alleys, side by side with the poorest of peasants, waiting their turn to enter the tent. Misery, fatigue and utter bewilderment lined their faces. To make way for all the newcomers, others must leave on work "commandos." Opinions varied among the Ravensbrück regulars as to whether one was worse or better off on "commando," but the majority of our group were of the same mind—we were willing to risk anything just to get out.

Our turn finally came! The evening of September 11th we were led off to the shower rooms to endure the same procedure as the day we arrived. Some of us had acquired a few precious personal effects from the Slav women who always had some stolen article—such as, a mirror, scarf or pull over, to give in exchange for one or two bread rations. But now everything had to be given up. Once again, we were back to comb and toothbrush. After the shower we were given clean clothes, but, to my amazement, nothing to assure a little warmth. I had hoped for a coat, but was not given even a sweater. I wore cotton underclothes and a pink cotton dress which had a blue green X sewn in the front and another in the back. I had one thing for which to be grateful—the sleeves were long! As we finished dressing, we went out in front of the building to wait. Darkness had fallen now and the air was chilly. Mother's adage of "Don't go outdoors after a hot bath without dressing warmly!" was useless. The proceedings took so long that they lasted all night. Having been given new prison numbers which we sewed on by candle light, we had hardly finished before the early siren sounded. After coffee, we left the camp.

Box cars were waiting for us at the station of Fürstenberg. We climbed in, fifty to a car, and our guards—an armed member of the Wehrmacht

10. With the advance of Allied troops during the second half of 1944, the number of transports to Ravensbrück from internment camps in both the west and east dramatically increased. Although solid statistics were destroyed by the SS, Morrison has calculated that "Ravensbrück and its sub-camps had a prisoner population of 45,000 to 65,000 at the end of 1944." Morrison, *Ravensbrück*, p. 277.

and a woman SS, rode with us. They sat on boxes in front of the door which, due to their presence, was left half open. The trip, they said, was to last three days, but they wouldn't reveal our destination. However, we were so relieved to quit Ravensbrück that we were in good spirits.

The afternoon of the third day we stopped in the station of Torgau. This was our destination.[11]

The town seemed to harbor hundreds of French prisoners of war.[12] They were on the streets; they hung out of windows; they stood in barbed wire confines. We called out to them as we marched along, as they to us. They were from France and we were too! We were so happy to see them, and though the guards tried to prohibit our communicating, they didn't succeed. Many of our questions were answered. We learned that the Allied armies had crossed the frontier into Germany! We remarked on the good state of health of the men and their gaiety. We were happier than ever to have left Ravensbrück!

After a good thirty minute walk, mostly through open country, we filed past a sentinel and into a guarded confine. Here were numerous stucco-buildings, built among trees and bordered with bushes, grass plots and neat cement walks. A high square tower reached up through the trees and was topped with a platform on which stood another sentinel. Janette, walking beside me, suddenly remarked, "This is a munitions factory."[13]

"Oh no!" I gasped, "Don't say that until you're *sure!*"

We crossed a railroad siding on which were several box cars. As we passed beside them we could read, stamped on their sides the word: "Ammunition."

Janette had been right. A hot sick feeling swept over me. I was afraid of bombardments, and I didn't want to make ammunition to kill just the

11. The Buchenwald subcamp of Torgau was about one hundred kilometers south of Berlin.

12. Most likely these were enlisted French prisoners of war assigned to Stalag IVD, at Torgau. In accordance with the 1929 Geneva Convention, enlisted POWs, unlike officers, could be required to work outside prison camps. In contrast to German labor and extermination camps, prisoner-of-war camps had at least some oversight by the International Committee of the Red Cross. See, for example, Angelo M. Spinelli and Lewis H. Carlson, *Life Behind Barbed Wire: The Secret World War II Photographs of Prisoner of War Angelo M. Spinelli* (New York: Fordham University Press, 2004).

13. The name of this munitions plant was Heeresmunitionsanstalt Torgau.

men I had been trying to save! How ironical it seemed. It looked as though we were going to live in the very center of the factory. We saw the familiar barbed wire, which this time surrounded a sandy yard, in the center of which was a moderately large rectangular building of light stucco. After entering the gates, we began to explore our new barracks. There were three small dormitories and one large one. The floors were of cement; the bunks had three tiers; there were steam heat radiators; the straw mattresses and pillows were new, and everything was clean. There were two washrooms, down the center of which ran two troughs and a water pipe, with spouts at regular intervals. Out-houses were the only unmodern feature. There was a kind of lean-to on one end of the building, which was to serve as an infirmary and a short narrow structure opposite—headquarters for a camp commander and the SS girls.

We were soon called for an "appel," and a short-statured, neat looking German officer began talking to us politely, using good French:

"I wasn't expecting you today. In fact I counted on only half your number, and was expecting Polish women, not French. However, we will make the best of it. You may lack sufficient food this evening, but from tomorrow on, you will have what you need. After the roll call, blankets will be distributed and you will begin work on Monday morning. The morning "appel" will be held at 6:00. You will be awakened at 5:30."

What a change from Ravensbrück! It looked as if we were going to be treated like human beings! We lined up for our blankets and were given two apiece—clean wool ones. Each of us had her own bed! That same evening food arrived, which included good fresh bread, not the black sawdust of Ravensbrück. There was sauerkraut soup too and a piece of sausage for each of us.

The following morning we went out to the "appel" robed in our blankets. Nothing was said. We had already observed that the Torgau commandant seemed unfavorably impressed by our lack of proper clothing. I believe we began to feel more important and confident than we had the right to. In this atmosphere of cleanliness, generosity and consideration, we became freshly conscious of our human rights. We decided that we were belligerents and that no one, not even the Nazis, had the right to make us work in the munitions factory. Perhaps the women who instigated this "Bill of Rights" and those who voted for it should be admired for their courage, but, when they announced their decision that Sunday morning to the alcoholic adjutant under whose direct command we had been placed, they did not realize that they had put a match to a fuse of dynamite. Now, those of us who are still alive know it. That drunken soldier played with us as a cat plays with a mouse.

"Of course, it can be arranged," he said. "Those of you who refuse to work in the factory will simple be sent back to Ravensbrück."

Ravensbrück! The word that struck terror every time it was uttered! Many of the women changed their decision at this threat, while those who were willing to take the risk were scornful of their comrades' cowardice. What a morning that was! There was no semblance of order, the adjutant lost complete control and he didn't seem to care; on the contrary, he seemed to enjoy it. Women were lecturing and arguing, fighting and weeping. Leaders were making lists, drawing up petitions. It was all madness; everyone was caught up in the wild excitement and nervous intensity of the situation. I didn't want to be a coward. Half-heartedly I signed up for Ravensbrück, but an hour later someone convinced me that it was lunacy, and I took my name off the list. "We haven't the right to dictate to the Germans; we'll suffer for it."

Someone else put forth another opinion: "The war is nearly over; the few munitions we might make will never even be used."

Another person added: "Ravensbrück is slow death; we must avoid going back there, at any price. We have parents and husbands and children in France who need us; the future France needs us. Our work isn't done yet. We have grave responsibilities for the future. Let's not forget it."

We all suffered that day. Friends, enemies. We were torn between courage and fear, idealism and realism, pride and shame. All the while the Germans were laughing at us, teasing us, torturing us, and in the end did exactly as they pleased.[14]

Monday morning, at the end of the "appel," the adjutant announced: "Those who are willing to work in the factory will form in a group near the front gate. Those preferring to work in the fields here in the center. Those who want to be in the kitchen, over on the right, and all willing to

14. For an account of the French protest at Torgau by one of its leaders, Jeannie Rousseau, see David Ignatius, "After Five Decades, a Spy Tells Her Tale; Britain Gained Warning of Nazi Rockets," *Washington Post* (December 28, 1998). Jeannie Rousseau arrived at Ravensbrück about the same time as Virginia. After Torgau she, like Virginia, was reassigned to Ravensbrück and then to Königsberg.

do the camp housekeeping, by the back gate. English and Americans stay together."

Two hundred were needed for the factory. The quota was there, but a few days later, when they decided to work us on the night shift, they took as many as they needed from the farming group. The Anglo-Americans, of whom there were seven, were relegated to the kitchen work. We prepared vegetables. Eleven and a half hours a day we peeled potatoes. Our fingers, hands and arms ached, and then became numb with fatigue. But I won't complain about the job, because it had its advantages. We were permitted, while working, to eat all the raw vegetables we wanted. We were forbidden to carry any back to camp, but we did it all the same, hiding as many as we could in our clothes to give to the factory girls, who needed vitamins even more than we. Nearly every evening we made a salad. At noon, in addition to the soup, we were given eight or ten small boiled potatoes. We saved half of them for the salad, to which we added cabbage, rutabaga, carrots grated on the punctured bottom of a tin can, onions stolen from the rafters of the cellar in which the vegetables were stored, and dandelion greens picked through the barbed wire. Once we managed to steal some tomatoes from the commandant's personal garden, and another time the French war prisoners gave us some of theirs. The French slipped us salt too and, though we had neither oil nor vinegar, those salads tasted mighty good to us!

We labored under quite ideal conditions. Early in the morning we worked seated on wooden crates, in the long, narrow, electrically lighted vegetable cellar. The cellar was built half underground, having an arched ceiling which, on the outside, was covered over by earth and grass. It wasn't in the camp itself, but just outside the factory confine, next to the large building which contained the dining rooms and kitchens where the Germans, working in munitions, were served cafeteria style, noon and night. What we thought at first was only a small factory, turned out in time to be a large one. The buildings were so scattered, so well hidden and so successfully camouflaged that we only realized their extent after being able to circulate in the confine enough to be able to observe more accurately. The French girls worked in only one of the buildings, the rest were occupied by Germans, mostly girls, working for the war effort. We never came in actual contact with them; we only passed each other on our way to work. The Germans started in as early as we did.

After the sun had chased away the dew and damp, we dragged our crates and vegetable baskets out into the fresh air. Here we were in close proximity to one of the barracks occupied by the French war prisoners. The men smiled at us and, whenever possible, called out to us. As that was forbidden and because we were always being threatened, we had to be careful. We had a hiding place nearby, known to us both, a regular post-office where we left and received notes and parcels. The men sent us, among other rare items: salt, aspirin tablets, paper and pencils, mirrors, combs and even prayer books. A few long distant romances sprang up and a special delivery service came into existence. We were very intrigued one day when the men asked us for our names and home addresses. They had, so they said, a secret radio transmitter and they were going to send messages of cheer to our families. They were to contact the Red Cross and make a demand for food and clothing parcels for us. As far as I know there was never any definite result though we mailed several duplicate lists to our benefactors. The fact of knowing that those Frenchmen were near us did an inestimable amount of good to our morale. They had considerable contacts with the outside world; they received mail from home, and although we were never quite sure what was real and what was rumor in the war news they passed us, still we knew that the conflict was progressing in our favor and, thereby, found the courage to work and wait.

One Sunday afternoon, four or five prisoners—a committee representing all the Frenchmen at Torgau, came to our camp. The purpose of their visit was to ask permission from our camp commander to share their food and clothing parcels with us. He gave his consent and the following Sunday, they came again with a truck loaded with boxes and sacks. Needless to say how thrilled we were. We embraced each other, laughed and cried, sang and shouted. At the arrival of the truck we were ordered to go inside the dormitories and shut both windows and doors, but as it was leaving, we broke out into the yard to cry: "Merci, merci beaucoup! Vive la France! Vive les Français!"[15] We liked these boys; they were good-looking and polite and, before coming to call, they shaved and dressed as neatly as they could. They brought us the marvelous comfort which one feels at being remembered and cared for!

15. Thank you, thank you very much! Long live France! Long live the French!

We could hardly wait for the distribution, which didn't come. During the delay we were constantly threatened of an imminent return to Ravensbrück! We tried to explain the situation in different ways: "We are too many; some of us are to be sent to another work camp, in a week, in ten days, in two weeks, which is the reason why the prisoner's gifts aren't being distributed; there is too little to divide among five hundred women; the SS are waiting until some of us are gone."—"The Germans themselves are taking what is meant for us."—"Some of the more privileged are profiting, the interpreters, the women in the infirmary." Yet, when the adjutant opened the door to leave his office, we could still glimpse the bags and boxes still piled high. We elected representatives to appeal before him, but without result. The cat was still playing with the mice: The Frenchmen were concerned too, but they didn't allow themselves to become discouraged; the following Sunday they came again with another truck load!

In the meantime, my worked changed. Our soups were originally prepared in the main kitchen, but now a smaller one within the factory confines was turned over for our special use. As a result, a new group was formed which worked exclusively in the kitchen and did everything from preparing the vegetables to cleaning up. So I, with most of those who originally prepared the vegetables, now turned to the back-breaking job of potato digging! We had to work fast! It was already the first of October and heavy frosts were imminent. The potatoes must be gotten in. Patches of them were scattered here and there all over the factory district and, sometimes, we had to walk fifteen or twenty minutes before reaching the spot where we were to work. In this way, we realized its extent. Everywhere were huge caves, much enlarged copies of our vegetable cellar. It was evident that they housed important stores of munitions. Small ventilators stuck their innocent-looking necks out of the carpet of wild grass studded with baby fir trees. Rail tracks branched out like fingers and well kept paved roads ran in all directions, but there was never a house, a civilian car, or a common pedestrian. The whole place seemed shrouded in mystery and secrecy.

I didn't dislike my work. The weather was fresh and invigorating during those beautiful fall days, but I was never cold because I wore my blanket. I felt good. I had a healthy color. The SS girl who guarded us was not unkind nor was the German officer who supervised our work. He came by on his bicycle, two or three times a day, to check on our progress.

He always appeared satisfied and went so far as to allow a French prisoner to cook us some of the potatoes we had dug. A token of his satisfaction!

The girls working in the factory weren't as fortunate as we. Many of them became very thin and their skins were turning yellow. They all looked tired. I arranged to replace one of them one day, because I was curious to see what their work was like. It all went on in the same long room and consisted in the recuperation of shell cases. It was chain work and the din of the acid bath cranes, the moving belts and the polishing machines was terrific. The noise never let up until work was over; never could one cease to be on the alert for there was always another shell case groping along on the sliding belt. I shared one of the most tiring jobs in the chain. Two of us directed a push cart due to receive crates of cases as the crane dropped them dripping from out of the acid bath. To avoid acid burns I was clothed in a heavy suit, thick boots and rubber gloves, but the thick sulfuric fumes seemed to sear my nostrils and lungs. All day long we received crates, pushed the laden cart to the revolving belt, and unloaded the shell cases onto it. They were heavy and their weight varied. They varied according to the date stamped on them and to the country in which they were made. If they were German and had been manufactured in 1938, they would be of heavy copper, but, as the dates approached 1944, they became lighter and lighter. Recuperated allied cases, however, were made of good heavy copper, every one of them, no matter what their year of fabrication. By the end of eleven and a half hours of bending, lifting and placing, I was exhausted. Give me potato digging any day! I understood why the factory workers looked so poorly. Those working at the acid baths should have had a special milk diet, but of course they didn't. I tried to judge that day what opportunities there were for sabotage. Only on the machines, I decided. I had heard previously that the polishing machines were constantly breaking down, and I was able to ascertain the fact.

We didn't work on Sundays. That day the Catholics held a mass, and the Protestants a service. Afterward, we washed our clothes, searched each other's heads for lice, and "went calling." I made the acquaintance of a large number of girls and made many friends. Janette had the bunk adjoining mine, third floor up. She was a loyal generous friend, and though only a few years older than I, treated me as if I was her child. We really had nothing in common prior to our meeting at Romainville, but she proved a selfless adoration for me, for which I shall always be grateful.

I was happy to have some English-speaking friends. There were two women other than myself who were of American nationality. One was Mrs. Jackson; I have never known a woman with such courage, will power and vitality. Born Swiss she was the wife of Dr. Jackson, medical chief of the American Hospital at Neuilly whom she married at the end of the war 1914–18. Both her husband and son had been arrested, and she was without news of them. There also was Mrs. Dixon, a charming French woman with a beautiful smile, married to an American engineer. Lin, Violet, Lillian, and Janette were the English girls. The first three had been parachuted into France on a mission. Lin was a tall, good-looking girl, who was very much in love with a well-known French automobile racing champion; she had dyed her curly hair black in order to escape identification, but, as the weeks rolled by, the hard black gradually gave way to a lovely auburn. Violet was young, charming and attractive. She used to stretch her limbs like a cat as she lay on her bunk not far from mine; to me, that stretch expressed a love of life and the desire to be back in the world of dancing and danger. Violet was always planning to escape and, night after night, her plan was to be culminated. Somehow, it never worked and, although she spent hours waiting for her chance, it never came. Lillian was a girl of 30, very quiet and sensitive. She was easily depressed and discouraged and suffered ill health almost from the beginning of her arrest. Lillian gave the impression of someone who has always had everything and does not know how to go without. We lost patience with her over things which, in those days, turned out to be of great importance. We tried hard to make her eat the little food we were given, but she wouldn't because she didn't like it. She appeared to be doomed from the start. The fourth girl, Janette, was very lovely. Angelic in her beauty, with fair hair and soft brown eyes; she was tender and sweet. She amazed me by her physical resistance which never seemed to give way before her sensitiveness and natural melancholy. Obviously she was a girl who had suffered and the kind of whom one says: "She was born to suffer."

The infirmary was always crowded, but we didn't realize that there were any serious illnesses until a death occurred one Saturday morning. It was Mme. Le Bart, whom I learned to know at Ravensbrück when she and her daughter, Georgette, shared a bunk next to mine. Her death came as a shock because it was the first, but the second came only twenty-four hours later, when the wife of a well-known professor passed away. We wanted these women to be properly buried, and after notifying the

French prisoners, they cooperated with us in getting the camp commander to acquiesce. The Frenchmen made the coffins of rough boards and the women fashioned wreaths and floral decorations from leaves and wild flowers. The bodies were laid out in the washroom, and a blanket draped before the door, while women took turns, keeping watch at night. On the Monday, a farm wagon arrived, the coffins were placed in it and, after a short mass, while all women stood around, the wagon drove off. Two women were allowed to accompany the coffins, Georgette Le Bart and the best friend of the other woman. At the cemetery there were representatives of the war prisoners and the burial service was conducted by a local priest. We all felt satisfied and grateful that the German command had been willing to cooperate.

The rumors of departures continued to grow and suddenly one day they broke into reality. Our number was to be divided: half were to leave the following morning; the rest, twenty-four hours later. The first to go were the regular factory workers, and rumor said that they were going to another munitions factory at Leipzig. Janette, though designated for departure, arranged somehow to stay because she didn't want to leave me. This breaking up of our group was painful. We had left Paris together and we had been together ever since. Already a strong attachment, born of the same ideals, the same suffering, the same hopes, had made us one. Small differences could not ruffle its grandeur. We wanted to stay together. There were many tearful faces and forced smiles that morning, as half of our number marched off. Those leaving had not even a part of the war prisoners' parcels to help console them. The parcels fell to those left behind. The same afternoon, all the articles were displayed on tables where they were divided up as equally as possible by a committee of girls. We were organized into groups of ten, each with a chief who was to collect for her group and make the final distribution. We found every excuse possible to walk past those tables. How thrilling to see those jars and cans and packages! Almost everything was from the United States: Klim milk, Kraft cheese, Sun Maid raisins, Jack Frost sugar—all the old familiar names and brands that I hadn't seen for years! It was a wonderful display! It is true that divided up among two hundred and fifty women, there was not actually very much for each—a few lumps of sugar, a quarter of a chocolate bar, ten or twelve crackers, a handful of raisins. But personally, the pleasure it afforded me far exceeded a banquet that I might relish today.

That evening we gloated over our new possessions, nibbling a little bit here, a little bit there, trying so hard to prolong our pleasure, glancing jealously at our neighbors who managed to hoard more than we. But we were happily diverted from thinking of what was coming next. We didn't know yet our destination, but we were afraid that it would be Ravensbrück.

The early morning dawned into a beautiful day. We had plenty to do it seemed, getting dressed, putting our meager effects together, and preparing to render our mess bowls, spoons, towels, and most precious of all, the blankets. Some women had cut off pieces of blanket and were wearing them under their dresses to help keep out the cold. We had already been warned of a strict search, so we were afraid to go too far. After having had coffee, we left the dormitories to line up for roll call, laden down with our blankets and possessions. It's amazing what one can collect even in a prison camp where one is not supposed to have possessions. Some of us had knives stolen from the kitchen, in our shoes—nothing was more valuable than a knife. As each name and number were called, we passed to the other side of the yard to line up again. On the way we dumped our blankets, towels and utensils in a heap on the ground, and allowed a woman SS to pass her hands over us to make certain that we didn't bulge in the wrong places! In the meantime a string of box cars had backed upon the track beside our confine, and I volunteered to help carry the sick to one of the cars assigned to them. We were glad to find plenty of fresh, clean straw on the floors of all the cars, which would guarantee a little comfort and warmth. There were a few war prisoners on hand to say good-bye, and others waved to us as we pulled out. We were delayed a few minutes in the station at Torgau, where there were more soldiers to give us the latest war news. Leaving these men was like being torn once again away from our families. They had been so kind. Thanks to them we had enjoyed some unusual advantages, and which is more important, they had furnished a moral uplift for which we were continually grateful.

Our route was strangely familiar. We were returning to Ravensbrück![16] The first time I passed through those deep green portals I was unprepared for what lay on the other side, and the shock was terrible. This time there was no mystery, but I felt a deep depression and foreboding over what

16. According to information provided by the United States Holocaust Memorial Museum, the trip back to Ravensbrück occurred on October 6, 1944.

was to follow. There were fewer of us this time, and we already "be-longed" to Ravensbrück, so the usual procedure of plunder, shower and clean clothes was completed more rapidly, and we were assigned to a "bloc" that same evening.

We were still without sweaters, coats and stockings, but I was glad to again escape the hair shaver's snare, and happy to find a good sweetened milk and barley soup waiting at the "bloc." It was about 10:00 and, after eating the soup, we went immediately to our bunks to sleep. Janette and I were on the top tier up against the front wall. It was impossible for us to sit up on our bunk without bumping our heads against the ceiling. We could only crouch. But we felt satisfied because we were out of the draughts, and whatever warmth there was, would rise. It was the end of the first week in October when we returned to Ravensbrück and, though the days were still pleasant, the nights were very chilly.

It was horrible to be awakened the next morning by the din of those terrifying sirens, at 4:00. It was dark; it was cold and we had no coats. A crafty-looking, black-haired gypsy screamed at us to hurry and get out for the "appel." I hated the woman. She was a witch, and she never missed a chance to strike a prisoner or do her a nasty turn. Having someone like that with authority over us, seemed to me a bad sign, and I was filled with apprehension. She shoved us brutally through the door, not even allowing us the time to swallow a bowl of coffee, which was now served in the "bloc" before the "appel," instead of after.[17]

As usual there was a long line for the toilets, but few managed to arrive before the "appel." To go out the door into the cold was like diving from a high platform into the icy water. It took the same courage. It seemed even more terrible because winter was only beginning and the early morning sorties stretched ahead endlessly into the future. There were times when we were convinced that the war would end in the fall but, as the weeks wore on, we nervously felt that only a spring offensive would terminate our misery.

When we were in line, we saw for the first time the woman SS who commanded our "bloc." I can't hate all Germans just because they are Germans. I find that unnatural and unfair, but I can hate individual Germans, such as this woman, who spent her time making other women

17. On the experiences of gypsies at Ravensbrück, see Morrison, *Ravensbrück*, pp. 48–53.

suffer. She was young, perhaps 25, but she was hard, mean and cruel. She beat us with her stick; she pulled our hair; she seized our miserable little sacks that we made out of whatever we could find, dumping their meager contents onto the floor, and she kicked us as we bent to pick them up; she stole our wedding rings from off our fingers; she threatened us; she punished us; she deprived us of what meager rights we had as human beings. I wish today that I could find her. I would point at her and cry, "*There* she is! Make her suffer! Make her suffer as she made us suffer! Strike her! Kick her! Starve her! That's all she can understand!"

Ordinarily we would have had ten days of quarantine before circulating in the camp or before being made to work, but this time it was different. Almost immediately we went through another superficial physical examination in the nude, following which we were sent to labor in the filling in of swamps. Surrounding the swamps were high sand dunes which we dug out, shoveling the sand into dump cars which we pushed on rails to the edge of the swamp, and dumped. There were high observation ladders, from which armed Germans and an SS in uniform who bossed our job, kept an eye on us. The latter was young, tall, good-looking, and flirted constantly with the SS girls; but he was quick-tempered and his face wore an expression of self-conceit and ruthless cruelty that made us fear and despise him. I was shoveling one day at the base of the high dune on which he was standing, observing our work. He didn't like the way I was shoveling, or at least misunderstood what I was trying to do, for, in a fit of temper, he leaped down the side of the dune in my direction; this started an avalanche and he and the sand swept everything in their wake, including me! He was so discomforted that he forgot to strike me, which I feared he was going to do. Instead, he became very red in the face, roared some ugly German at me, and brushed the sand off his uniform. As I write this now I am amused, but when it happened, I was frightened. I knew that dungeons existed at Ravensbrück, where women were punished by being made to stand in water, ankle deep, for days.[18]

Another time, at the dunes, a dramatic episode took place that reminded me of the construction of the tower of Babel, as a Hollywood film

18. Virginia is probably referring to the Bunker and its seventy-eight primitively furnished cells. According to Morrison, "To be sentenced to the Bunker was to experience the most severe form of official punishment that Ravensbrück had to offer." Morrison, *Ravensbrück*, pp. 231–232.

director would probably see it. The narrow gauge rail track for the dump cars had to be moved without being demounted. There must have been three hundred of us women, and two hundred men, Poles and Russians in striped blue and grey prison uniforms, working in the same area. The ties were heavy and the track was long, so all of us were needed for the task. We lined up on the track between the ties, and when the order was called, we bent down simultaneously to grasp the rails. It was a sight! The endless line of slaves in convict clothes, straining as they lunged forward, grasping the weight of wood and steel, against a background of uneven dunes topped with pines, vast low swamps, and dump cars temporarily derailed!

Another high light of that week was Janette's soup. One day, just after the ladle had been dipped down into the huge soup kettle and emptied into Janette's soup bowl, she discovered that it contained great hunks of meat. She could hardly wait to climb up the three flights into our bunk, where I was already ravenously devouring my soup which was entirely meatless. She passed up her bowl, exclaiming: "Look, Virginia, my soup, it's full of meat! I've never had such luck. Isn't it wonderful?" She reached the bunk breathlessly and crouching over her soup, plunged and re-plunged her spoon in it to bring up the luscious morsels. It was true; there were at least seven or eight pieces, but big pieces, each about the size of a silver dollar.

"Here, Virginia, let's divide," and she began ruthlessly serving meat into my bowl. I'm certain I had more that half. But that was Janette, always sharing, always giving the biggest portion to those she loved. We often talked of that soup afterward.

Our regime at Ravensbrück was far tougher than the first time. All Janette and I prayed for was to leave again. We had been so well off at Torgau, and even if we weren't to be so fortunate as the first time, we believed that nothing could be worse than Ravensbrück. We felt that we would lose our minds if we stayed on much longer. All of us were despised by the "bloc" captains and we could not have a meaner or crueler SS in charge of us. It was bitterly cold and we had no place to go when we were not at work. There was a stove in the common room, but it was for the captains and their "clique." We were not allowed to stay in the room. Circulation in the camp was forbidden, and so there remained only our bunks. We were miserable. Early morning roll calls were a nightmare, although, after a week, some of us, the younger ones, had been given coats and so suffered less from the cold. It was frightful to see the older women standing and shivering for two long hours. I was fortunate to have been given a fairly warm imitation fur coat. We, younger women should have unselfishly surrendered our coats to the older ones who must have felt the cold even more than we, but already we were beginning to suffer from the deprivations and strain of this unnatural existence. We knew, though perhaps unconsciously, that we were fighting to sustain life. Realization of what this regime could eventually mean was gradually coming over us. The laws of self-preservation and of the survival of the fittest became something real, no longer only titles in a psychology text. Were we sinking to bestiality? Perhaps. Unselfish gestures were becoming more and more rare. No one wanted to die, especially in Germany, and the war would soon be over, we knew that. To resist the cold, the hunger, the deprivations, until then, was our only aim.

8
Internment at Könisgberg

In the early morning of the 16th of October, we left Ravensbrück once again. We waited for hours previous to our departure, standing in line, first for galoshes, then for a shower bath and the change of clothes. The galoshes were heavy, shapeless and wooden-soles, and never fitted to the foot, they rubbed and made blisters. Usually blisters developed into vitamin sores, ugly sores that never healed. Although my shoes, the same pair I was wearing at the time of my arrest, were in bad shape, with the soles worn through the heels worn off, still they fitted my feet, and I decided not to ask for galoshes. A few hours before leaving the "bloc," my coat had been rudely yanked off my back by one of the "bloc" captains. I had to shiver for hours, out under the clear starlit sky, waiting for my turn to enter the shower rooms. All I was looking forward to was having another coat. Almost all the women had their coats seized before leaving the "bloc" and it seemed inconceivable, after a hot shower, that we should be handed only cotton underclothes and a dress; no stockings, no sweater, no coat. I inherited a two-piece affair, a light beige skirt, part wool, and a pink cotton machine-made pullover with a short zipper down the front, and then was sent out under the shaded camp light to sew on my new prison number. Soon after the early siren, we left the camp. I begged God never to let me see it again.

We were full of hope as our long column wound its way to the waiting box cars at Fürstenberg. But this time there was no straw and we were obliged to sit on the cold dirty floor. We had two armed guards, elderly soldiers of the Wehrmacht, who established their bulky persons in the midst of us, seated on a couple of empty crates. They were kind enough and jolly, but they were licentious old men, who appeared to enjoy the overcrowded conditions of the box car.

Our trip this time was a short one, and we reached our destination the following morning shortly before noon. We had asked our guards where we were going and what our work was to be, but they wouldn't tell us.

Of one thing we were certain, we couldn't be unhappier any place than we had been at Ravensbrück.

It was impossible to see out of the car as the doors had been shut, but when the train stopped, we were deafened by the din of airplane motors at very close range. We stood in suspense, listening and waiting, when suddenly the doors were shoved back. The vision was far from encouraging; huge green sheds which were airplane hangars; the vast terrain of an aviation field; a miserable grey sky through which planes zoomed at low altitudes, and that which held the most significance of all for us, a long line of dump cars on the far side of the field. We sensed what our work was to be, and we became silent.[1]

Now, we were being ordered out. We climbed stiffly down and lined up on the paved road that ran parallel with the railroad siding. Everything was ugly and bare. There was not even a tree, only stubby grass and dull grey sand.

As we advanced, we could see for the first time what lay on the other side of the track. There, in the near distance, appeared a concentrated group of buildings not unlike a college campus. As we approached, we could count twelve or fifteen large two-storied frame structures, built in regular formation around an open rectangular area. They were slate-roofed and painted dark green. With their white window facings and broad steps I found them rather attractive. A few had stone porches with great square stone columns supporting the overhanging second stories. All were charmingly landscaped with lawns and beds of bushes and evergreens, while paved roads ran around and across the great rectangular confine. We skirted the back of the camp, turning abruptly to cross the far end of it and to stumble down a rough dirt path which gradually led us from the high ground of this stronghold of Nazi power and pride, down into the mire and misery of our prison camp.

I have never seen a place uglier and dirtier than our narrow confine. It could have been compared to an old-fashioned pigsty, with its familiar barbed wire, unpainted, unkempt sheds, and mud. We were in deep hollow here. The aviation camp was up back of us to the South and West,

1. Virginia and the other 250 French prisoners who had been at Torgau had been transferred to a smaller subcamp at an airstrip near Königsberg Neumark, about eighty kilometers east of Ravensbrück, where roughly eight hundred women worked mainly at enlarging the airstrip.

while to the North and East ran cultivated fields. Over a rise in the distance could be glimpsed the grey towers and red roofs of the town we were told was Königsberg, picturesque and charming, the only touch of beauty on our immediate horizon.

On the inside of our electrified barbed wire cage were seven long, narrow, wooden barracks. Each contained two identical units, and each unit consisted of a short hall into which opened three dormitories, one washroom and a small room for the "bloc" captain. In each dormitory there were twenty to thirty two-story metal and wooden bunks. Each of us should have had her own bed, but there weren't sufficient straw mattresses for all, so we had to double up. One just couldn't lie on six or eight wooden slats. There were approximately two hundred and fifty French women in the group, that is all of those who had returned from Torgau to Ravensbrück, and about the same number of Russian and Polish women. However, a few days after our arrival, three hundred more came, bringing our total number to eight hundred.

The first day, after our dormitories had been assigned to us, we rushed madly from one "bloc" to the other trying to find the cleanest of the straw mattresses, but they were all so dirty, it made little difference. We grabbed all the slates we could from other bunks, and filled up the gaps in our own; then we took straw from abandoned mattresses to plump up our thin ones. No one seemed to be guarding or bossing, so it was a regular "free for all." Close friends tried to share the same bed; groups of friends fought for adjoining bunks, and congenial groups even claimed entire dormitories. Once the bed question was settled, we turned to the room. Everyone shared in the washing of windows, scraping of tables and benches and scrubbing of floors. Polish men prisoners had recently occupied the "blocs"; we could read their names written on the wooden partition and the sides of the bunks. They had left their dirt behind them too, but, even without benefit of the proper brooms and brushes, we managed to make the place feel and look a little more hospitable.

We were glad to find a small stove in each room, and although we didn't know what we would have to burn, we were optimistic. Some of the women had already discovered dandelion greens growing in unfrequented places between the "blocs." They were gathering and washing them in the washroom, where a trough ran down the center of two cement slabs over which was a pipe with faucets at regular intervals like at Torgau.

Four of the seven "blocs" were being used as living quarters, one was being turned into an infirmary, another contained the kitchens, store room and work rooms, while the seventh had been so pillaged that it was of no immediate use. There were other buildings like ours outside the barbed wire confine. They contained offices, sleeping quarters for the SS and the Wehrmacht, as well as supplementary store rooms. There was one long narrow building which we passed every day on the way to work, which housed Italian war prisoners, while another contained kitchens and dining rooms for workers and personnel of the aviation camp.

From the very beginning, we felt the startling contrast between this work commando and that of Torgau. The atmosphere here was brutal. The contacts we had with the Poles and Russians were for the most part unfortunate. There was the language barrier and the constant irritation caused by the differences in the character of the races. Where the French woman liked to lash with her tongue, the Slav woman preferred her fists. In any relationships between the prisoners and the Germans, the French always remained proud and aloof, while the Russians and Poles were far more pliable and cooperative. The Germans despised the French whom they considered the stubborn, arbitrary trouble makers of a defeated and prostrate nation, but they proffered a "régime de faveur"[2] to the Russians whom they respected and feared because of their victorious armies. As for the Poles, they amicably supported them because they were good fighters and hard workers. English and Americans were so few that they were given no special consideration either way or the other. We had been arrested in France, were deported with the French, and so were always considered a part of that group. One principle of deportment which I learned very quickly was that if one refused to collaborate with the Germans, one should be as self-effacing as possible. It was neither the place nor the time to be aggressive. The least one was noticed, the better.[3]

After three days we started to work, and we started without stockings, sweaters, coats or even blankets. All we had was what we had been given upon leaving Ravensbrück. The cold was creeping upon us. The lights flashed on in our rooms long before daylight and it was still dark when we were called to the "appel" held in the open space in front of the

2. System of favorites.
3. For information about nationality conflicts at Ravensbrück and its subcamps, see Morrison, *Ravensbrück*, pp. 86–91.

"blocs." There we stood shivering until the first streaks of dawn reflected enough light into our miserable world, so that the guards would be sure to see any attempts at escape once we left the camp to go to work. We were organized into different groups depending on what we were ordered to do. Some worked in the forest through which a route was being cut; others were aiding Germans in the construction of garages and barracks, but the great majority were laboring on the aviation field which was being enlarged. There were a few good jobs in the camp, including those in the kitchen, the infirmary and the shoe fixery, but they fell to the lucky or favored ones, who were in the great majority of cases either Polish or Russian. The Poles and Russians had ganged up together to keep out the French. My job, along with fifty or sixty others, was one of "Reisendecken"[4] on the aviation field. We re-laid slabs of sod which had already been cut and removed by other prisoners, leaving the terrain free to be dug up and leveled. I didn't mind the work itself. It was the impossible conditions under which we worked, the cold and the damp, and the fact that we were under clothed and underfed. I saw signs of physical and even mental deterioration in many of my companions. Personally, I wasn't ill. I had contracted no special malady. The only actual sign of positive change in my system was that menstruation had stopped, but so it was with nearly all the women. I noticed too that I tired more and more easily and was beginning to lose weight. But what else could one expect? We were doing manual labor from dawn until dusk, with hardly anything to eat. What is a daily ration of a pint of thin soup and half a pound of poor bread, with an added tablespoon of liquid honey, or white cheese, or a square inch of margarine, but a teasing mockery of the actual needs of the human body?

Starvation causes suffering, but freezing temperatures are still more unbearable. It was around the first of November when the first snow came, and we were still unclothed. There was a real storm which resulted in several inches of snow, much deeper in places where it had drifted. Laying slabs of sod in the snow is by no means a picnic. Ordinarily I thought the work rather fun, not unlike a picture puzzle, because the slabs were all sizes and shapes and had to be fitted in; but in the snow, which first had to be swept away, and especially during the thaw, it was

---

4. Virginia, who was unfamiliar with the German language, meant *rasendecken*, the German word for sod slabs.

a muddy, sloppy job. The water stood every place in puddles, but we had to lay the slabs anyway, right in the water. It was ridiculous. Of course the work was poorly done, and the terrain which was supposed to be level was, in these places, a crazy quilt; but the fairly decent German civilian foreman who bossed our job couldn't say anything. He knew the impossibility of doing it any better under the conditions which existed.

Between the 15th of November and the end of the month, extra clothing began to arrive. My winter garb finally consisted of my Ravensbrück outfit plus a coat, a pair of hose knitted with an ersatz yarn, some underpants of ersatz flannel, mittens of the same material and a bonnet with the famous blue and grey stripes. My old cotton panties I put around my neck as a scarf. My shoes were in a pitiful condition by now, but were not considered bad enough to be replaced by galoshes. When the worst cold came, I pleaded for a sweater because my pink cotton pullover afforded little warmth, and I was finally given a short sleeveless wool one which I wore under the other. We didn't have any blankets. A few were distributed shortly after our arrival, but they had been stolen immediately by the Polish and Russian women and had never been replaced, although we pleaded and begged all winter long. We were not given any towels and only obtained a tiny piece of heavy latherless soap twice during three months and a half. Nor did we ever have a change of clothing, nor an opportunity to wash our clothes. As a result we became infested with head and body lice. I found the courage somehow to rise out my underslip from time to time and to wash the bottom of my underpants, holding them against the stove to dry. It was impossible to wash them completely because they would never be dry in time for work the next day. As we had no nightgowns or any protection from the dirty prickly cord mattresses, we slept in all our clothes. Janette and I used to take off our coats, however, spreading hers over our feet and mine over our shoulders, which gave us the illusion of snuggling beneath woolly blankets. Of course we never opened the windows, but even so, icicles formed on the interior of the window ledge. It was the body heat of forty women in a small room that made the nights bearable. We always slept because we were exhausted.

When we returned from work, we lighted our stove with coal stolen from the aviation field and wood gathered in the forest. Nearly every prisoner took it upon herself to bring back something that would burn.

During the period of bitterest cold, the suffering we endured on the aviation field is impossible for me to describe. Even our foreman, realizing our agony, sometimes allowed us to make a fire and, when we reached the end of our endurance, to approach it for five minutes of warmth. We tried to take it in turns, but there were always those who, once they came to the fire, refused to leave it, and though our foreman threatened to strike them, he never did—he only stamped out the blaze. That was the worst blow he could have given!

I shall never forget those early morning sorties from our dormitory into the dark and the freezing cold, after having had nothing hot to drink and nothing to eat unless one had managed to save a little bread from the ration of the day before. The "bloc" captain served the usual pale, tasteless "coffee" each morning, but having been made the evening before and not re-heated, it was only tepid and could not serve as a comforting bulwark against the cold that we had to endure. As the moment of the "appel" approached, a brooding silence prevailed in the room. We were seated in the benches besides a long table over which dangled a dim electric light. Many of us had already been up for well over an hour, in order to have time to search our clothing for lice and we were still working on our coats when the gong sounded, giving the order to file out. We had to face it—sometimes a cold, steady, grey rain, or again a driving blizzard of brilliant snow, or what was beautiful but unbearable because of the intensity of the cold that accompanied it—a clear deep blue sky with a myriad of stars gradually fading away before the growing glow of a rosy dawn. We lined up in rows of ten deep, under the guidance of the "bloc" captain. Then we stood and waited. Janette usually was in front of me, and I used to put my arms about her, hoping that some of our bodily warmth could be transferred and held those endless minutes until we heard the call "Achtung!" when we must separate and stand at attention. The camp commander arrived, along with her cohorts.

When we first came to Königsberg, a German officer was in control, but he was soon replaced. We weren't surprised. He was weak and ridiculous-looking. His face was a mask without character and without expression; so pale was his coloring, he gave the impression of being an albino. His beautiful uniform, great height and erect stature could not make up for his lacking the qualities of leadership and discipline. He was replaced by a woman. Rumor said that, while on the Russian front, she had been shell-shocked and had only recently been released from a hospital for mental cases. Even now she wasn't normal, at least not what I considered normal, but one thing was certain, she possessed all the qualities that her predecessor lacked. Physically, she was extremely good-looking and perfectly groomed; about thirty years old; tall and slender, poised and erect, stern and unsmiling, she inspired respect and obedience, not only in us, but in all the men over whom she was in command. She talked little but knew what she wanted; she had the power of decision and she used her power. But how cruel she could be; how hard; how relentless and ruthless! She didn't seem a woman. I tried to imagine her being kind and tender. It was impossible.

Directly under her command, her vassal was one of the most comical men I have ever seen. He afforded us many smothered laughs without desiring to. He wanted us to take him seriously, but we couldn't. He looked and acted like a poker-faced comedian. I guessed his age at about 55, skinny, perhaps tall, but impossible to tell how tall because he always was hunched over. He had heavy eyebrows and a bristling mustache, and could never talk to us without doubling up and bellowing. It may have been his desire to frighten us as he waved his stick in the air, stamped his feet and roared out his orders and threats. Our indifference never discouraged him, and even during the frequent absences of his superior officer, when he was in full command, he didn't change. However, the camp discipline ran riot.

Those early mornings, as we heard the firm steps of our woman commander as she strode across the confine to the "appel," we stood rapidly at attention; she arrived, dressed in a grey coat and hood, boots on her feet, notebook under her arm, her vassal—Badine, we called him—running along at her heels. Her coming was always preceded by the SS girl guides who checked up on our number, alignment and discipline, before her arrival. Afterward, the "bloc" captain gathered around her, for detailed instructions, and items of special importance for us all were called out in French, Polish and Russian, by a prisoner who served as interpreter. Then, as the name of each work group was called, we separated from the ranks in order to line up with those with whom we worked, and, as the grey dawn grew and the electric lights faded out, we marched out through the gates into another day which stretched endlessly ahead.

So winter came on and the cold grew bitter. As we climbed up out of our hollow, crossed the camp and followed the inclined road to the aviation field, we were filled with the dread of that cold and the fierce blasts of icy wind that blew continuously across the high broad plateau, with nothing but ourselves to break its force. It penetrated and pierced every garment. Straw served as an added protection. Every morning, Janette and I robbed our mattress. I stuffed handfuls of straw up under her sweater, front and back, and then she did the same to me. We looked like powder pigeons. Our foreman laughed at us. We worked all morning as close together as possible, trying to forget our suffering in conversation. As the noon hour approached, we scanned the horizon for the soup wagon and, once it crawled into sight, we became tense and only pretended to work until the whistle blew. Then we threw aside our instruments of work, grabbed our bowls and dashed madly down the field to try to be among the first in line. Once served our soup, we crowded into a wooden hut to eat it. We found a lighted stove there and protection from the wind. It was heaven! But how terrible to have to leave it! The cold seemed fiercer than before. We had to be driven out by the foremen who threatened us with their sticks.

One day, in the hut, I had a remarkable surprise—I had a great wing-shaped piece of tendon in my soup. It was *meat*! It practically covered the bottom of my soup bowl! But I wasn't the only one to see it. All my neighbors saw it, and all those who were my more intimate friends drew closer, staring hungrily at my prize. I held it up, and they tore strips of it off, almost without asking, and it was quickly gone. One day we had boiled potatoes which were badly distributed so that there weren't enough for all. When my turn came to be served, there were no more, but each of my friends gave me one, or two, or three of hers and, in the end, I had more than anyone else. Once a girl fell while hurrying across the rough slippery terrain from the soup wagon to the hut, and she lost all her soup. The Germans wouldn't replace it, but her friends offered her one, or two, or three spoonfuls of their own, and her bowl was soon full again. It had to be that way. The greatest act of unselfishness was to give of one's food. It was the giving of one's life, because we were starving. Eyes were becoming dull, cheeks were getting hollow, skins were turning grey, limbs were no longer round, and strength was ebbing. It was a shocking sight to see, the change in those around one. For example, there was Mina, a beautiful, robust young Swiss woman, who, in two months' time, became a wrinkled, bent and haggard old lady; she lost her morale and all power of decision, and had to be led about like a very young child.

The toilets on the aviation field were short ditches dug in proximity of our work, around which low board fences were built. All day long, girls crouched there, huddled together, hiding from work, in order to avoid the cold winds.

There was a potato patch off the end of the field and, sometimes, we managed to steal some of the potatoes. It was a day in late October that a Polish woman creeping there was seen by one of the guards; he warned her to come back, but she went on. Perhaps she didn't hear, or perhaps she was partly mad. It was said that the guard thought she was trying to escape. Anyway he shot her in the back and she died right there on the ground.

Women whose hearts could not stand the cold had as many as three or four attacks a day. They were carried off the field by fellow prisoners, but as soon as they regained consciousness, were forced back to work. I have never seen such human suffering. Janette couldn't bear the cold either; very often I found her crouching behind the stacks of sod, weeping and repeating desperately over and over again, "I want to die, I can't stand it any longer, I want to die!" Her morale that was so high at Romainville sank lower and lower. It was a bad omen and although we tried constantly to divert her, we never succeeded for long. The only help for her was a fire. When she returned to the camp after work to find a place close to the stove, she smiled and relaxed and purred. She would hug me and say: "You see, Virginia, I'm a different person when I'm warm. I just can't stand the cold."

I was beginning to wonder if I could stand it much longer myself. We had ceased to look for the end of the war, because we couldn't know when it would be. Instead, we centered our hopes on the end of winter, because we could count on it. The war might last through this winter.

The girls who worked in the forest said that there it was less cold—less cold because the trees served as a protection against the wind. On the other hand, there was an hour's march to and from work, the labor was more strenuous, no fires were allowed, and there was no hut in which to eat the noon hour soup. It would seem that all that would frustrate one's desire to change jobs, but not if it were less cold. One could bear anything else. So Janette and I, along with some others, decided to go to the forest. It was easy to make the change as more workers were needed there and they were being supplemented from the plateau.

I suffered less at the forest for it was true that it was less cold. However, the march was long and tiring, more so at night after the end of a hard day and because we always carried armfuls of wood for the stove. The walk was nearly impossible after the snowfalls, because the snow clung to our wooden soles, gradually caking until the thickness of it raised us several inches from the road's surface. Then our ankles turned and we would fall. We made jabs at the caked snow with sticks we carried for the purpose, or even with our soup spoons. We had to do it quickly as we marched along, because if we fell out of line we were likely to be struck over the head. Our way to work crossed the length of the camp rectangle and then followed an asphalt road which paralleled the aviation field about a half mile to the north. On that road in the early morning, when the temperature was exceptionally low and the wind was particularly biting, I was grateful to know that soon we would dip down into the protection of lofty pines and into an atmosphere of natural beauty. The aviation field was ugly and bare, man made and noisy with the roar of plane motors, the chugging of the locomotives and the groaning and grinding of the steam shovel. But in the forest, there was only a track with dump cars which we pushed ourselves, and the Nazi Germans shrank like unimportant midgets before the greatness of the pines, while our suffering took on some of their grandeur.

We built a road through the forest, which was in conjunction with the aviation field. It was a wide curved road that branched off from the far end of the huge terrain and circled around through the forest to meet the field again farther on. This road was to serve as a runway for planes and, at regular intervals along it, large hangars were built by German air force personnel. They were carefully camouflaged among the trees to avoid discovery by enemy bombers. The country was hilly and the road must be level, which obliged the taking of earth from the high ground and putting it on the low. The path for the road's foundation was first cleared by "free laborers," Russian peasants—whole families of men, women and children, who cut down trees and hauled them off with the aid of horse teams.[5] Every day we saw them. They stared at us and we at them. They looked healthy and were warmly dressed, and every night they returned to their own fireside. We were not of the same "species"!

5. These were Polish—not Russian—civilian forced laborers.

As the trees were felled and lugged off, we dug out the stumps. They were so huge that the foreman usually put six of us to work on each one. We gradually sank out of sight, along with our picks and shovels, as our hole deepened and the earth we flung out piled up like a mountain range all around. When all roots were cleared, except the tap root, we chopped it off as far down its base as possible and then all of us grappled with the stump, dragging it up and out of the road. It was hard work but not unpleasant, and it was easy for six congenial persons working in such a limited circumference to talk and try to forget.

As the stumps were pulled away and if the ground was high, we next dug a trench down the center of the roadway, a trench which sought the level of the road bed and varied in depth. Often the ground level was over our heads. The ditch must be wide enough for the narrow gauge rail track and for the broad girth of the dump cars. As the ditch was cut through, we laid the rails. This was the most strenuous work of all. The rails came in sections; they were of steel and the ties too. It took twenty girls to carry a section, but so few of the twenty were capable of doing their full share. It was in doing this work that sometimes I thought I must give up. The effort of grasping steel rails with frozen hands, stumbling along rough ground on frozen feet, bending under a weight that sometimes literally brought us down on our knees, was too great. When the sections were laid together, end to end, down the trench, it was time to pull the dump cars along and station them at regular intervals, a yard or two apart. Now, we were divided into groups of six and each group was assigned to a car. With picks we dug out the sides of the trench and shoveled the earth into the cars. We had to work quickly because the Germans deliberately placed the fastest workers—that is, the husky Russian and Polish women—at the head of the line, and when the first car was full and ready to be pushed off, the whistle blew and we too must be ready. We had to push our heavily laden car, fifty to one hundred yards ahead, to the place where the road bed must be filled in, and dump it there. Then we had to drag it back to begin again. As the roadbed widened, we shoveled the earth from one pile to another, over to the cars. The grass and moss which grew between the trees were never dug out and shoveled into the cars with the earth. It first had to be hoed up and raked back, but this was the least strenuous work of all.

We were about two hundred and fifty girls working on the road, and we were scattered along an area of perhaps five hundred yards. Our job was not always the same. As the foremen were pressed to the completion of the road, they took more and more of the French girls off the dump cars and put them onto the moss and stump digging jobs. Naturally they couldn't expect the same output from cultured Parisians that they could from Slav peasants! Personally, I took part in every phase of this road building, but as time went on and I became weaker, I did all I could to avoid the dump cars. The Russians and Poles scorned the French for their weakness. The Slav women kept their flesh and color and strength far longer, as well as their bright, gay and brutal energy. They seemed born to the situation in which they found themselves.[6] But though the French women lacked the physical resistance for this life of deprivation and suffering so foreign to anything they had ever known, still they never lost the natural charm, spirit and intelligence common to their race.

It was while working at the forest that we first became definitely aware that French war prisoners were in the vicinity.[7] On our way to and from work, there were always two or three of them sauntering nonchalantly along the road. Communication was of course "verboten," but that, as usual, didn't hinder us from obtaining the latest news of the war. All the time the men kept "feeling out" the woman SS who was in charge of us at the forest. We were governed by a young woman of about thirty. She was of heavy build and comfortably attractive—the kind one describes as the "maternal" type. She smiled easily and never raised her voice. It seemed miraculous to be guarded by one with a character such as this, but, contradictory as it may seem, we had little respect for her. Her attitude expressed not only kindness but weakness, and, while she was with us, discipline hardly existed. However, her presence afforded us opportunities of contact with the French prisoners that would not have been possible otherwise. The men quickly realized what type she was. They flattered her into cooperating with them in the distribution of food and clothing. So, for several days, every morning Frenchmen were on the road with biscuits and sandwiches, and toward 10:30, our "guardian angel" distributed a bite of something to everyone. A pair of green wool gloves

6. On the strength and stamina of Soviet women who had "borne the brunt of physical labor in Russia for centuries," see Reina Pennington, *Wings, Women, and War: Soviet Airwomen in World War II Combat* (Lawrence: University Press of Kansas, 2001), p. 32.

7. Most likely, these were enlisted French prisoners of war assigned to Stalag Luft 2, located at Königsberg Neumark.

that came to me during the distribution of wearing apparel brought me even greater joy. I wore them under my mittens and they were a great added protection from the cold. Unfortunately, we were not lucky for long. Wind of what was going on got back to camp and to the ears of the commander. Our SS disappeared overnight and was replaced by someone who quickly made up for the laxity of her predecessor. But this didn't discourage the men. They went straight to the head of the camp and, though we heard that permission had been granted them to share their food and clothing parcels with us, as at Torgau, nothing ever came of it. They had been given false promises.

Christmas time was coming, and New Year's. We knew that the holiday season for us was going to be just the contrary of everything it usually stood for. The women who had children at home were the saddest of all. There was Tita who was the mother of three little boys—aged seven, five and two. She told me all about each of them; of the Christmases they had enjoyed together, and the gifts they had received. Allen loved mechanical toys, while Chris preferred animals, especially farm animals, and then there was the youngest, but he was still just a baby. Chris had not yet been baptized. Tita asked me to be his future Godmother, and I accepted. Although we all knew that Christmas would be sad, we decided to do all we could to make it the least sad possible.[8] One thing, for which we were thankful, was the three day holiday at Christmas and again at New Year's. Six whole days away from work and the cold! We brought back a baby fir from the forest and decorated it with bits of cloth and paper. Yvonne, so clever with her hands, filled a little pine twig manger with the Holy Family, the members of which she shaped from clay found on the aviation field. We decorated the bunks with pine branches and our dangling light as well. We all made a great effort the last days before Christmas to carry back as much fuel as possible so that we would have a comfortable reserve. We divided the members of our dormitory into groups, and each group planned to make a "cake" or Christmas pudding! For this, we painfully put aside, during the week proceeding Christmas, parts of our bread, margarine and honey rations, as well as pieces of potato out of our soups. Our mouths were watering for the Christmas "goulash" promised us by the Germans, for we had visions of a good thick stew!

8. For information on the 1944 Christmas parties organized by the prisoners at Ravensbrück, see Morrison, *Ravensbrück*, pp. 267–270.

On Christmas Eve we "went calling" on our friends and we made visits to the other dormitories to esteem the different versions of holiday decoration. There was even a tree, a fairly large one, in our confine between the "blocs" where the "appel" was held; the Russians girls had decorated it with bright paper. At first it looked garish and out of place in that ugly hole but, after midnight on that same Christmas Eve, I went out alone to find it brilliant under the arc lamp, glorified by a dazzling white gown of freshly fallen snow, the broad train of which stretched out all around untrammeled and untarnished by human footprints. During the days that followed I often wished it could have disappeared at the height of its beauty, so that we would not have to see it become like one of us, stripped of its freshness, blanched and blown by the merciless wind until it could no longer stay erect.

Christmas day was very sad. A heavy nostalgia settled down upon us and it took an immense effort to throw off the memories of past Christmases. Besides, discouraging news of the war had seeped through to us. The Germans were making a successful break-through in the Ardennes.[9] Our lunch, to which we had looked forward with such eagerness, was a tragic disappointment. It was not served until 3 P.M. due to the breakdown of one of the stoves and we were obliged to wait in line for it, outside in the freezing courtyard. We wouldn't have minded waiting so much though, if the so-called "goulash" had been what we imagined. The delicious recipe for Hungarian goulash, as found in my Boston Cooking School book kept coming back to my mind. But what they finally served us wasn't at all like that. Instead of a thick stew of meat and vegetables, we were given a handful of boiled potatoes and a ladle of a thin watery sauce, with a little ground meat floating about in it. "Why didn't they give us a good thick barley soup instead of this?" we kept asking. By the time I had crossed the freezing compound, my lunch was no longer hot and, by the time I had peeled my potatoes, both sauce and potatoes were definitely cold. With time and patience we could have re-heated the lunch on the stove, but there was room for only one bowl at a time, and we

9. The battle in the Ardennes, popularly referred to as the Battle of the Bulge, represented Hitler's last effort at driving the Allied forces out of Europe. It began on December 16, 1944, and ended on January 7, 1945. It was the largest battle fought on the Western Front during World War II and resulted in a decisive victory for the Allies.

were forty! I couldn't have waited anyway; having had nothing to eat since the evening before, I was ravenous. Although the "goulash" was a bitter disappointment, our puddings were not. The one our group made was *delicious*! After having mashed the potatoes which we mixed with the margarine, honey and bread crumbs, we cooked it on the stove, stirring constantly, until well agglomerated. When it cooled, it became firm and truly was worth tasting!

We sang carols that evening and held a prayer service. Afterward, Tita's sister, Nanine, a writer of children's stories, climbed upon one of the high bunks to relate some of her charming tales. I recall very well one of them. It was about the beautiful Lady Moon who was so very tired of wearing the same gown; so she went to the dressmaker to order a new one; however, each time that she went for a fitting, the dress had to be re-cut and refitted, for the size of Lady Moon was always changing. She was very unhappy and wept about it for she was so anxious to have something new. But when her family and friends heard about it, they convinced her that her old gown could never be surpassed in beauty and that never could another be found that would fit her so well.

Our New Year's Day was not like Christmas. There was a kind of uncontrolled nervous excitement about everyone. Very early in the morning we began receiving visits from girls of the other dormitories, who, dashing into the room, cried out over and over, "Happy New Year! Happy New Year," weeping and laughing and embracing all at once. 1944 was over! 1944, the year of arrest and torture and deportation. This was 1945—the *New Year*! A new year that would bring peace and liberation, and home! We laughed a lot that day. We argued over turns on the stove as everyone wanted to heat water to wash, or to stir up a New Year's pudding. We industriously searched our clothing and each other's heads for lice. The hours rolled rapidly by and we pushed aside the ever-recurring thought that the freezing bleak days of January stretched ahead of us—days of cold and hunger and heavy work.

The "appels" after New Year were heavy with misery. The cold was unbearable.[10] Women were constantly falling unconscious on the snow and, if no one moved to carry them to the infirmary, they just stayed there. Everything became an effort. Now, when a woman dropped unconscious, one's first reaction was "I won't move; I can't help carry anyone;

10. The winter of 1944–1945 was one of the coldest in German history.

I'm so weak, I must save the little strength I have, or I shall fall myself." Then, there followed whispers of "who is it? who had fainted?" and, if it happened to be a friend, one struggled out of a state of lassitude to step forward and clutch at the dead weight which, after all, *was* a human being that demanded sympathy. The camp director always allowed us to take the fainted women into the infirmary but, before all the work groups had left the camp, she made a tour of the building and, if there were more there than she believed had a right to be, she screamed and beat at those who were regaining consciousness and forced them out to work. Rarely did a morning pass that I didn't help to carry at least one woman to the infirmary. There were never enough cots or even benches. We had to lay them on the floor. It was a fearful sight to see them huddled there, one against the other whimpering and moaning—such grey, haggard, shrunken things they were, half alive, half dead. I was eternally grateful not to be ill. The atmosphere at the infirmary was terrifying. There were practically no medical supplies, no heat, not enough blankets. A woman was only considered ill and allowed to stay in the infirmary if she had a temperature 3 degrees above normal. However, she could really be very ill but, with the freezing weather, it was rare that her body temperature rose in indication of the seriousness of her physical condition. Many of the women wished to fall ill. They did everything they could to go to the infirmary. Their desire was engendered by physical weakness, fear of the cold and dread of hard labor. Janette wanted so badly to get the grippe and, in spite of her amazing physical endurance, she finally did manage to attain a 100 degree F. temperature. It was forbidden to visit the sick, but I could see Janette through the window and each time I found her looking relaxed, her face wreathed in smiles, just because she was out of the cold. But Janette and other women like her at the infirmary lived in constant fear of being put out. As soon as their temperature dropped below the 100 degrees, they had to leave and go back to work. A short period of convalescence at the "bloc" was not even permitted. As the month of January progressed, this ruling was relaxed, however, as the general physical condition of most of the women was so poor that they had no resistance left. If they were not fit to return to work, they fainted or fell ill again, and this tried the patience of the foremen. Those leaving the infirmary were finally given a paper which allowed them to stay away from work during a three to ten day period of convalescence. More and more women fell to the state where they could not work at all—for example, those who had acute heart or lung trouble and those whose feet and legs were so covered with festering vitamin sores that they could not even walk. Some of the more serious cases were loaded into a truck and returned to Ravensbrück; very soon, the news of the death of many among them found its way back to us at Königsberg. But all who remained at camp, unable to work, excluding those in the infirmary, were required to attend "appel." One evening, on returning from work, we learned that the commandant, in one of her fits brought on by the fact that so many women were remaining at camp, made them all stay at attention from the time the rest of us left, until noon. Five hours in that cold, standing in the snow! It is amazing what human beings can stand!

As we were starving, we could talk of nothing but food. We lived from one soup to the next, from one distribution of bread to the other. At work we repeated menus and recipes. We invited each other to fictitious dinners and week-end parties, during which we did nothing but eat. "Now, it's my turn to have you" I would say. "You're invited to Nesles for the week-end. You will arrive on a cool, crisp Saturday in October, but you will find the house deliciously warm and a great log fire burning on the hearth. It is about 4:30 in the afternoon and the tea is ready to be served. There is tea, of course, and chocolate for those who prefer it; there are sandwiches of anchovy, caviar, chicken salad and cream cheese; there are fruit tarts, hot biscuits with jam, chocolate cake and a luscious Lady Baltimore Cake of which I'll give you all the recipe once I get home and find my cook book. After tea, you may like to go and dress for dinner which will be served at 8:00. We will begin with oysters on the half shell, then a cheese soufflé, followed by roast duck with orange sauce." This orgy would continue until Monday morning when the guests would leave for home. Then it was another's turn to do the inviting! Sometimes we would look at each other and say, "We are going crazy. It isn't normal to talk like this!" and it wasn't.

At the forest, the soup was delivered in a truck. We heard and recognized the sound of the motor when it was still far off. We had developed a new sense. In the morning, we did everything we could to work in close vicinity to the spot where the soup was served so at the blowing of the whistle we could manage to be among the first in line. This was important, because it might mean a second helping. We lined up in rows of five as usual, but although we might be at the head of the column at first, we rarely stayed there because the Russians and Poles usually succeeded by brutal methods to push in front of us. Disorder reigned. There was pushing and hitting and rude things said in at least three tongues, but the Germans rarely intervened to settle the disorder promptly and fairly. Sometimes they appeared amused, sometimes helpless, and sometimes they threatened punishment. The situation was never ameliorated, due to their inconsistency. However, everyone knew that the guard would not permit the soup to be served until there was order, so, eventually, grievances were forgotten in the cause of hunger.

It amuses me now to think of the importance I gave to each little detail regarding my daily pittance. They were of momentous importance: "Is my soup thick? Is it thicker than yesterday's? Can I manage to save a few of the potatoes with which to make sandwiches tonight? If I do, I must save as many as Janette and she always manages to save quite a few. Should I eat it slowly so it will last a long time, or shall I try to finish it before it gets cold? Do I have as much as my neighbor? I wonder what tomorrow's soup will be like. Perhaps I'll be luckier than today." There was always a question of luck, as some of the barrels contained thicker soup than others.

The twenty-five or thirty second helpings were supposed to be served in the same manner as the first ones. Order reigned until the server tipped the barrel, proving that there was but little left. At this point, there was a riot always started by the Poles and Russians. They broke forward, a thundering herd, fighting to take the barrel and to dip into it with their bowls. It was all over in three minutes, but during this time those who should rightly have been served, had nothing, and the Germans only stood by and laughed. One rarely saw French women in these mad fights. They had too much pride and dignity to show their hunger in front of the Germans. Once, however, we caught Janette scraping an empty soup barrel. We scolded her severely, which resulted in her weeping all afternoon. A month before she would not have done it. In her case, it was a sign of physical exhaustion and lowering morale.

On the way back to the camp, we scanned the road for any rutabagas or sugar beets that might have fallen during the day from overloaded farm wagons. We would make a dive for them whenever we were afforded the opportunity. The price we paid was usually a good rap on the head, but it was worth it. It was good to eat something raw, even if after the first few bites it turned bitter in the mouth. When we reached camp, we would sometimes race for the kitchen garbage heap. There, we found potato peelings (until the potatoes for the soups were no longer peeled), carrot scrapings, rotten vegetables of which parts were edible, the wilted outside leaves of cabbages, and sometimes whole potatoes purposely thrown away with the other refuse by prisoners working in the kitchen. We washed the potato peelings pieces and roasted them on the stove, while the edible pieces of vegetables and carrot scrapings we ate raw. Sometimes, Janette and I, when particularly hungry and daring to claim the stove for a half an hour, would combine all we found in order to make a soup! I was tempted to do it often, but the idea of fighting for refuse on a garbage heap, was repugnant to me. Instead, Janette and I became ardent "panade makers."[11] To make a "panade" you break bread up in little pieces which you put in cold water with some salt; this mixture you bring to a boil, and allow to cook about five minutes, or until it becomes thick like porridge. Serve at once while hot! To make our "panade," Janette and I each sacrificed three or four quarter inch slices of our bread. Once it was cooked, we ate it together out of the same bowl, dipping and filling our identical spoons simultaneously, so one would not have a drop more than the other. Who scraped the bowl? The one who had not scraped it the evening before! Being hot and thick, a "panade" seemed to pad our stomachs in a way four slices of bread could have never done.

As our hunger became more and more acute, a crime wave started—a crime wave of bread stealing. Perhaps the word "crime" seems too severe when used in conjunction with starving women, but the stealing of bread, under the circumstances, was the taking of life itself. There were some women who claimed to be hungrier than others, but who could prove it? The stealing took place all day long. Many of the women saved a portion of their bread so that they could enjoy little snacks during work. They kept it in their little sacks, on which they had to keep their eyes every minute, or they would disappear. At the "bloc," there were constant breaks in the electric current and, when the lights came on again, it was rare to find everything intact. One evening, I had my sack at the foot of my bed; the lights went out and, when they came on again, it had disappeared. I found it the next morning in another dormitory, nothing missing from it except that which was edible.

11. A soup made of bread, water, and usually butter and egg yolks.

We were very upset on returning from work one night to discover that one of the most attractive and best-liked girls of our room had been caught in the act of stealing bread. From that moment to the next, no one spoke to her. She was ostracized completely. A few days later, she called me over to her bed to say:

"Virginia, I swear to you on the head of my little boy that I didn't steal the bread. I want you to believe me because it would mean so much to me to know that you had faith in me."

I would have liked to have believed her, especially as she had always talked to me of her baby and I knew she adored him, but others among my friends in whom I had confidence, had caught her in the act of stealing of bread and, when apprehended, they had seen her trying to hide it under her dress.

After New Year's I became in desperate need of another pair of shoes. Six weeks before I had been given a pair of wooden-soled galoshes to replace by Parisians pumps, but the tops were made of bits and scraps of cloth and canvas sewn together in patch work style, with ordinary thread that had soon rotted from the dampness of the snow. Although I tried to tie them on with whatever I could find, including strips of cloth and pieces of string and wire, still my primitive methods could not resist the strain of the hours' rapid march to and from work. Every night I came back to camp with my feet soaking wet and snow caked under my toes. My stocking feet were full of huge holes, for the ersatz wool dissolved with the dampness, and I had nothing with which to darn them. I was practically barefooted. I had asked for another pair of shoes, but was told that there were no replacements. I believe it because there were other women in as critical condition as I. Already a new group was beginning to form at the "appel"—those who were prevented from going to work because they were without shoes. The climax came for me one evening, on the way back from the forest. My galoshes kept coming off my feet and, as my efforts to put them on broke the regularity of the marching column, the woman SS made me take them off for good and walk in the snow in my stocking feet! At the camp, one of the French girls, who had vitamin sores on her legs but which were not considered serious enough to allow her to stay at camp, came to me with an offer:

"I suffer terribly with my legs, but the infirmary won't give me permission to stay at camp. Let's exchange shoes and I'll risk the shoeless group at the "appel."

I could have stayed away from work myself, using my shoes as an excuse, but I thought it would prove a lack of courage. Besides, I noticed that the women who stayed in the "blocs" all day had a far lower morale than the others. So I took the girl's galoshes which were still in good condition and returned to work.

A few days later, about the 20th of January, I woke early one morning in excruciating pain, such as I had never suffered in my life. I doubled up on my bed and rolled from side to side, helpless to stop the tears which ran down my face. It would have been impossible for me to work, but I had not the right to go to the infirmary because I had no fever! At the hour of the "appel" I felt a little better, but when my work group was called, I refused to join it. Instead, I slipped into the infirmary and took a place among the prostrate women with whom the room was full. I was feeling nearly normal by now, but I wanted to avoid work that day for fear that the intense cold would bring a return of the insupportable pain, so I doubled up on the bench and tried to look as I must have looked two hours before. Just at the moment the camp director entered, she stopped to take a slow steady glance about the room. She was looking for the "regulars"—those whom she found there every morning and who she was certain were feigning their daily attacks. All those who could still stand, she shoved out the door. I was frightened, but when she looked at me I knew what went through her mind: "I've never seen that one in here before, I'll let her stay." And so I stayed. Later, the Polish nurse gave me a couple of white pills and sent me back to the "bloc." I was happy that day. My pain was gone so I could appreciate my hours of freedom. I made a decision too; I was perhaps proving a certain courage in going to work, but I was not saving the little remaining physical strength I had, by doing manual labor all day long in temperatures such as we were obliged to endure during the bitterest of all months. I decided to reclaim my shoes and join the shoeless group. The next morning, I was chosen with eight or ten others to pay a visit to the director. She looked at my shoes and gave me a ticket signifying that I was to go to the shoe fixery, but there I was told very firmly that my galoshes were irreparable. I was glad because it gave me an excuse to stay at camp. As the shoeless group grew, the temper of the SS grew too. I saw many women with shoes as bad as or worse than mine driven off to work. The picking was done by "bloc" captains among whom was one who, fortunately, liked me enough to overlook me when it came to reducing the number of women staying at camp.

The last week in January was one of the coldest we had experienced. Women came home from work, in tears; others, with wild haunted expressions on their faces. Their resistance was at the breaking point, and they knew it. They were fighting not to lose their minds. It was as if they were struggling to hold on—to hold on just a little longer until relief would come. Relief did come, thanks to the great Russian offensive. We knew the Russians had struck and we knew also that they were not far distant. We felt a new strain in the Germans who guarded us, and we saw civilian members of the air camp personnel, packing up and leaving. The road to the forest was lined with over loaded vehicles of all sorts, heading West—German refugees running from the Russians. We were delighted and almost hysterical in our excitement. "Chacun son tour! Chacun son tour!"[12] the French cried over and over again. News came to us that the French war prisoners had been evacuated from Königsberg. This frightened us, and our excitement subsided. We were afraid that we would be evacuated too. It would be terrible; without transportation we would have to take to the roads. In our weakened condition we could never live through it! We had always imagined that, if we were liberated at Königsberg, the Frenchmen would be there to help us celebrate. How many times had we already discussed and planned the party we would throw, and the sumptuous dinner we would serve! We would take over the air camp and play host to the Russian troops. We were going to move out of our pigsty too, up to the fresh clean quarters on the rectangle.

The Germans became more and more agitated. Rumors ran riot, but we knew for certain that something definitely was brewing when we saw the women arrive back from work in the middle of the day on January 31st. They had been told abruptly to drop their tools where they stood and to line up for the march back to camp. During the afternoon, the director was seen to drive off in a car, bag and baggage, with a young officer from the aviation camp whom gossip had already singled out as her "boyfriend."[13]

12. To each his turn.
13. The Soviet army was then within eighty kilometers of Berlin, but it was not until late April that the city was completely surrounded; Berlin surrendered on May 2.

It was just after dark when we heard wild excitement in the confine. The Russian girls who, for days, had been nearly uncontrollable, had now literally broken loose. We ran outside to see immense flames leaping toward the sky. The aviation camp was on fire! Not only that—our gate was open and there was not a guard in sight! I felt as if I were going crazy—that I was living in a kind of nightmare. Was it true? Could I actually go through that open gate? Was there no one to stop me? The Slav women were already streaming through, in both directions, and those coming back were loaded down. Plundering had started! I hesitated a second. I was alone and I remembered that before leaving the "bloc" some of the women had warned me: "We don't know just what this means yet. It's dangerous to go out. The Germans may come back and shoot us all, especially if they find us outside the confine." But I was at the open gate. I lost all sense of danger and wisdom. I had to know what it felt like to make a decision and act on it; I intended to go out that gate! To be *free* again! Oh heaven, what mattered what happened after! The sky was alight with the dancing flames. It was melodramatic to see the women running here and there like strange witches in the shadows; to hear their cries of joy in tongues I did not understand. I passed before the quarters of the SS. They were lighted and I could see that everything was already turned upside down—papers, furniture, drawers everywhere,—a frightful mess. I reached the long "bloc" where the Italian war prisoners had lived. They were gone now and, in their place, were women—numberless women, opening cupboards and drawers, ransacking everything, grabbing whatever their hand touched. There was a mad race. The early comers had the spoils and when I arrived, there was nothing of value left. It does not take long for several hundred women to pillage a "bloc." But there was still wood and coal—plenty of it, piled in boxes beside the stoves. I discovered a bucket and a big basket, and was soon struggling back to my dormitory, loaded down with fuel. I found nearly all the girls there. I never have been able to understand how few of them found the courage and strength to take part in this amazing liberation. It was due, no doubt, to their depleted physical state—they were just too exhausted. But they were thrilled to see the wood and the coal. We cleared a corner of the room for it and, when I said there was plenty more where that had come from, several of the girls went out to bring back more before it was all taken. We decided that it was not right to steal everything, but that it was fair to take fuel, food and clothing, for it was those things of which the Germans had deprived us. Tita came with me the next time; we brought back another load of wood and coal, after which we went out again. There was a steady stream of Slav women coming back from beyond the Italian "bloc." They had their arms full of tins and boxes—it was *food* they were carrying! We tried to find out where it had come from but they made signs to us which we interpreted as meaning that we must not go as it was too dangerous. But we quickly observed that, once they left their burdens in their "blocs," they returned in the direction from which they had come. They didn't want us to be in on this because they wanted it for themselves. But we followed! As we mounted the incline, we realized that the fire was dying down, and that only some of the hangars and the huge clerical building had been put alight. The buildings on the compound were unharmed. No one walked, everyone ran. Tita was too exhausted. She told me to go on without her. The main body of women headed toward one of the longest structures at the far end of the rectangle, and I followed. Lights were on and I could see through the windows, great dining rooms and kitchens. I followed the others down a wide cement ramp which led to the cellars. There I witnessed the most amazing sight, endless corridors onto which gave numberless rooms piled to the ceiling with crates, cans, boxes, sacks. Women were swarming everywhere. There were a few German soldiers too. They motioned us on, and made passes, and tried to grab hold of us, but we ignored them. All we wanted was food. I suddenly felt paralyzed. I only had two arms—what from all this hoard of plenty could I take? What *should* I take? My eyes lighted on gallon tins of jam. We all craved sweet things, so I grabbed one of the heavy buckets. In my other arm, I took as many large size cans as I could carry. I hurried back to camp and, when the girls saw what I had brought, they became hysterical. They cried; they kissed me; they praised my courage! But there wasn't time to lose. I described hurriedly the hoarded treasure that was to be had for the taking, and the result was that a good number set off for the cellars. Competition was growing. If we wanted our share, we must hurry. Tita was not back yet, so I went off to find her. I was curious to see the kitchens and it was there that I found Tita. But we couldn't stay. A German patrol had arrived. The men were brutally driving the women out, threatening them with their rifles and extinguishing the lights. We had to leave, but we managed to grab a dairy can of fresh milk with which we arrived safely at the "bloc." In the meantime, all the bread and margarine left in the canteen at our camp was being evenly distributed. The distribution was being made by the only guard who had remained behind. He wasn't German; he was a Pole who had deserted the Wehrmacht.

We had a wonderful supper that night. Lovely slices of bread spread with margarine and jam, and delicious fresh creamy milk. But our joy was soon interrupted. Two of the girls who had left for food were long in returning. We were rightly apprehensive, because when they finally did arrive, one of them had blood showing through her coat. She had been shot through the shoulder! It was Georgette, the courageous young girl who had lost her mother at Torgau. She was just as courageous now. As one of the French women who was a doctor began dressing her wound, she calmly told us her story:

"Marcelle and I were in the canteen. We heard the Germans shouting up on the compound, and we could tell that they were approaching. We were frightened and ran out in order to get back here as quickly as possible. They saw us and yelled at us, but we didn't understand and just kept on running. Then I heard an explosion and, then I felt my shoulder turn hot, I knew I'd been shot. But don't worry; I'm not very badly hurt; it will be all right in no time."

An examination of the wound showed that the bullet had passed under the shoulder blade and had left a clean trace. We had no disinfectant, no proper bandages, but Dr. Perity washed the wound with boiled salt water and protected it with a piece of clean linen. She had hardly finished when we were warned that a German patrol had entered the camp. Quickly we hid the unopened cans under the mattresses, camouflaged the vestiges of our earlier feast, and put the semblance of order in the room. Georgette hid in the shadow of her bunk. It would never do to have her wound discovered. Suddenly we heard the stamp of heavy boots in the hall. We all tried to adopt an air of innocent repose, although we were quaking with fear inside. A tall, brutal-looking, energetic German officer strode into the room. He had the camp interpreter with him. He spoke forcefully: "Since the evacuation of the aviation camp late this afternoon, thievery had been committed by prisoners from this camp. Are any of you here responsible for what has taken place?"

He waited, but only utter silence answered his question. We wondered if he would search for evidence. He went on: "Don't forget that you are still prisoners and under German jurisdiction. Military patrols will continue to survey this district and anyone caught and guilty of pillage will be shot."

He paused, looked about the room, and then added, "I will return in one hour; when I return I intend to see this room clean and in perfect order."

As the door closed behind him we breathed with relief. The girls who had not been "guilty of pillage" cleaned the room. They washed the floor and arranged the mattresses after hiding carefully all the cans. At the end of the hour, all was in readiness, but the officer had not returned. After thirty minutes, a messenger arrived to say that the officer was delayed and that he had ordered us to go to bed. We were glad, and climbed with relief on to our bunk. When he came later, we all pretended to be asleep. He paused to look in for a few seconds, seemed satisfied and went away. When we were assured that he had left the "bloc," we all sat up and everyone started talking at once. The hidden cans miraculously reappeared and, when opened, were found to contain either mixed vegetables or asparagus. After eating my share, I fell asleep nearly happy.

We woke up early the next morning because we were too excited to sleep. Already the Poles and Russians from next door were passing before our windows. Many of them had already been up to the camp because we saw them go by with their arms full. Evidently the patrols were not active yet. If we intended to have something to eat we must hurry! It was essential to find something to drink some place, as the water mains had been blasted. All our bread was gone too; we wanted to find something to replace it. There was the housekeeping to be done. In fact, there was a great deal to do, so we all volunteered for the various chores. We discovered beer in the civilian canteen just outside our barbed wire confine. We brought water from an open reservoir found in a hollow in back of the camp. The Russians discovered a deserted truck full of bread, but they would not share any of it with us. However, we did not mind after coming across an attic room full of crackers and sweet cookies!

Some of us had to risk going up to the main camp for food. A group from one of the other rooms had gone and, although they had fallen on a patrol and had been shot at, they managed to get back safely. The patrol was evidently stationed at Königsberg because the Germans always arrived in a military truck coming from that direction. They drove into the camp by the main entrance, which was on the side of the compound opposite the "bloc" where we found the food supplies. Thus we could see the arrival of the truck before it was actually upon us, giving us time to escape, or at least to hide.

Toward the middle of the afternoon, several of us decided to risk it. As we climbed up to the camp, we saw very few women and no signs of patrols. We crossed the length of the rectangle to the canteen and went into the immense dining hall where there were tables enough to seat two to three hundred men. We were amused to see that the order of evacuation had come when the Germans were in the midst of a meal. Everything was just as they had left it. Their dinner, consisting of meat, boiled potatoes, peas and carrots had been only partially eaten. We tasted it and, finding it good, we emptied the serving dishes into one big receptacle to take back to re-heat. In the kitchen we discovered immense cooking kettles such as we had known at Ravensbrück and Torgau. One of them was full of boiled potatoes, with which we filled a basket, and started back to our dormitory. Our successful venture encouraged the others, and more and more girls went out after food. Our reserves grew. For lunch we prepared a mixed vegetable salad, and heated up the Germans' interrupted meal. For dessert we ate jam and crackers. We were no longer hungry.

Before lunch we had visitors—two French prisoners of war! They had escaped when they learned that they were to be evacuated, because they wanted to join the Russians. They told us that the Russians were not more then ten miles away and advancing rapidly. We too had considered escaping and had weighed the pros and cons of it. The Polish deserter who had distributed the bread had offered to lead away any of those wanting to go. A good number of women had put themselves under his protection, but they were all Poles who were deathly afraid of the Russians. We were not afraid of the Russians and, as they were so close, we thought that the Germans would not dare to evacuate us. At Königsberg we had food and a place to sleep. If we took to the roads, where would we go? In our weakened physical state we could not go far; we would probably be arrested and shot. No, it was best to wait. We believed that our liberation by the Russians was not far off; we could hear the cannon in the distance and a Russian fighter plane had shot up the aviation field that morning. If only the Russians would *hurry*!

That afternoon, Yvonne and I went up to the canteen. We still needed food, especially as we did not know exactly how long we would have to wait for our liberators. We wanted a considerable reserve. If we waited until everything had been taken by the Poles and Russians, it would be too late. Six hundred women consume a lot of food. Yvonne and I were within ten yards of the canteen entrance when we saw the German patrol drive up at the gate entrance. What could we do? It was too late to go back. We would have to run the whole length of the rectangle and the Germans would have plenty of time to shoot at us. Our only choice was to hide some place in the building. We were frightened because we knew the men had seen us. We ran into the hall and down the steps into the cellar, after which we heard the truck drive up and the sound of the men as they leapt to the pavement. We sought desperately a good place to hide, but without success as we had no time to spare. Already we heard the clamp of heavy boots in the kitchen over our heads. Other men were coming down the ramp. We ran into a small room, dark except for a feeble reflection from the room across the corridor which had high windows looking out on the camp. Our hideaway was a small room full of beer kegs. We wanted to get behind the kegs, but they were too heavy to move and being round offered poor protection for hiding. We had no other choice; boots were already stamping down the corridor. We dared not make a sound. At the last extremity we crouched down beside the kegs, our heads between our knees. A German with an automatic flashlight which he worked with the thumb came into the beer cellar. He was so close to me I could easily have touched him. It was only the humming sound from the lamp which kept him hearing the loud beating of our hearts. I was trembling with a strange kind of exhilaration and, although I was conscious of the danger, I was not really afraid. As the man flashed his light up, around and over us, without seeing us, it was with an effort that I kept from laughing. He went out, but returned again after a minute or so, to repeat the same unsuccessful operation. It amused me to think about efficient Germans having such inefficient flashlights! This time he left for good and we only straightened up from our cramped positions when we heard the truck drive away. What a relief!

That evening, we ate something that I had hardly tasted since the beginning of the war. It was rice! It was a task to cook rice for forty women on a small stove. The kettle extended over the edges of it! It was late by the time we had all been served, and we were so tired by all the excitement and strenuous exertions that we were anxious to get to bed. We knew that the two French prisoners were still in the camp some place.

The French girls in one of the other "blocs" had invited them to a "liberation banquet."

We had a comfortable bed now. We had made it up with sheets, pillows and soft blankets which we found in the aviation camp dormitories.

I woke up two or three times that night. I was too happy to sleep, and every time I woke, I ate a little lunch of jam and crackers. Nicole was awake too and we discussed our plans of the future. Ann was mumbling in her sleep and Nicole mentioned that she had carried on rational conversations with her as she slept. She spoke to her:

"What are you saying, Ann?"

"It's the cold, Nicole, I can't bear the cold."

"But you don't have to bear it any longer now. Your suffering is over."

"Is it, Nicole? I'm not so sure. It's so terrible to be cold and hungry."

"Don't worry, Ann, you'll soon be going home now."

"Oh, will I? If only I *could* go home. I wouldn't be cold and hungry any longer."

It was heartrending to hear her speak so. It didn't seem right to penetrate into the secret soul of this sensitive child. I say "child" for, although she was twenty-five years old, she had never known what reality could mean until now. She had always lived in dreams. We knew she suffered, for we had seen it on her face, but she never complained, except in her dreams. We were unwilling to continue the conversation. It was too sad and frightening, and perhaps prophetic.

We were awakened early the next morning by shocking news. During the "liberation banquet," a German patrol had arrived in our camp. The Germans entered the banquet hall and, without preamble, shot the two Frenchmen as they sat at table. They died at once. The girls who witnessed these murders were stunned by the shock. It was a frightful experience. The patrol left immediately after the shooting.

The Russians were too long in arriving. The strain of waiting, along with the murder of the Frenchmen, made the women more and more uneasy; they were beginning to despair. I felt as if I must get away from the atmosphere of the camp. Janette felt as I did, so, during the morning, we visited some of the other buildings that gave onto the rectangle. Having seen them daily while marching by, we were anxious now to satisfy our curiosity as to what they were like inside. One consisted of beautifully furnished private offices, all of which contained bright flowering plants. I had always heard of the Germans' love of flowers, but it seemed incongruous to me at the moment. In another "bloc" was a very harmoniously decorated little bar and buffet, while, in the cellar of the same "bloc" were cubicles evidently allotted to individuals or families. In one, there was a trunk full of what we decided must be wedding gifts. They were perfectly new and, packed away with them, were baby clothes. Being sentimental about weddings and babies wherever found, we replaced everything as we had found it. We visited the men's quarters too. Everything was in disorder. Beds were unmade and military equipment, maps and pieces of clothing were strewn everywhere. The tables were covered with empty liquor bottles. The whole scene told a tale of rapid departure. The women's quarters were in far worse disorder, but almost entirely the result of plunder. There were letters, pictures, pieces of clothing, half-emptied bottles and boxes of beauty preparations, summer paraphernalia including straw hats and sun glasses, but there was nothing of value left. The climax of our sightseeing tour came when we fell on an attic room where women's uniforms were stored. Here was a chance to get rid of our lice-infested clothes! There were undergarments too. What fun we had! Among other things, I chose two blouses, light blue in color, a grey skirt, a very smart double-breasted grey gabardine, and a pair of sturdy black shoes. I could hardly wait to get back to camp to wash and dress. I was going to take pride in my looks again!

At the "bloc" we were greeted with the latest news—the Russians were only four kilometers away! The women had become cheerful again. It was the 2nd of February—"le Jour des Rois." This is an old French fête day which one celebrates by eating pancakes, and our splendid cook was busy in the frying of big French "crêpes."[14] There was to be one for each of us! A long time was needed to make the pancakes, so lunch would necessarily be late. I had ample time to wash and put on my new clothes. I found some hot water, filled my bowl, and sought a little privacy back in the

14. *Le Jour des Rois*, the Day of the Kings, is a national religious holiday in France that is celebrated on January 6. Also known as the Epiphany or Twelfth Night, it commemorates the coming of the Magi with gifts for the baby Jesus. February 2 is also a religious holiday and called *La Chandeleur* in French and Candlemas in English. It is a Christian festival that commemorates the ritual purification of Mary forty days after the birth of her son. Candles are lit on this day to symbolize that Jesus was the light, the truth, and the way. It is celebrated in France by eating crêpes. Virginia probably mixed up the names of these two holidays.

corner beside my bunk. I could see Tita from where I stood. She was ill with dysentery and looked very bad. Janette too was suffering from the same thing. Although, for months, the majority of us had it mildly, it was primarily these last two days, since we had started eating unwisely, after the long period of starvation that our conditions had grown worse.

I mused as I went on with my washing.

I knew that several volunteers were out digging graves for the two Frenchmen, while others were making flags from pieces of red, white and blue cloth. When all was ready we would hold a burial service. How sad life could be! Here had been two young men for whom the love of liberty had brought only death. Such was their fate. What was ours to be?

9

Return to Ravensbrück

My musing was violently interrupted by a great clamor in the court-yard. Men were shouting and women were screaming. Shots were being fired. Was it the Russians? Had they come at last? I must hurry! Why did I have to be undressed just at a moment like this? My hopes soared as the deafening sounds reached my ears. At the same moment, one of our girls ran in, but looking as though she had seen ghosts. "It's the *Germans!*" she cried. "The SS from Ravensbrück. They've come to *get* us! They've or-dered us to line up outside!" The joy that had welled up into my throat now became something that choked me. In silent despair, the women stared at each other. There was more misery to bear. Would it never end? How could we go on and on like this? Yes, it had been too good to last. We had always thought so. We could see the SS through our windows. They were threatening the women outside with their rifles, trying to herd them into line. The women acted stunned. The soldiers acted like mad-men. They were dashing crazily about, chasing the women. There seemed to be no one in charge and not one of the Germans seemed know how to obtain order. One of the men suddenly burst into our room, and what he saw did not appear to please him. However, he realized that, considering the various stages of undress in which he discovered us, he must accord us a minimum of time in which to be ready to leave.

"All those not outside in five minutes will be shot," he roared out. "Bring what food and blankets you can carry." Then he disappeared.

We knew this man meant what he said. We were horror-stricken. I tried to hurry to put on my clothes—all except the gabardine and the shoes; if I had been seen wearing a German uniform I would have been shot at once! During this time, Janette gathered what food we could into a blanket and tied it into a sack. Everyone else was doing the same. If only we had more time! The SS came back into the "bloc." He ran from room to room, threatening, bullying, and brutally forcing everyone out, whether they were ready or not. In the courtyard, there were many more of these madmen, running along beside the stricken women, herding them out through the open gate and onto the road where we stopped to form the usual column. We wondered what would happen to the women in the infirmary. They were unable to walk and we saw no trucks ready to take them.

It was clear that the men were in a desperate hurry. They evidently were afraid of being trapped by the Russians. They acted like brutes being tracked down by hunters. They snarled and they raged. They knew they were finished—but they still had us on whom to mete out their vengeance and despair. We knew that with men such as these our lives were not secure. Knowing the reason, it pleased us to see them in such a state. The Russian army must be very close. Perhaps we would be liberated en route!

As the column was forming, a rifle shot broke through the confusion. It came from the rear, near the camp entrance. We became tense for we sensed another tragedy. The news, in staccato whispers, rapidly echoed its way along to us. "It's Monique. She started back to the 'bloc' for something she had forgotten. They shot her as she ran!" It must have been true for we never saw her again.

We were silent and depressed as we started forward on the road toward Königsberg. We approached the picturesque old gateway which led into the town, we circled off toward the West, taking a road from which we could see the roofs of the aviation camp, two or three miles across the plowed field. We were suddenly attracted by a great column of smoke which, rising slightly to the left, was without doubt the site of our confine. What was burning? Our camp? But the smoke would have risen from over a greater area. There must be only one building in flames. Was it the infirmary? We were filled with anxiety. (Since returning from Germany, I have learned for a fact that the SS had put fire to the infirmary, but it was poorly and hurriedly done thus giving everyone time to escape. The women buried Monique and the two Frenchmen, and waited for the Russians who arrived three days later.)[1]

We were not yet out of sight of the smoke when we heard another rifle shot at the end of the column. Who was it this time? We soon knew. It

1. According to the records of the International Tracing Service in Arolsen, Germany, the final evacuation of surviving prisoners at Königsberg, with the exception of some ill prisoners, occurred on March 3, 1945. I would like to thank Gerry Schwab of the Division of the Senior Historian at the United States Holocaust Memorial Museum for providing this information.

was Nanook. Nanook who, upon her arrival at Ravensbrück, had her head shaved; Nanook who, at Torgau, intervened to protect a friend from the brutal blows of our drunken sergeant and, in turn, received a blow which opened a great gash over her right eye; Nanook who, at Königsberg, led the Protestant service at Christmas time, helping to heal our hungry lonesomeness with just the right word of courage and hope. And now it was Nanook who was dead! She was too exhausted to go on, so they just shot her and left her there beside the road where she fell.

We had left the camp about 1:30 in the afternoon and before having had lunch. We were beginning to feel hungry. Most of us had brought along tinned food, but it was impossible to open cans for the present. Fortunately, one of the girls in our group had hastily grabbed a large box of crackers, which we distributed right and left. The weather was overcast, but it was neither raining nor snowing, and it was not unbearably cold. After an hour or so, our road dipped down into a forest. We knew it was a part of the same one through which we had been constructing our road. We came suddenly to a halt. A pleasant surprise awaited us. There was a truck up ahead, out of which climbed all our old guards—the ones who had run off and left us. They were harmless, so we were happy to have them back, especially when we realized that they had come to replace the SS, who climbed into the truck and drove off.

From time to time we halted for five or ten minutes. We were obliged to walk rapidly because the energetic Russians were leading the column. The farther back in the column one went, the more straggling there was. Some of the women were making an extreme effort to keep up. There was something strange about the end of the column—something hypnotically dangerous about it; it seemed to draw you back in spite of yourself and, once there, you felt panicky and lost, as if never would it be in your power to catch up again. But you just had to make an effort, a supreme one, not only to keep up but, from time to time, to run up ahead, way ahead to the center of the column.

There was a little worn-out lady of about 55, whom we called "Tante Marthe," who could walk no longer. Without help, she too would have been shot. We knew now what to expect. It was her friends who supported her, mile after mile, dragging her along between them, her arms thrown about their necks.

It was amazing that there were not more like her. Many of the women had been very ill at camp, but they found the strength to keep going.

Looking at them I was convinced that, for many, it was a last effort. Women, whom I knew to be very ill, such as Tita and Janette, seemed to be draining away little by little. We were fairly heavily laden too, a fact which tired us all the more quickly. Janette and I walked together, our blanket swinging between us. In contrast to us were the Slav women who had arranged packs on their backs and had enough provisions to last for days.

There were practically no refugees on the roads; they had already gone by, several days before. But none of the hamlets through which we passed were completely deserted. As we were going West, we knew that sooner or later, we would have to traverse the Oder River, and we presumed that there we would find the German defense. About 5:00 in the afternoon, our road began to mount and, on the summit of a broad plateau, we saw the first German guns. An hour later we came to the river. It was wide at this point and we crossed over several miles of bridge and causeway before we reached the town of Schultz situated on the opposite bank.[2] In crossing the river we were disappointed to see that, due to the recent thaw, the river was no longer completely frozen over. We thought this would delay the Russian advance.

A constant stream of military vehicles, tanks and cannon passed us, going in the opposite direction. It was dark when we dragged into Schwedt. The town was in a state of great excitement. The streets were crowded with people. A barricade had been thrown up at the bridge entrance. It would have been so easy to disappear into the black of the crowd. Why did not some of us try to escape? It must have been the fear of the unknown, our complete physical exhaustion and the shootings which had unnerved us. I know that I felt so tired—all I asked was to be able to lie down and sleep, any place, it didn't really matter. We could hardly stay in our column because of the pushing crowds and the complete black out. After crossing the center of town, we halted before a tall barn-like structure into which disappeared half of our number. The rest of us went a few hundred yards farther on, to another one like it. The barn or granary, was full a straw. Janette and I quickly found a good spot and, with our blankets, tried to arrange a comfortable bed. But it was difficult because we were too crowded. However, we lay down, more or

2. The town was Schwedt, not Schultz. Schwedt is on the western bank of the Oder River. All further references to Schultz have been changed to Schwedt.

less on top of one another and, after being assured that no one else would try to crowd us out, we sat up long enough to borrow a can opener. One tin contained peas and the other asparagus. We shared them with Ann and Nicole who had no food at all. During our five minute evacuation, Ann had just had time to dress, while Nicole had been caught at the infirmary, having her vitamin sores dressed. Mme. Jules Henri was beside us, but was too exhausted even to eat. As I gazed at her narrow pale face I though of the tragic contrast of her life. Wealthy widow of the French Ambassador to Brazil and, later, to Turkey, she was now lying lonely and ill on a bed of straw. The following morning we lounged around, waiting for the signal to leave. While waiting, we tried to resist the temptation of eating our remaining provisions. There was a heap of cabbages at the far end of the barn and, whenever the guard's eyes were averted, we stole as many as we could. We ate them by dipping the leaves into a can of cooking oil we had unconsciously brought along. We knew that this wasn't a diet for dysentery, but we had nothing else, except some black bread distributed by the Germans. They gave us only bread, as the women appeared to have all they needed. It was true of some of the women, but others of us were already going hungry. It was unbearable to look about and see food to which we had no right. One group of girls had come away from Königsberg with a ten pound tin of powdered milk. It was all they had and they were already sick of it, but it was very valuable for bartering and in that way they were able to have other things. I craved for some milk, but I had nothing of interest to exchange. One friend made me an onion and margarine sandwich, and asked for nothing in return. This was such a rare gesture that I shall never forget the woman who offered it.

We left our barn in the early afternoon and went to join the other girls. We passed building after building like the one in which we had spent the night; huge brick structures with geometrical ventilators high up under the eaves. Schwedt was evidently the store-house of an extensive grain belt. Curious onlookers stared at us as we passed. On and on we walked. As the day advanced, we saw more and more German army vehicles going East. The weather started to change. It became much colder, due to a strong wind from the North. As the sullen grey afternoon disappeared into a heavy black night, the wind became a gale laden with snow and sleet. The cold was unbearable. We bowed into the wind and plowed through the snow which was rapidly deepening and drifting. We huddled together in our column, walking as closely together as possible for protection and warmth. On and on we stumbled, hour after hour, silent in our misery, extenuated by our fatigue. Janette was of great concern to me. She was dragging more and more on my arm and had started to mumble and weep. She was sobbing: "I can't go on any farther, Virginia, I just can't. I want to die. Oh, I want to die here, beside the road."

It was just after midnight when we came into the outskirts of a town, and it was whispered that a guard had indicated this place as our destination for the night. Again it had happened! Each time that we felt as if we could no longer resist, something occurred to give us new hope and the spark of strength necessary to carry on. We entered the town and, though the black out was complete, a dull glow from the snow outlined the buildings for us and we realized that we were in a place of some importance. At any second we thought our straining ears would hear the command to halt, but on and on we went. We crossed the center of the town and, soon, found we were again in the outskirts as the houses dwindled in number. Now a protest of despair began to rise from the women. There were sobs and cries from those who saw their last hope dwindling. Some started to drop out of the column while attempts were made by others to drag them back. At just this moment, we made a sudden turn into a dirt road which widened almost immediately into a railroad yard. We knew what this meant—we were going the rest of the way by rail. Words cannot describe our joy. We still were able to react and now, as I write this, I wonder how it was possible. The human spirit is an amazing thing.

We came to a halt and lights flashed on. There were deserted-looking cars on the siding, and no human beings but ourselves. As our train was not made up, we threw ourselves down on the snow to wait. After an hour or so, some box cars backed up beside us, into which we climbed with difficulty. We traveled very slowly the rest of that night and the following day, and it was in the middle of the next night that we stopped beside the familiar siding of Ravensbrück.

By now, Janette was but half alive. It was horrible for me to see her in such a state, a shapeless heap lying in her filth, unable to talk and no longer reacting to either hunger or cold. There were others like her, but this was my friend. As we stopped at the siding, I put on her shoes and hoisted her up. She could barely stand and, as soon as we were out of the car, she collapsed at my feet. I protected her as best as I could with the blanket and let her lie there until our column started moving toward the camp.

Our third arrival at Ravensbrück was unlike the others. We were allowed neither a shower nor change of clothes. Our heads were not even examined for lice. This breakdown in the system was unprecedented. We went directly to our "bloc" which, this time, was the tent which we had seen constructed in August and out of whose dim interior there had seeped such stories of misery. The tent was rectangular, with frame sides and a canvas roof. It was divided by a partition into two sections, one of which contained four story wooden bunks, while the other was empty. When we arrived, the bunk section was already occupied by Russians and Poles, so we had no choice. We were approximately six hundred women, and we were all obliged to crowd into that cold, damp, airless compartment. Nicole, Ann, Janette and I had managed to stay together. As we were herded through the narrow entrance at the end of the tent, we had the impression that already there was no more room for anyone. Each prisoner was trying to make herself as comfortable as possible on the paved floor, the choice places being along the walls which would serve as support for the back when sitting down. But all the choice places were already taken and the rest of the women were installing themselves as best they could. Janette fell into the first vacant spot she found. Nicole and I decided to go into the bunk section to see if, by chance, there would be room for us. This was the wrong thing to do because we found conditions there extremely overcrowded, with even the floor between the bunks covered with sleeping women, and, when we returned to our side, there was not a vacant spot left. At the end of the tent, near the door, was a section barred off for the Polish "bloc" captain and her friends. The captain had a bed, while her friends slept on the tables and on the floor. The electric light was burning, but everyone was already installed for the night, and all was quiet. We crept silently into the forbidden sector, carefully spread out our blanket and lay down, but almost immediately one of the women turned over and ordered us to leave. When we hesitated, she started to kick us. How could she be so mean? She was a prisoner too, and we had not bothered her, nor even touched her. We crawled away for fear that the Polish captain would be awakened by the din. We were so exhausted we could have slept any place! But even the center aisle that had originally existed was now filled with sleeping women. When we tried to recline on our sides in a crack between two bodies, we necessarily disturbed the sleepers and they struck and kicked us, forcing us to leave. We were miserable. Wasn't there anyone who would try to make a little room for us? Eventually, it was a group of our friends who in squeezing together made it possible for us to have some sleep that night.

The next morning there was an "appel," after which we were ordered back into the tent. We were among the first to enter and, so, we were able to get one of the best places, next to the wall. Janette was very ill. Her eyes were expressionless and her skin was yellow. Before leaving Königsberg she had become bloated, but in twenty-four hours the swelling had subsided and now she was like a limp rag. We tried to feed her soup, but she had lost all interest in food. Her hands were cold and I knew that she was dying. It seemed cruel to let her stay there on that cold hard floor, without any care. It would be terrible to wake up the next morning to find her dead beside us. The only solution was the infirmary. I appealed to Annie, our interpreter, to get the "bloc" captain's permission to take her there. She came over to look at Janette. I thought she must be made of steel. Not once did she show any sign of kindness or sympathy. She was a great husky brute of a woman, hard and cruel; she refused to allow Janette to leave. But Annie understood how I felt. She went to the infirmary and came back with a paper which would officially admit Janette. It was dusk when two of us found a stretcher. We brought it into the tent and lifted Janette, who was only half conscious, on to it. I took off her galoshes and wrapped the blanket about her. We managed to leave the tent with our burden, unseen by the Polish captain. I thought we would never reach the infirmary. Janette seemed so heavy because we were so weak. When we arrived, we went in by a side entrance which led into a room where the diagnosis would be made. A nurse in white uniform took one look at Janette's emaciated face and then pulled back the blanket. She said nothing, but I knew by her attitude that my friend was condemned. We picked up the stretcher to carry it farther down the corridor to the main entrance hall where numberless other stretchers, each with its human wreck, were posed on the floor. My stretcher bearer left now, and I was alone with Janette; I stopped beside her, knowing and trying to realize that this was good-bye. The sadness and the tragedy and the horror of it all shocked me. Janette's eyes, which shortly before were expressionless, now seemed to glow with recognition and adoration as she gazed up into my face. I knew she loved me. I wondered whether she realized that she was dying. She was not suffering now. She was no longer cold, nor did she feel her hunger. I wanted my last words to her to give her hope: "Goodnight, Janette. Now that you are in the infirmary you will be properly cared for. Soon you'll be well and then it will be time to go home to St. Front and to your mother. Remember how often we have talked of it? We will be there in time for the cherries. Goodnight now. Sleep well."

A slow smile crept over her face. She couldn't speak, but she tried to make me realize that she wanted to kiss me. I bent gently over her. With an effort, I rose and stumbled out into the night.

The eight days and nights we spent in the tent were fraught with misery. This was the first part of February and the weather was cold and wet. Most of us were ill with dysentery; lying on a damp brick floor only aggravated our conditions. At night it was frightful. Our situation was unimaginable; a long tent with one narrow exit at the far end; a tent housing several hundred miserable women, the majority of whom were suffering from dysentery—an illness humiliating and enervating; the night during which all those who were ill were obliged to go out at least once, and not the slightest light by which to make their way. I was awakened several times by women stepping on me while trying to find the door, and I know that I did as much to others when I was obliged to go out. I would crawl over the bodies, groping ahead with my hand to find a place for my foot, but often was unsuccessful and I would lose my balance and fall on someone's stomach or face. Between sobs I uttered an apology. If I had stepped on someone who knew me and recognized my voice, my apology was accepted, but if it were a stranger, I received kicks and blows which sent me sprawling on to someone else. It was a nightmare. By the most amazing self-control, the women usually were able to get to the door before it was too late, but, once outside, it no longer mattered. The area between the "blocs" was found each morning in a state of indescribable filth. Prisoners were relegated to clean up. During the day, there were such long lines of women waiting to go to the toilets that many were unable to control themselves until their turn came to go in. Then, the Germans ordered holes to be dug about three feet in diameter, at regular intervals between the "blocs." There, without protection of any kind, women, two or three at a time, were to be found squatting around the same hole. Living in these unsanitary conditions, with no medical help of any kind, our conditions became worse and worse. The morale of women fell lower and lower. Some no longer tried to leave the tent when necessary, and sleeping here became unbearable. Others were so weak they were unable to move but, though they were not forced to attend the "appel," neither were they moved to the infirmary. During every night and every day deaths occurred, but the bodies were not taken away until hours afterward. The neighbors covered them over with what they could find. I saw all my friends about me growing weaker and weaker—and I knew that I was like them.

Three days after our return to Ravensbrück, there was an "appel" which was to send some of us on a new work commando. We lined up in a column, and the first sixty girls were chosen. The rest of us went back to the tent. A few days later, there was another "appel" for the same purpose. The work was said to be the digging of trenches around Berlin. Nicole and I felt incapable of lifting a spade, and decided that we would feign illness in order to miss the "appel." We lay prostrate on the floor. There were others like us, pretending to be more ill than they really were, and the necessary number needed for the commando was not being reached rapidly enough. An SS woman with her stick strode into the tent and began beating the women to make them go out. We determined to resist. The minutes passed. Now she centered her blows on us. We were lying on our stomachs and it was our heads and shoulders that received the blows. It was too painful, we were forced to give up. Climbing to our feet, we gathered up our few possessions and went out. But we were too late, the others had gone! (Now I know the truth about this commando; not one of the girls who left that day had been heard of since. It was a "black convoy"!)[3]

The days under the tent dragged on. We were weak and listless, drugged by the horror that surrounded us. It was forbidden to visit the other "blocs," but we made an effort all the same in order to see the other girls whom we knew. The greatest risk was of being caught and forced to work. We went too in order to wash; we wanted to avoid our own wash-room which was in a separate building beyond the end of the tent, in

---

3. "Black convoys" were transports of women, usually too weak to work, from Ravensbrück to extermination camps, where they were killed. By the early months of 1945, a gas chamber just outside the gates of Ravensbrück was in operation. Between five and six thousand women from the main camp of Ravensbrück, thinking they were being sent to a camp named Mittwerda, were victims of this gas chamber. The Ravensbrück gas chamber was destroyed before the liberation of the camp in late April 1945. Morrison, *Ravensbrück*, pp. 289–291. See also Tillion, *Ravensbrück: An Eyewitness Account*, p. 40.

which there was a stove ruled over by another one of these brutal Poles and her faithful followers. They did not allow us to even approach the stove, much less heat water on it, or toast our bread. There was an SS too who spent much of her time there and before whom the Pole and her group fawningly catered. Whenever we entered the washroom, they looked at us with horror and disgust: we were the untouchables, the filthy lice-infested occupants of the tent. The German stole everything she could from the prisoners, many of whom still had in their possession objects pillaged at Königsberg. I saw her take food from them, as well as blankets and soup bowls. One day she observed my wedding ring. At Königsberg I had replaced it on my finger but, as a result of all the hard labor, my knuckles had swollen and I could no longer remove it. But now this woman ordered me to get it off. I showed her the condition of my hands, but that made no difference; she motioned that I was to do it with soap and water. I pretended to try, using the little piece of ersatz soap which I still had in my possession. I took my time, waiting for a moment to escape, but the opportunity never came and, in the meantime, she kept goading me. She was cruel and I hated her. I saw her strike the women with her heavy rod if they passed too close to her—she didn't want their lice! Tears started running down my cheeks. I felt as if I could bear no more. My wedding ring was all I had left, all I had of Philippe, of love, of life. I turned to one of the women who was beside the stove, whom I had heard speaking French, and I blurted out: "I am an American. Does she steal the wedding rings of Americans too?"

The woman, who I believe was Austrian, appeared surprised, "Are you American? One moment."

She turned to the SS and spoke to her in German. The German looked at me as though she had seen me for the first time. I felt as if I suddenly had an identity—that I was no longer just a stinking skeleton good only for the gas chamber. She looked startled—even concerned. She said a few words to the Austrian, who nodded to me and said, "You may keep your ring."

The number of deaths increased. I was worried about Tita and Nanine who, along with Mina and Mrs. Bertrand, lay opposite me at one side of the tent. They never went out now. Mina was bloated and half uncon-scious; she had reached the horrible disfiguring condition, the final state prior to the rapid collapse followed so swiftly by death. The others were skeletons. Their eyes were immense and lifeless. I had had such delightful conversations with Tita. I thought of the many exciting projects we had planned together. Now it seemed impossible. Her personality had gone; she had become something frightening and revolting. This horror was not Tita.

Yvonne and I, together outside the tent one morning, were horrified by the sounds we heard coming from the interior of the washroom; long wails punctuated by piercing cries like those of a trapped animal. Suddenly the door was opened by the SS who, seeing us, ordered us to enter. By gestures, she indicated that we were to carry out the creature uttering those horrible sounds. We pushed through the crowded room to the far end where we discovered that it was Vera—a young white Russian woman who had been with us ever since Romainville. She was horribly bloated, writhing on the floor in delirium. "Au rever, au rever! To the infirmary, to the infirmary!" she kept crying.

Poor Vera! We struggled to lift her, but she was a dead weight and we were so weak. Half carrying her, half dragging her, we finally reached the door. No one helped us; no one cared. We were to take her to the tent, to the other side of the partition where the bunks were. When we entered, we were shocked by what we saw: everywhere were bodies of dead and dying women. They were piled together in heaps on the floor and in the bunks. The sight made my flesh crawl. Where would we put Vera? We looked frantically about for a vacant bunk and, with a great effort, we dragged her over the prostrate bodies and lifted her into it. She was lying in a tortuous position, but we could do nothing to help her. We ran away from her cries and from the horror of that stinking tomb!

Following the departure of the second convoy, we were moved into a "bloc." There must have been approximately a hundred of us left. Those in a dying state were moved directly from the tent to the infirmary. In the "bloc" we were comfortable. We were no longer obliged to go to the daily "appel" and we were not required to work. This was an annex to the infirmary. The "bloc" assistants served us our soup and bread in bed. More women came to join us, principally Russians and Poles evacuated from the camp of Auschwitz. There were some children too.[4] After we

4. Following the Soviet army offensive during the second half of 1944, the SS began evacuating prisoners from Auschwitz, as well as other camps, to camps located within the interior of the Third Reich. Orders for the final evacuation of Auschwitz came in mid-January 1945, when some fifty-six thousand women and men prisoners were led on a forced march out of Auschwitz and its subcamps. Many of these prisoners died during this evacuation. On January 27, 1945, the Soviet army liberated the

had been lying there two or three days, the "bloc" captain made an announcement early one morning:

"Those who want a shower and a change of clothes, come immediately."

Personally, I felt as if that was just what I needed to feel right again, but some of the women said it was dangerous. While in the tent, the lack of light had made it impossible for us to search each other's heads for lice and we risked having our heads shaved. I felt willing to take the risk however. I pulled myself wearily from my bunk to make my way with others across the camp. I should have consulted my horoscope that day! It was an unlucky one for me. I returned to the "bloc" thirty minutes later, with a hairless head! I can laugh about it now, because I am no longer bald; today I have several inches of hair, and it is curly, whereas before it was very straight! But that day, the 16th of February, I felt as if I had reached the lowest depths. I had suffered the final humiliation. I was hairless, and still covered with lice. They had allowed me neither a shower nor clean clothes. My friends were very sympathetic. Nicole said: "Most women are ugly without hair, but you are like a charming little boy!" I wanted to cry. I ran my hand over my bristly head—"Just like a Mexican hairless," I thought, "How awful!" My head was cold too, so with an extra pair of underpants from Königsberg, I arranged a turban.

I was growing weaker and weaker. We were not encouraged to leave our bunks as it made too many people under foot and, besides, there was nothing to do. Nicole, Ann and I shared the same bed. Nicole was very thin but not really ill. She was as courageous and energetic as ever. Ann was sick with dysentery and very weak. There was a stunned air about her; she was the victim of an extreme lassitude. Nicole and I decided that we must force ourselves to get up once a day. We realized that we were on the border line of life and death. We were losing our friends, one by one; Tita and her sister had gone; Mina too, and Mrs. Bertrand. Every day we saw dead bodies being carried out of the "bloc." So we made the extreme effort of getting up once a day. We got up to wash and to try to find extra food. Our Danish friend, Süni, was convalescing in the infirmary. We had seen each other through the window one day, not long

---

few thousand prisoners remaining at Auschwitz. The arrival of prisoners from Auschwitz and other camps at Ravensbrück during the winter of 1944–1945 compounded the already overcrowded conditions there.

after returning to Ravensbrück from Königsberg. Four months had passed since our last meeting and, when I saw how she gasped unwittingly at her first sight of me, I knew that I must have changed. She carefully opened the window to whisper that I must return in half an hour—she would be able to pass me an extra soup. Every evening from then on, she did the same thing and even shared her food parcels which she received from Denmark. I owe a great deal to Süni. She not only gave me nourishment, but the incentive to leave my bed.

The 25th of February, the "bloc" captain came into the dormitory to call out, "Will the American who was at Königsberg, come immediately."

What did this mean? I gathered together my galoshes and climbed over my neighbors to reach the aisle. In reaching the other room I found a woman distributing clean clothes. After ordering me to undress, she gave me an anti-vermin powder to rub on my body, and then she gave me a whole new outfit including a beautiful coat. When I returned to the dormitory, no one recognized me. I felt very set up! A new person! I thought at first that my nationality had brought me this favor, but though I was one of the first to be given clean clothes, I was not the last.

10 Liebenau

The twenty-eighth of February dawned just like any other of the cold damp ones that had preceded it. I was taken aback when one of our neighbors, a Pole with whom we had been friendly suddenly remarked, "Virginia, I have the feeling that something extraordinary is going to happen to you today."

She hesitated, and then added, "Something good."

I smiled and answered but without conviction: "I hope you're right."

Half an hour later, the "bloc" captain came in. "Madame d'Albert is wanted at once," she cried out.

Everyone turned to stare at me. I felt panicky. My heart began to pound. I nervously gathered my clothes together and started to dress. Before I had finished the woman came in again. "Hurry, Madame d'Albert, the office doesn't like to be kept waiting."

I grabbed my coat and shoes and crawled over the other aisle. At the door, a woman who was waiting for me indicated that I was to come with her. She walked rapidly across the camp. I struggled to keep up with her. My legs were so weak; at every step I felt that my knees were no longer going to support me.

When we entered the office, the woman seated behind the desk smiled and stared at me with interest. Their arm bands showed that they were prisoners, but privileged ones, designated for secretarial work. I was offered a chair—an unbelievable consideration! After a few minutes I was called into an adjoining office occupied by a woman SS. She smiled agreeably and, though she evidently explained the new situation in which I found myself, I could not understand a word she said. Shortly afterward an SS officer came in. He shoved a bundle of grey and blue striped uniforms into my arms and ordered me to follow him. I was frightened. I thought the uniforms were for me and that a new and greater trial lay ahead. I was shivering all over now. By sheer determination I managed to keep at the heels of this man who was rapidly leading me in the direction of the main gate. We crossed in front of the kitchens and shower rooms, before which were prisoners waiting to carry the soup kettles to the "blocs." Why did they stare at me so?

After going through the gate, we made a sudden turn to the right where cement steps led us up a steep incline. When we reached the top, we crossed a grove of pines and entered a long frame building. The officer led me into another office, abruptly seized the striped garments, and went out. Now I found myself alone with two SS women in uniform. The older of the two was an officer; the younger woman was evidently her secretary. They both turned to stare at me—just like all the others. I fell back in amazement as the officer addressed me in perfect English:

"You are Mrs. D'Albert? You are an American?"

"Yes," I murmured.

"Give me the place and date of your birth," she continued.

She wrote down my answers. The younger woman smiled at me and said in halting English, "I can speak a little English." She hesitated as she groped for words. "Tonight you will be happy. You are going away."

A great surge of hope and excitement rose in me. But could it be true? Were they playing with me? Were these more Nazi lies? I felt frightened and apprehensive again. I wanted to ask questions, but I felt stunned and tongue-tied. The secretary led me outside into the hall, and locked me alone into a cell, but not before she had said, "Just for five minutes."

I was really shaking now. I felt as if I could never wait for the five minutes to pass. I began muttering to myself: "Is it true? Is it true? Am I really leaving? Oh, God, is it true? Are they lying? No, it's true? I know it is? Oh, hurry! Let me out of here!"

The door of my cell was opened again by the same man who had led me out of the camp. I must follow him again. We took the same path by which we had come—down the steps, and back into Ravensbrück. Why were we going back again? Where was he taking me? Wasn't I going to leave? My spirits fell. How long could I stand this strain? We crossed again in front of the kitchen. The same staring women were there. I was gasping for breath as I struggled to keep up. We entered the original office where I was immediately handed over to a Czech prisoner. She motioned to me to follow. She seemed in a hurry too. We crossed to the infirmary, where I was told to undress. Afterward I entered a room where there were two persons in white uniform, whom I presumed to be a doctor and a nurse. As I entered, bald and naked, my emaciated body covered with lice bites and vitamin sores, they turned to look at me. I saw only disgust and indifference in their expressions.

The man turned away, while the young woman, superciliously, asked me in French, "How do you feel?"

"Fine," I answered. That was all. I was dismissed.

The Czech was waiting for me outside. She spoke neither French nor English, but she clearly indicated by her attitude what I must do. I must dress now—quickly. No use putting on my stockings or even my dress; just throw on my coat. We hurried out to another "bloc." At the door, we pushed through a crowd of women carrying valises. Inside was a big room with a long counter behind which were shelves covered with clothes. Wearing apparel was being thrown across the counter to women who were undressing and dressing as rapidly as possible. I must do the same. I threw all of my soiled things into a big box of dirty clothes. Now the Czech was rapidly piling clean things into my arms. I put on a girdle, a brassiere, two pair of underpants, two underskirts, a crepe dress, a sweater, a red jacket, an orange velvet coat, a pair of gloves, a scarf around my neck and another around my head. I put on everything they gave me so that I wouldn't be cold. The most amazing thing about all my clothes was that they were not marked with crosses! I was the last to dress and, when I was ready, the Czech led me outside where I joined the group of waiting women, after which she disappeared.

I observed those about me. These women were German. They were wearing their own clothes and carrying their personal valises. I had heard that German internees in the camp were being liberated to work as "free laborers" for the Reich. This must be one of the groups being liberated. But why was I a part of it? We were ordered to line up and be ready to march off. There were approximately sixty of us. For the second time that day I went out the gate of Ravensbrück. For the second time I climbed the steps to the long frame building. We waited in the hall, where each woman answered present as her name was called. But my name was not called, so I went into the office where I had been brought earlier that morning.

"Oh, *there* you are!" cried the older woman. "Sit down, won't you, there, beside the stove. You will have a short time to wait. Your train leaves at 4:30."

"But where am I going?" I asked.

She lowered her voice. "I'm not sure, but I think you're going to a Red Cross camp near Lake Constance. I heard two officers talking about the departure of two persons—Geneviève de Gaulle and an American. They mentioned Liebenau, and I know that at Liebenau there is a camp where exchanges of prisoners are made.[1] You will be well off there and perhaps you will soon be going home."

I felt as though my heart could not stand the joy brought by her words. I sat on quietly, thinking of the miracle which was becoming a reality!

While waiting, I watched the woman as she checked her files. I watched her eat a meager lunch of bread, margarine and honey, which she washed down with a cup of coffee. I asked her where she had learned to speak English.

"In New York," she answered. "I spent several months there with relatives of mine. They have a factory in Brooklyn, and a beautiful home on Long Island. I want to go back again as soon as I can. America is a wonderful place."

How strange it seemed to find a German woman here in this lost hole of Ravensbrück, who had known the same world as I.

She told me that, until two weeks before, she had been at the camp of Auschwitz. The Germans had evacuated the camp before the Russian advance. "There was no transportation. We had to take to the roads. For two whole days we marched without food. Terrible people, the Russians. If only it were the Americans who were advancing in this direction! I'm afraid of the Russians. The Americans are kind, but the Russians are murderers," and she drew her finger across her throat to show what procedure the Russians took with Germans. Then, to my amazement, she shook her fist at the portrait of Hitler which hung on the wall over her desk: "To think that *that* man is responsible for all this!"

I said nothing; one never knew; she might be setting a trap for me.

A door to my left suddenly opened and a girl and two SS entered. The girl was Geneviève de Gaulle. It was not the first time I had seen her. After my arrival at Ravensbrück in August, she had been pointed out to

1. Liebenau was not a Red Cross camp; it was an internment camp for enemy nationals, including American and British Commonwealth civilians as well as other prominent figures. Geneviève de Gaulle, the niece of General Charles de Gaulle and the greatly respected *résistante*, wrote a short memoir about her experiences at Ravensbrück. See de Gaulle Anthonioz, *The Dawn of Hope*.

me. I knew that she had been arrested and deported for her work in the "Resistance." Many times I had heard of her charm and kindness and courage. Everyone who knew her loved her. Her features definitely resembled those of her uncle, but, unlike him, she was short in stature. Her straight brown hair, expressive dark eyes, pale skin and easy smile, combined to give her an appealing charm. I was thrilled to know that Geneviève was to be my traveling companion. We left immediately, with three SS to guard us—two men and one woman. Six days of traveling followed.[2] I have never known such fatigue. Hope and despair were intermingled. I struggled on believing and living for one thing—my arrival at our destination. I grew weaker and weaker. I was constantly stumbling and falling. I could hardly keep up with the others. The two men were not unsympathetic, but the girl was impatient. She took hold of me roughly and pulled me along. The first evening we arrived in Berlin and we boarded the subway to change stations. Our SS were unfamiliar with the city, and their errors resulted in our having to retrace our steps. The interminable stairways in the subway became a nightmare. I had to pull myself up by the banisters. At one time there was an air raid warning. The crowds became panicky and rushed madly into the underground shelters. We followed, but there was not room for all. We were left in the underground tunnel, with gaping holes and falling timbers overhead—the result of recent bombings. We stumbled over wood and plaster not yet cleared away. It was raining and the water leaked through, making muddy puddles through which we waded. It was not possible to stay there so we went down beside the tracks where we waited for the end of the raid. Berlin was not the objective. We finally reached our station, boarded our train and traveled all night. I slept fitfully in my corner seat.

We continued in the same train the whole of the next day. It seemed wonderful to travel in public coaches after knowing the misery of overcrowded box cars. The Germans spoke neither French nor English, but Geneviève knew German. I saw that they liked her and I am sure that it meant a great deal in the treatment and consideration we received from them on this trip. We had enough to eat. Before leaving Ravensbrück, we had been given bread, margarine and sausage rations, and Geneviève shared the personal food parcels she had received before leaving camp. The last four months she had been given special consideration by the

2. See Map 2 for the route that Virginia and Geneviève traveled.

Germans, due evidently to a political move. She was placed in solitary confinement, was obliged neither to work nor attend the morning "appels," and was given the same food as the SS themselves. As a result of the new regime, her health had improved and the horrible vitamin sores with which her legs were covered the first time I saw her were now healed.

It was after midnight of the second day that our train stopped in a station outside of Munich. We boarded a crowded trolley car which took us half way into the city, but to reach the central business section we were obliged to walk. It was a brilliant moonlight night. We followed an important thoroughfare lined with bombed-out buildings. The walls which remained had weird shapes, like giant fingers; black silhouettes against the moonlit sky. The street was clean, with all the debris neatly piled as high as two stories on both sides. After half an hour's walk, we reached a large square where a tall building still stood erect, though badly pock-marked by exploding shells. It was a recreation and information center for the Nazi troops. On entering, we found it brightly lighted and crowded with soldiers. A broad staircase led upward, under a high dome, to the mezzanine floor, which was crowded with men sitting around tables, eating, and drinking beer. They appeared very young and very tired. We tried to find a vacant table, but without success. There was a small empty room at one side, which we entered, only to be ordered out immediately. The room was reserved for the dead and wounded!

After hurriedly drinking a glass of beer, we went out again among the ruins to search for the Munich Gestapo. We found it eventually, opposite a great two-spired church which miraculously was still standing. The Gestapo Headquarters had been damaged, but were still fairly intact. We entered a building composed of stairways and hall onto which opened numberless doors. Geneviève and I spent the rest of the night in a locked cell where we shared a narrow cot. It was very early when a uniformed matron came to wake us. "Dress quickly," she ordered. "You are to leave in half an hour." It was strange to hear the key turn in the lock. This was the first time since Fresnes that I had been in a prison cell. The early morning light was coming through the bars of our tiny window. It must have been about 7:00 when we left.

While walking to the place where we were to take the street car, we passed in front of the severely damaged Opera House and the destroyed

beer house of Nazi party fame. I had always heard of Munich's picturesque charm, but now the city was only a mass of rubble. It was strange
to see so many people in the streets. I wondered how they could continue
to stay in such a place. Where did they live? I studied their faces which
wore expressions of strain and exhaustion, but I no longer wondered how
people could bear up under the horror of such bombing; I had already
learned something of the remarkable resistance of the human mind and
body.

We boarded a train which was to take us to Ulm. When nearing our
destination, the train suddenly stopped in the middle of a vast prairie.
The SS said that it was the sign of an air raid, and it was not long before
we heard the throbbing motors of American bombers. The train was
crowded, but everyone remained quiet. There was nothing to fear here.
The raid was a long one and from the direction of the explosions, we
were certain that Ulm was the objective. We had waited at least two hours
and, though the bombing had ceased, the train showed no signs of moving on. The SS were becoming restless. They decided that we should walk.
We were always having to walk. It was dreadful! We followed the tracks
as far as the next station, a tiny one belonging to a small village. We
inquired about trains.

The station agent could only be vague. "Ulm has been severely
bombed. There will probably not be any trains before tomorrow."[3]

Our guards held a long discussion. They decided finally that we would
try to spend the night here. I believe they were enjoying themselves. This
trip was an adventure for them and, besides, once Geneviève and I had
been safely convoyed to our final destination, they were to have several
days of leave before reporting back to Ravensbrück. This little town was
charming; neat dirt paths ran around and between attractive frame
houses and barns painted in pastel shades of pink, blue, yellow and green.
There did not seem to be a commercial center, but a passer-by directed
us to the Mayor's farm, which was the most elaborate one in the community. He, in turn, sent us to the inn. We entered the big, low-ceilinged
dining room which was so clean that it glistened. Fresh white curtains
decorated the small windows. A long bunk ran around the wall under the

3. Allied bombing of Germany's cities and industrial centers intensified during
the spring of 1945. The city of Ulm, in southwestern Germany, was severely damaged
by Allied bombing.

windows, before which shiny tables were placed at regular intervals. A big high rectangular stove made of tile was opposite the windows. I almost fell onto the bunk—I was so exhausted. We were the only guests, but an old grandmother sat darning socks on a low chair in one corner. A little boy and a little girl stared at us as they munched big red apples. Their aproned mother bustled in and out of the adjoining kitchen. She brought us beer in big glass mugs. I began to relax in this atmosphere. This was a home. There was a radio and an orchestra was playing beautiful music, the first I had heard in months. I had forgotten what music could do, and I wept. Our girl SS became quiet friendly. She showed us amusing photographs of members of her family, all standing in stilted poses with frozen expressions on their faces. Our sergeant, who had gone out, came back after a while, smiling delightedly and carrying a big package. I'm sure that there were butter and eggs in the package. He must have paid another visit to the Mayor.

The five of us ate around the same table that evening. We all had a good hot soup, after which the SS were served scrambled eggs and fried potatoes. Geneviève's plate and mine remained empty. We realized that we were not eating eggs because, after all, we were prisoners and could not expect to claim any, but we were not without fried potatoes simply because we had no ration tickets. After offering our hostess the margarine we had with us, we soon were enjoying fried potatoes with the others.

That night, the girl SS, Geneviève and I shared the same room. There were twin beds; Geneviève and I were in one, our girl guard in the other. She locked the door and slept with the key under her pillow!

There was a train for Ulm the following morning about 8:30, but we were obliged to get down outside the city due to the bombardment of the previous afternoon. After walking about two miles we reached the city limits. It was at this moment that the air raid sirens started wailing, but we continued into the city. A frantic old lady passed us running in the opposite direction:

"Don't go any farther!" she screamed. "An air raid warning has sounded. We were bombed yesterday; it may be for us again!"

The streets were emptying quickly. We entered the first under ground shelter we found. After the 'all clear' sounded half an hour later, we continued our way into the city. The bombing of the previous day was the first that Ulm had suffered. Smoking ruins were everywhere. It was frightful the amount of damage that one raid had caused. Men and women were pulling little carts, loaded down with personal and household effects saved from tragedy. As we went along, we kept asking the way to the station, but we arrived to find that it no longer existed. An information booth had already sprung up along the ruins and, there, we learned that to reach Stuttgart we must walk to a small station five miles north of the city. I wondered if I could walk five miles. We had already walked as far and I was exhausted. But there was no other choice. There were many other people, soldiers and civilians, men, women and children, on the road, walking toward the same objective. It was early afternoon when we arrived. The station was the only structure on the open countryside and all around it, on the grass, were travelers.

We reached Stuttgart late the same night. Like Munich, this city was a mass of ruins. We walked the deserted streets in search of the Gestapo Headquarters. Up to now the SS had never told us our final destination. They claimed to be ignorant of it and said it was only at Stuttgart that they would receive final instructions. Geneviève and I slept on benches that night, in the front office of the Gestapo. We were not locked in, but were constantly guarded by the night watchman.

The next day, we left Stuttgart, following the visit of a very dapper, polite little gentleman, who was the director of the camp where we were to be taken. We dreaded the trip that lay ahead because we must retrace our steps to Ulm. There was no way to avoid those endless miles of walking. To make matters worse, snow fell heavily all afternoon. The SS, fearing that Ulm might be bombed, wished to avoid passing the night there. In the train, they made conversation with a stranger who suggested that we spend the night in his town. It was dark when we left the train to walk quite some distance along a country road which led into a broad street lined with large sturdy houses. We sought out the Mayor's residence, and it was he who was responsible for our having a bed that night. The town was overcrowded already, due to the exodus of people out of Ulm following the bombardment.

Early the next morning, we boarded a train which took us to the little station in open country from which we must make the long trip to Ulm. I stumbled along, hardly conscious of what I was doing. This was our fifth day of traveling and we had had very little sleep. Would we never arrive? On reaching Ulm, we went again to the station to inquire our way. Trains were not yet established on a regular schedule, and we must walk five miles south of the city in order to make connections! Another five miles!

I remember very vaguely that long "supplice."[4] I was always dragging behind the others, straining, struggling to keep up. There were many people on the roads, refugees from Ulm, carrying heavy suitcases, pushing baby carriages and pulling wagons. After an hour of this, I saw that we were about to enter a small town.

I signaled to Geneviève. "Geneviève, ask them to let me rest a while in this next town. If they won't, I can't go on."

"Don't worry, Virginia, I'll talk to them."

The SS turned to look at me. I guess they realized that I meant what I said, and they assented. It was too cold to stop on the road, so we entered the first inn we saw. We sat down in the dining room, which was crowded with refugees. There was a stove in the corner, and I was able to have a chair beside it. I became warm and relaxed; such a wonderful feeling! There was no order in the room. The people were crowded around the stove, talking loudly over the din of the radio. But, suddenly, they became very silent; the radio had announced an air warning; an announcer was giving the position of the planes:

"A—formation—is—over—Ulm. Ulm—is—being—bombed! The—formation—is leaving—Ulm—going—South. The formation—is—over—"
Suddenly the whole inn shook with thunder explosions. Chairs were overturned, glasses fell to the floor. People ran for the door, others fell flat under tables. There was another explosion, and still another! Bombs were falling all around us! Only two people remained in their original positions: a soldier who, with his chair tipped back, seemed to be inviting a bomb to fall in his lap, and myself—too exhausted to care what happened. I was comfortable beside my stove, and all I asked was to stay there. But the SS were badly frightened and showed it. They wanted to get out and as I was their responsibility, I must go along. We all crowded out through the door. As we left the inn, I was conscious of a smoking bomb crater just across the street. People were running madly in all directions. But I was incapable of running; I tried, but I couldn't. My legs would not obey. I saw the SS running for protection from one tree to another which grew along the ditch beside the highway. They kept urging me on. And I went on, but slowly, down the center of the road. I felt no fear.

I finally joined the others in a cement shelter. Columns of black smoke were rising over the hill in the direction of Ulm. The city had received its

4. Agony.

second bombing. At the end of the raid, we went out on the highway to continue on our way. During the next half hour refugees passed us continually, some on bicycles and others in trucks and wagons, eyewitnesses to the recent raid. Excitedly they called out to us the horrors they had seen. How grateful I was when we found a driver who had room for us in the back of his truck. We had to drive around bomb craters in the middle of the highway, and at one place, military police made us get out and walk, as there was an unexploded shell up ahead. Our driver got around it successfully, and we climbed in again fifty feet further on.

It was at the next town that we were to board a train for the last leg of the journey. It was almost one o'clock now and, as the train was not due until four, we entered an inn opposite the station. It was Sunday and the dining hall was crowed with middle-class families having their lunch out. It was warm here and I began to relax again. I was hungry too, but I craved something other than sausage and black bread. Geneviève felt the same as I. She had been saving a big box of fifty sardines from one of her food parcels. This being Sunday and our last meal with the SS, she decided to open it. All eyes in the restaurant turned to look, as the fragrance of the fish permeated the room. Those people must not have seen sardines for years!

There was a large mirror in the restaurant. I mention this because it presented me the first opportunity of seeing my reflection since leaving France. Never in my life have I received such a shock. I shall never forget it. What ugly creature was this? A woman, yes, but neither hips nor breasts; great lusterless eyes staring out of the grey countenance, the skin stretched like parchment over the skull and high cheek bones, beneath which were empty holes; no hair line showed under the sagging turban. I turned away in horror. It was 10:30 that night when we arrived at the station of our destination, which we knew now was to be Liebenau. One of our SS phoned immediately to the camp which had already been warned of our arrival. There was no means of transportation at that hour, so the person who answered the phone suggested that we walk the three miles from the station to the camp. Must we walk again? It had been snowing since early afternoon and walking was very difficult. We trudged on through the black deserted streets, pausing from time to time to knock at a door to ask our way; the houses became fewer and fewer; the white road seemed endless. Our girl SS said that she was too tired to go on, so the men stopped at the next dwelling and arranged for her to spend the night. How I envied her! On we went, never certain whether we were on the road, or off it. The houses disappeared all together, and we could no longer ask our way. After we had gone what we thought must be at least three miles and since the camp was not in sight, the men decided that we should go back to the station. It was 2:30 A.M. when we reached it. The station agent lighted a fire in the public waiting room, and we lay down, exhausted, on the wooden benches, to wait for daylight.

The camp supervisors came to meet us at 8:00 the next morning—dignified elderly gentleman in civilian clothes.

We all walked to the camp together and, judging by the trees and road turnings, I realized that we had taken the right road the night before, but had turned back too soon—half a mile farther on we would have found Liebenau and the gates—of Paradise!

The gates of Liebenau marked the border line between life and death. The moment I entered I knew that I was saved. From that day, March the sixth, until our liberation by French forces on April twenty first, I was given the care I so desperately needed. Each morning when I awoke to find myself in that heavenly place, I could hardly bear the joy that nearly suffocated me.

Liebenau was a Catholic institution for the feeble-minded, but during the war, the greater part of it had been turned into an internment camp for English and American women. It consisted of three large modern buildings built in conjunction with a farm on which the degenerates were employed. The setting was charming—a rolling country side of fields and orchards, with Lake Constance and the Swiss Alps in the near distance.

I had a clean comfortable bed in a large room, shared with four other internees, including Geneviève. The camp food, plus American and English Red Cross parcels allowed no one to go hungry. The "appel" consisted of rounds made in the evening after curfew hour, by one of the guards who visited each room to make the count. The only work included minor household chores. Daily walks were permitted outside the confine and there was a well stocked library. Does it seem strange that Liebenau seemed like heaven?

Geneviève and I had hardly arrived at the camp before we found ourselves famous—Geneviève, of course, because of her honored name; I, because of my appalling physical state. I gave the impression of being an old woman—one of sixty-five years, as an acquaintance later told me. The two weeks following my arrival, my dysentery continued, and I was too weak to walk. I was eating anything and everything, waking in the night to nibble at delicacies I had forgotten existed. After two weeks, I entered the sick room, where I was cared for by internees who had volunteered for nursing and who were under the direction of the German camp doctor. He prescribed a special diet, medicines and sun baths. Before I entered the sick room, I weighed 76 pounds and, when I left it three weeks later, I still weighed 76 pounds, which is 50 pounds under my normal weight; but, during that time, my dysentery was cured; I lost and regained my appetite, the dancing flecks before my eyes and the roaring in my ears gradually disappeared. I regained little by little my nervous stamina. I began to read and was allowed visitors. My vitamin sores healed and my swollen feet and legs, reduced to normal. I was so very happy there. Every evening, the head nurse would come in with her map to point out to us the amazing Allied advances and then, because she knew I was aching for love, she kissed me goodnight.

On the afternoon of April 21st, the first Allied troops came into Liebenau. We heard the roar and grind of the military vehicles long before we saw them from our observation posts on the roof tops. The women who had been interned for five years were nearly mad with joy and excitement. But, for me, this was an anticlimax which brought a serene quiet happiness born in the realization that this most horrifying of wars was nearly over, and that soon I should find myself buried in the arms of those I loved.

The intensity of the situation suddenly increased when a Jeep broke away from the endless line of vehicles to turn down the secondary road leading to our camp. The old soldier guarding the gate slowly pulled it open, the dejected slump of his shoulders proving how painful was the task. There was not the slightest opposition from any part of the camp and the soldiers drove in as if they had been invited. There were four of them, an officer and three men. As they came to a halt in the courtyard, a mass of women rushed over and surrounded the Jeep, shouting and cheering. Quite to their dismay, they discovered that their liberators were French, not English or American as they would have preferred, but even so, their disappointment did not appear to dampen their ardor.[5]

Following a short interview between the officer and the camp director, the men drove off, but they and others returned the next evening as our

5. Free French troops who had joined the Allied forces liberated Liebenau on the afternoon of April 21, 1945.

guests of honor at a liberation dance. They were delighted to have liberated a camp of women, many of whom spoke French and as they were not to continue to advance but to stay and occupy the surrounding region, they were free to visit us. I have always been fond of dancing, but that evening I danced as never before. I discovered with amazement that my emaciated body still retained an extraordinary source of energy stimulated by a new love of life. After each dance, I fell exhausted onto my chair, furnished with my personal cushion. It was still unbearably painful to sit on fleshless hips!

This gay evening led to many others both inside the camp and out, at least for those of us who found escorts among our new acquaintances. We sometimes dined in restaurants, at others we attended parties in German homes which had been requisitioned by the occupying forces. What fun we had and how marvelous it seemed to be among the victors instead of the vanquished! These good times eased the period of waiting for repatriation which still seemed so far away. We had been made to realize that weeks of waiting probably lay ahead, not only for us, but for thousands of liberated prisoners all over Germany.[6] The retreating enemy had left devastation in its wake. Highways and railroads needed repair, rolling stock and buses remained to be found and each prisoner must take his turn passing through the bottle-neck of a repatriation center before finding himself on home soil. In the meantime we all wrote endless letters while waiting impatiently for replies which never seemed to come, until one day I finally heard from Philippe.[7] Never shall I forget the thrill of it! He wrote that he was moving heaven and earth to bring me home and since I was considered a "special case," I could hope for an imminent departure from Liebenau. It seemed too wonderful to be true but should there be delay I could easily support it, for I would have more time to regain my strength and especially my physical appearance. I believed that I was still too ugly for Philippe to be able to love me!

Approximately two weeks after our liberation, Geneviève was repatriated by air. This seemed perfectly normal to us, for was she not the niece

6. With millions of liberated prisoners and refugees to be repatriated, it would be another four weeks before Virginia received authorization to depart for the repatriation center at Strasbourg.

7. For a transcript of Virginia's first letter to Philippe, written on March 8, 1945, see Appendix 10.

of our great deliverer, the General de Gaulle? We all crowded around the car that was to take her from the camp and gave her a joyful send-off. We loved and admired Geneviève and knew that we were going to miss her. Two weeks later came my turn to leave. I believe that my repatriation seemed perfectly normal too, to the anxious women I left behind, for was not I the skeleton so miraculously saved from the death of Ravensbrück? I wanted to feel their sympathy for although I had been disillusioned by the many feuds, the jealousy and the meanness that existed between so many of them, I could understand. The camp of Liebenau, which to me was a paradise, was for the women interned there, a purgatory of mental suffering.[8]

8. Following a brief interval at the repatriation center at Strasbourg, Virginia arrived in Paris on May 27, 1945.

11 Epilogue

The low-swung Citroën was approaching Paris . . . May 27th, 1945 was to be yet another important date in my life, and the glowing sunset could not reflect all the joy that stimulated my entire being.

After many weeks of impatient waiting I was at last entering the city I love. A French colonel had driven me all the way from the repatriation camp at Strasbourg. He was kind and full of thoughtful attention for the fragile object that I was. I had been silent most of the way partly on account of my extreme physical weakness and also because of my confused emotional state which intensified as we drew nearer to our destination. I had never experienced such joyful anticipation, but the joy was mingled with fear, fear of the unknown awaiting me. What was I to find in reaching home? What had become of those I loved; my husband, my family, during this long year of unbroken silence? Our little cottage at Nesles, our flat, and all the belongings to which one gets so attached; did they still exist after the storm?

The car was now hurrying along the old familiar streets of Paris; they seemed unusually calm in comparison to my troubled state of mind. Was it possible that eleven months earlier I had driven along these very same streets in a German prison van? It was hard to realize that after those days of frustration, of green uniforms, and of Nazi vehicles, freedom had returned and that the uniforms were khaki and the vehicles Jeeps!

After having crossed the Place de la Concorde and followed the Boulevard Saint Germain, the car was now turning sharply into the rue de Bellechasse. In a matter of seconds it would reach the rue Vaneau and I would know. I would know whether it had been worthwhile clinging on to life, or whether it might have been preferable to let myself sink quietly into the unknown which was constantly inviting us under the tent at Ravensbrück.

It was my mother-in-law who was the first to greet me. The colonel stood beside us beaming, as if he were totally responsible for this happy reunion. I was reassured at once of Philippe's safety, but when I enquired after my family in America, a heavy silence indicated that something serious had occurred. Mother had died! She had passed away on the eve of my liberation, after having battled incessantly to save my life.[1] I learned that it was thanks to her efforts and to those of my husband that I was liberated from Ravensbrück the last day of February 1945.[2] Mother had died without knowing that I was alive and safe, but also ignoring the horrors of the Nazi concentration camps.[3] I also learned that my brother who was with the Forces in the Far East, and who had been given special leave owing to Mother's condition, had arrived too late. Poor Mother, who experienced only pain and anguish during those last days, and never knew that her efforts had not been in vain.

I only saw Philippe the day after I returned, for he no longer lived at rue Vaneau, having taken a small flat at Neuilly with Pierre.[4] Strangely enough, Marshall Crouch, the American aviator whom I had caught sight of while being deported, had returned to Paris the same day. He and Philippe went out to celebrate. Later that evening, Pierre, coming back to the flat, went immediately to Philippe's room to ascertain whether he too had learned of my return. When in the half light he saw two forms peacefully sleeping, he tactfully backed out, satisfied that Virginia and Philippe had been reunited. But of course Virginia was Marshall and this explains why I saw my husband but the following day!

Philippe had experienced many adventures following my arrest. Returning to Paris immediately, he gave warning, and when the Gestapo searched our home, they remarked, "It's no use looking; they have already been here and we shall find nothing of interest now." No one else was arrested because of me, and "Comète" was able to carry on with its work.

At the end of June 1944, the Châteaudun camp was still without liaison with London. The supply situation was becoming critical and more airmen were arriving every day. As Philippe was now "brulé" or "cooked"

1. Edith Roush had died of leukemia just days before Liebenau was liberated.

2. Virginia's release from Ravensbrück had occurred largely because of the efforts of her mother, Edith Roush. See Illustration 8 for a copy of Philippe's cable to her and Appendixes 2, 3, 4, 5, 6, 7, and 9 for transcripts of relevant letters.

3. Just before her death in mid-April, Mrs. Roush had received a brief letter, dated February 23, 1945, from Major John F. White Jr. of MIS-X, which informed her of her daughter's whereabouts and indicated that she was in good health. See Appendix 8.

4. Pierre was probably Pierre Robert, who had worked with Philippe on the Comet escape line.

as we used to say, and since his presence could only endanger others should he be caught, Jean de Blommaert decided to send him first to Spain and then to England, in order to explain the situation. Philippe confided his responsibilities in Paris to Pierre Robert, and left for Spain with Bob Camus, another member of the line, who was to return to Châteaudun in order to report.

Their trip was hazardous, but they reached the Spanish territory and contacted the British authorities. Cables went back and forth to London, and a few days later a parachuting of supplies, cash, and a radio transmitter was virtually promised. The allied authorities were cautious regarding parachuting of supplies, and although Jean was their agent and the story of the camp appeared to be genuine enough, it took a certain amount of convincing before they agreed to act as required.

After a short stay in Gibraltar, Philippe flew to England and it was only then that he heard that liaison had been reestablished with the Châteaudun hideout, and the necessary supplies sent. The last weeks of the camp were glorious ones. Nearly 200 Allied airmen who had been hidden in the Forest of Fréteval, within a district heavily occupied by the enemy, were liberated by the allied advance on August 13, 1945. This event meant that "Comète," even though stopped by mass arrests four times since 1942, ended its gallant career by a climactic success in which both Philippe and I had a share.

Philippe was now a member of the Free French Forces, and I found him in uniform working for the French Intelligence in liaison with the British and Americans. As for my mother-in-law, she had escaped arrest by hiding in a maid's room on the top floor of our building.

None of my intimate friends from Königsburg have returned. Of our group of 250 women, only 25 of us are living to-day. Some were shot, others were gassed; the three English girls parachuted over France were shot. However the majority died of cold and starvation. Of the twenty-five who returned, nearly all are suffering from tuberculosis, heart trouble, or some other physical or mental disorder resulting from the privations they endured. Many have lost all their material possessions or have come back to find their homes completely broken by deportation and death.[5]

5. Virginia was fortunate in that she had recovered her health within a year and gave birth to her son, Jean-Patrick, on May 27, 1946.

Some weeks ago I attended the Salon des Artistes Français in Paris.[6] While wandering about the exhibit I was drawn by a life size reclining bronze statue in the center of one of the rooms. I suddenly felt sick with horror. It had been unnecessary for me to read the title "Buchenwald" to realize that this prostrate image was that of a human being dead of starvation. I had recognized the sinister skeleton at once. It was Janette; it was Tita, Ann, Nicole,—it was all or any of my friends, for they had all looked like that at the eve of death. I was hypnotized by the statue. Unwittingly I stooped nearer and involuntarily closed my thumb and index about the upper arm of the horrible effigy. The room with its pictures and people suddenly swam before my eyes. Time's merciful veil tore apart and I saw myself as I had been a year ago. This stark arm was my arm, this ghastly withered body was my body. For the first time I realized to what extent I had walked "through the valley of the shadow of death."

6. This would have been in the spring of 1946. The prestigious Salon des Artistes Français was founded in 1663. The Salon holds major exhibitions and awards several important prizes. The works of many famous artists have been featured at the Salon.

Afterword

Jim Calio

The first time I met Virginia d'Albert-Lake was in 1989. I was living in New York City at the time, and I was watching the evening news on ABC. I had tuned in late, but just in time to catch the last half of a story about a remarkable American woman who had received the French Legion of Honor, the highest award given to civilians in France. It was for her heroics during the Second World War as a member of the French Resistance. Of course, what made the story compelling—it just jumped off the television screen—was that she was an American fighting with the French Resistance, and an American woman at that.

I knew I wanted to write a story about her.

I called information in France to get Virginia's telephone number. I didn't know if this would work—she could have been unlisted—but sometimes the most direct way is the easiest. I quickly got the number in Brittany, and then I made the call.

"Hello," came the warm, plummy voice from across the ocean. It is one of those voices that you don't forget, and I can still hear it to this day.

I introduced myself; we chatted briefly, and soon we were off and running. Of course, Virginia spoke English, so there was nothing lost in translation. I explained that I had seen the ABC story on television and that I was a journalist and that I was interested in coming to France to interview her.

"When do you want to come?" asked Virginia, getting right to the point.

"As soon as I can," I said, still unsure of where I would get an assignment but knowing a good story when I saw it.

"How about next week?" she replied.

That was a little sooner than I had expected, but I was not going to let this opportunity pass me by.

"Sure," I said. "Just let me make a reservation and I'll call you back."

"All right, dear, just let me know," said Virginia.

But before we hung up, I had a question I couldn't resist asking, even though I knew I would see her in a week. I had seen enough of the ABC piece to know that she had suffered terribly in Ravensbrück and other German concentration camps and had walked out barely alive.

The question seemed obvious, and I was sure she'd been asked it many times before. "How did you survive the concentration camps?" I asked, hoping the question was not naïve or insulting, since I hardly knew her.

"Well," she said without pause, her voice steady. "It was simple, really. You could never give in. The women who cried at night were usually dead in the morning."

Those words sent a shiver up my spine. They do to this day. I knew that I had a great story. And I knew that Virginia's story would change my life.

I flew to France the following week. I had no trouble getting a magazine assignment, and I hooked up with a photographer who was as enthusiastic about the story as I was.

Virginia had given us directions to Dinard, the seaside resort in Brittany on France's north coast where she and her husband, Philippe, lived. They had moved from Paris many years before and now lived in a cottage on his family's estate. I say "cottage," but it was quite large—a house, really, in the style of most buildings in Brittany, with thick stone walls and a sloping, grey slate roof. It was set on a small hill overlooking an estuary off in the distance. The house was technically in a small village just to the south of Dinard called Pleurtuit, but Dinard was the nearest big town.

It was a long drive from Paris, about five hours with several stops to eat and stretch.

Finally, late in the afternoon, we pulled into the long gravel driveway that was marked on two sides by slightly leaning stone posts, exactly the way Virginia had described it in her directions.

As we pulled up in front of the house, our car tires crunching the gravel, a small, white-haired woman walked slowly out the front door. We got out and introduced ourselves. She looked exactly like anyone's kindly, eighty-year-old grandmother—except for one thing. When she took my hand and greeted me, she fixed me with her incredibly clear blue eyes. It was as if she was looking right through me. And in an instant, I understood where she got the steel to survive the horrors of capture by the Germans and months at hard labor in concentration camps. Those eyes, it was all in her eyes.

Over the years, I made many visits to Dinard to see Virginia and Philippe. They were living in quiet retirement, enjoying occasional visits from friends and, even at that late date, old airmen they had helped rescue. They were always gracious and generous with their time.

That first visit, of course, and several thereafter were journalistic. I was gathering information for my story, taping Virginia's and Philippe's recollections of their wartime experience and reading through their voluminous scrapbooks. They had kept an incredibly detailed record of the Second World War and their exploits in it, right down to the Western Union telegram Philippe sent to Virginia's mother announcing that she had been captured by the Germans. They even had the original scrap of paper on which she had scribbled a note to Philippe as she was being bused off to the train that would take her to Germany.

But after a few visits, and after I'd written my article, I found that I was making the pilgrimage to Dinard for another, more personal reason. I simply wanted to get to know them better. They were, to my mind, real heroes, people who had risked their lives for something they believed in. It was as simple and powerful as that. In an era when the word "hero" has become debased, when it often comes to mean simply surviving an ordeal, these two people did something more. They risked their lives, they took a chance, and they expected nothing in return. They actually *did* something.

We corresponded over the years, usually short notes and postcards. I learned that they had friends in Lisbon, and they made the trip there by car, even at their advanced ages (they were both in their eighties). I would tell them about my life in Los Angeles (I had by then moved there to work for *Life* magazine), although it always felt kind of puny compared to the lives they had led.

Whenever I was in Dinard, I would take Virginia and Philippe out for lunch or dinner, often to Cancale, a fishing village just a few miles up the coast, where we would gaze out at the colorful fishing fleet and feast on seafood platters piled high with fresh-caught *langoustines*, clams, shrimp, and mussels. They offered me their guesthouse when I visited, but I declined, not wanting to crowd them or wear out my welcome.

At the end of each visit, I would sneak off to a favorite *pâtisserie* in Dinard and buy them some baked treats, usually fruit tarts, which I knew they loved. Unfailingly, I would get a letter when I got back to the United

States thanking me for taking them out. They always asked when I was coming back.

In 1997 I saw a story in the *New York Times* that said American civilians who were interned in concentration camps during the war were entitled to reparation money from the German government. The money was to be distributed by the U.S. Justice Department in conjunction with Germany, but applicants had to fill out the necessary paperwork first. I knew that Virginia qualified, so I got the forms and flew to France.

By then Virginia was not well. She had suffered a stroke and according to Philippe was failing rapidly. He warned me that she would not be the same person I had known on previous visits and that I should be prepared.

He was right. When I arrived at their house in Pleurtuit, Virginia was in the back bedroom on the first floor. I went in to see her and sat beside her in a chair next to the bed. I don't know how much of what I said she understood. She seemed to be in and out of consciousness, sometimes speaking in English, sometimes in French. Nevertheless, I talked to her as if everything were normal, telling her about my trip and about the German reparation money.

Later, Philippe and I filled out the forms. Since there were no real records of Virginia's stay at Ravensbrück or the other camps she was sent to, I had to dig through their files and come up with the Red Cross paperwork that detailed when she was released. I hoped that would do the trick.

But when it came time to sign the forms, I was at a loss. Clearly, Virginia was in no shape to do it. I explained to Philippe that I needed her signature to make it all official. "Don't worry," he said as he took my pen. "I've been signing for her for years." Eventually, the reparation money came through.

The next day, as was my custom, I went to the local *pâtisserie* to get Virginia and Philippe some goodies before I left. Because of Virginia's condition, I was just going to drop them off before driving back to Paris. But when I got to the house, there, to my amazement, was Virginia sitting up on the couch. Although wrapped in a blanket, she was smiling and perfectly coherent, and she insisted that I stay for tea. We all chatted merrily as if nothing was wrong, and then I left.

That was the last time I saw Virginia. She died a few months later at the age of eighty-seven. Several years later I visited the tiny cemetery in

Dinard where she is buried. She is in the Anglo-American section, where American soldiers are also resting. It seems fitting. I stood for a long time at her gravesite, not believing that she was gone. I still don't sometimes.

Philippe died in January 2000, the long days and nights without Virginia finally over. I know it was very hard for him and he was very lonely. Until his death, he continued to live in the stone cottage he and Virginia had loved so much. He is buried next to her in the small cemetery.

After that last time I saw Virginia, when she was so incapacitated, I got a note from Philippe. It said, "Virginia and I wish to apologize for the reception you got with us when you drove all the way from Paris. We knew it could not be like previous times, but you fell on a period that was even worse than others."

I was astounded. That's the kind of people they were. I wrote back:

"You don't need to apologize to me for anything. It's an honor just to know you both." And I meant it.

In the years since then, and actually for the entire time I knew her, I have often thought of the words Virginia spoke to me that first day on the phone. "You could never give in," she said. Indeed, if Virginia could do what she did, who am I to complain about anything? Whenever I'm in a tough spot or I think that things are going badly for me, I think of those words. "You could never give in." It gives me courage. It always gets me through. And I can still hear her voice.

Report from Philippe d'Albert-Lake
Nom de plume: Paul Blanc
Activity: December 1943/July 1944[1]

In December 1943 my cousin Michel de Gourlet (201 rue de Genelle Paris) asked me if I was prepared to see a certain Jean LEDUQUE (RUTLAND) that I might be able to help. Jean came to my house one day (1 bis rue Vaneau PARIS) and explained that he had just arrived from London on an evacuation mission. He added that I had been recommended to him and asked me whether I was prepared to be his righthand man, as he had as yet contacted nobody to fulfill that post. It was immediately understood that I would take his Radio Operator Louis to Nesles La Vallée and then return to Paris in order to help Jean to find further contacts, convoy workers, people prepared to shelter, and landing grounds for future operations. This was done. I kept Louis at my house at Nesles for a few days and then arranged for Marcel Renard, Baker, at Nesles to shelter him. I had already and previously to my meeting Jean helped Renard on one or two occasions while he was sheltering some U.S. Airman and needed someone who could speak English. From then onwards I kept active between Nesles and Paris, helping Jean to prepare the ground for evacuation operations. Jean's mission, however, was not a success owing to his Radio Set being captured by the Gestapo in circumstances independent from our group (arrest of Martin and escape of La Fleur) and both Jean and Louis were called back to London Jan./Feb. 1944.

Upon leaving, Jean told me of his intention to return to Paris as soon as possible. He asked me to carry on the work with Lilly Du Chaila, 36, rue d'Artois PARIS and also mentioned that in the event of his not being able to return, I would be contacted by COMETE who would ask me to help them.

A week or two after Jean's departure I was contacted by Lilly (Michou) who explained that COMETE was unable to function owing to numerous arrests in Paris (Gerome etc.) and that owing to the Paris link being broken the Belgium section and southern France could not work effectively, she being the only one left that knew the contacts on both sides. She added that a certain MAX had gone to London to report and that before leaving he had ordered that no further evacuations should be made until his return. Michou, however, was of another opinion and asked me whether I would take care of the Paris link until MAX and DANIEL returned from London. I told her of Jean's orders, but, added that I would do all I could for them. From then onwards and until the return of JEAN, DANIEL, and MAX, who all came back approximately at the same time March/April 1944, I served as link

1. National Archives and Records Administration, RG 498, Records of Headquarters, European Theater of Operations, United States Army (World War II), MIS-X. A copy of this report is in the d'Albert Lake Family Papers.

between Belgium and Southern France, nevertheless, few evacuations were made during that period.

At a meeting held upon JEAN and DANIEL's return, meeting attended by JEAN SARMANT from BELGIUM, it was decided between us that the following responsibilities would [be] bestowed upon each one of us.

BELGIUM . . . JEAN SARMAN

PARIS . . . DANIEL

SOUTH . . . MAX

CAMPS . . . JEAN DE BLOMMAERT

I was to remain JEAN's righthand man, but, was also to help DANIEL who was a newcomer to PARIS, and open a centre in NESLES La Vallee for twenty-five men in order to avoid congestion in BELGIUM. Both COMETE and the camp were to draw on this lot which was to be continually renewed from BELGIUM. Everything worked well and evacuations were going successfully until two men were caught between PARIS and BORDEAUX and the Gestapo got on COMETE's tail once again. After a pretty narrow escape at the GARE D'AUSTERLITZ in which MICHOU, MONIQUE, DANIEL and I were involved, DANIEL thought it wise to stop evacuations towards the South for a period. This was April/May 1944. It was then that something went wrong in BELGIUM. JEAN SARMANT left for England and DANIEL decided to return to BELGIUM to sort things out and get a camp going there. JEAN and DANIEL were consequently both away from PARIS and I thereupon became responsible both for COMETE in PARIS and filling of the CHATEAUDUN Camp that was almost ready, thanks to JEAN. LUCIEN and his Radio Operator FRANCOIS had also arrived to help in the creation of Camps and both LUCIEN and JEAN decided to pool their efforts. At that stage, the BELGIUM FLOW OF MEN had greatly been hampered by the lack of transport owing to allied bombing and we had to look for further sources of men. DANIEL upon leaving had given me several resistance contacts, but, only one proved to be good. I will call it the "YVONNE–MRS. RAVALOWITCH SOURCE." It was understood that for all the men rescued and passed on to us, we would pay the above mentioned source a hundred francs per man, per day, dating from the time of their rescue.

The Camp was ready, at least JEAN was prepared to have men sheltered around CHATEAUDUN and we started sending some. At the same time MAX was prepared to take another shot at the South and he and BOB started making trips down South with a party of five men at a time. NESLES was proving difficult, always on account of bad communications, so Virginia and I moved into PARIS with the men who were being sheltered at NESLES at the time. We kept on sending men both South and to the Camp until D-Day.

I now must mention the PIERRE LE BOUTEILLER, BOLTER, GROUCH incident that took place in May. I had a party of seven men that had come together and were most anxious to get away together. Accommodation on trains was very scarce and I could only send five men with MAX on a particular day, knowing too well that rail transport towards the South might break down at any time. It so happened, that at that particular time, the Camp was without Radio Communication with London owing to LUCIEN and FRANCOIS having left their Radio Set in BAYONNE. Someone had to go and get it rapidly. I suggested to JEAN, a friend of mine, PIERRE LE BOUTEILLER who had been asking me for some time for an introduction to JEAN and had from the very start authorized me to use his name in order to rent one of the Premises which we required for our work. PIERRE was interviewed and accepted to go, I then begged him to take down the sixth man CROUCH as there was an extra seat available in his coach, and I could send BOLTER a day later on his own (he could speak French) and have him met by TANTE who was to have been warned the previous day by PIERRE's safe arrival in BAYONNE. However, this plan did not work OUT OWING TO PIERRE not being able to establish contact with TANTE. L'Abbé URRESTI who was to be contacted first took PIERRE for a Gestapo Agent and refused to recognise him. PIERRE then lost his head and instead of staying in BAYONNE for 48 hours which would have enabled him to receive BOLTER the next day and then meet MAX, due to arrive the following day with his five men, he abandoned CROUCH, stating that this man being so near to the border refused to return with him to PARIS, and started making for CHATEAUDUN in order to report. Before boarding his train at LE BOUCAUT he suddenly remembered that one of the men with whom he had been a prisoner of war in Germany lived in LE BOUCAUT. He located him, got him to promise to meet BOLTER the next day (PIERRE had a photograph of BOLTER) gave him twenty thousand francs and received an assurance that should BOLTER and CROUCH turn up, they would be got across the border (there was still a possibility of CROUCH turning up to meet BOLTER as he knew that he was due to arrive the next day by the same train that he and PIERRE had taken the day before). BOLTER turned up and was met by this friend of PIERRE's who got him across to SPAIN, but, we have never heard of CROUCH since. MAX and his five men crossed the border safely.

On D-Day we were caught in PARIS with sixteen men on our hands and no means of transport. It had been agreed that on D-Day we were to join the Camp ourselves so we decided to attempt the trip on foot. Virginia and I left PARIS on the 7th June with three convoy girls and eleven men. The girls were ANNE-MARIE, MICHELE, and ANY. VIRGINIA, myself, and one of the boys, started out on bicycles, the others took a suburban train that still ran to DOURDAN 25 miles from PARIS. We all met at DOURDAN and started to walk towards CHATEAUDUN in small groups of two or three. It was not an easy job and even the weather was against us. The second day owing to our procession of sixteen people being spotted all the same, we decided to split up in small groups which would individually reach a rendez-vous point short of CHATEAUDUN where we hoped that JEAN could have us picked up by some vehicle. VIRGINIA, one boy and myself took the bicycles and went ahead in order to establish contact with the Camp. We established contact with the first intermediary at CHATEAUDUN. He said he could arrange for a cart to go to our rendez-vous point the next morning and could also have me and the boy accompanied to the Camp first thing in the morning. It was agreed that

VIRGINIA would go with the cart in order to identify the men at the meeting point. The next day the cart met seven men and MICHELE at the rendez-vous. ANY and two others had gone direct to a certain farm that she knew, and ANNE-MARIE and one man had walked straight to CHATEAUDUN. Six of the men and MICHELE got in the cart. VIRGINIA and one man cycled a short distance ahead. At the bend in the road a German Police Car was stopped and one of the Germans asked our boy an indication as to the whereabouts. VIRGINIA realizing that they had a chance to get away with it, also stopped and started talking to the Germans, nevertheless, they were unlucky because one German Officer spoke French perfectly and realized that VIRGINIA had an English accent. They started questioning them, checking their papers and soon took them off to German Police Headquarters. While this was going on, the six men in the cart took to the woods, so that when the Germans came to have a look at the cart, they only found MICHELE and the young driver. They suspected nothing further and as we understand that VIRGINIA told them she was trying to reach the Spanish border, the Camp remained secure. VIRGINIA had over 100,000 Francs with her and a small piece of paper which gave indications as to how to contact the Camp. We had some anxious moments but, later were told that VIRGINIA swallowed that paper when the German Police asked her what it was. All six men in the cart were recovered within 48 hours, thanks to the French resistance, which means that out of a total of 16 men that left PARIS (BOB and petit PIERRE brought down five within 24 hours of our leaving PARIS) only one was lost!

After spending a couple of days in the Camp that gave me an excellent impression of security and welfare, I returned to PARIS with BOB and petit PIERRE, establishing a relay system on the way in order to be able to bring to the Camp cigarettes, blankets, and more men if possible (our trip had proved that it was still possible to continue evacuation towards the Camp).

We knew that the Gestapo would sooner or later come down on our PARIS premises and we were anxious to warn our friends and get out our documents before hand. This we had time to do and when the Gestapo came they found nothing except one gun that we had overlooked at NESLES. They knew, however, that approximately seventy men had come through the rue VANEAU premises and said that it was a very serious affair. This was reported to us by the Concierge.

It had now become necessary for security reasons that I should leave PARIS, and as JEAN had asked both BOB and myself to go to SPAIN, contact MR. CRESSWELL, and try to obtain an immediate Parachute Operation for the Camp, sending them a Radio Set (they still remained without contact with LONDON) cash, and various supplies, it was arranged that we would go together, but that he would return to CHATEAUDUN while I went on to ENGLAND.

Before leaving PARIS I left petit PIERRE in charge who turned out to be very devoted and successful. I also asked MAX who evacuated PIERRE LE BOUTEILLER for security reasons, he was at the time staying in my house at NESLES where I had sent him after his unsuccessful mission to BAYONNE. Both he and MR. AND MRS. BLANC were in the house when the Gestapo arrived at NESLES although they had been warned to get out. They were not arrested, however, but, summoned to Gestapo Headquarters for further enquiries. PIERRE never went of course and the BLANCS were not troubled as far as I know.

It took BOB and I five days 25th June/1st July to get from PARIS to BORDEAUX. Our passing the border was uneventful and when in SPAIN MR. CRESWELL obtained from LONDON that the Operation should be attempted at once. I heard upon my arrival in LONDON that it had been successful. BOB was to wait in SPAIN until the results of the Operation were known and then return to CHATEAUDUN.

Mrs. F. W. Rush to Honorable Cordell Hull[2]

4689 Lakeview Avenue
St. Petersburg, Fla.

August 24, 1944
Honorable Cordell Hull
Secretary of State
Washington, D.C.

Dear Mr. Hull:

Our daughter, Mrs. Virginia d'Albert-Lake of Paris, France, is in extremely serious trouble. She married Philip d'Albert-Lake, a French citizen, seven years ago, and has been living in Paris ever since. She has retained her American citizenship.

We have just received an air-mail letter from our son-in-law, under date of July 31, and post-marked London. He says in part: "Virginia was arrested by the Gestapo in June while doing some valuable work for the Allies. We both have been doing our spot of work for sometime. Of course, after Virginia's arrest the Germans came down on us like flies. They have taken over Nesles (their summer home) and the Paris flats with all our belongings. Mum had to escape, and I do not know where she is. I had a rather adventurous escape, but here I am! I cannot describe how I feel about Virginia, but I believe her American nationality will somewhat protect her and everything is being done in order to help her as far as possible. I don't know where she is, but I'm afraid it is somewhere in Germany. Of course, I cannot go into details. I plan to return to France at the earliest possible moment and help knock hell out of those bloody Germans. The prospects are good. When I leave England, I'll send you a cable."

He gave the P. & O. S. N. Company address, 14 Cockspur St., London S.W. Prior to the German invasion, he was publicity man in the Paris office of this company.

I might add that Virginia is Gentile, which may be in her favor in view of Nazi standards. She is 34 years of age, intelligent, and personable. This is true also of her husband.

I suspect that Virginia's case might come under priority classification, and I trust that you will give her your special and immediate attention.

Most sincerely yours,

Mrs. F. W. Roush

2. D'Albert-Lake Family Papers.

APPENDIX 3

Department of State to Mrs. F. W. Roush[3]

Washington
September 4, 1944

My dear Mrs. Roush:

I have received your letter of August 24, 1944 and can well understand your desire to do everything possible to obtain the release of your daughter, Mrs. Virginia d'Albert-Lake, who is reported to have been arrested by the Germans in Paris.

Before receipt of your letter, Mrs. Colson of the American Red Cross informed the Department of your daughter's case. In view of the exceptional circumstances, the Department sent a telegram to the American Minister at Bern instructing him to request the Swiss authorities to endeavor to ascertain your daughter's whereabouts and to report concerning her arrest and removal to Germany. You will be informed as soon as any information is received concerning your daughter.

Sincerely yours,
For the Secretary of State:
Albert E. Clattenburg, Jr.
Assistant Chief
Special War Problems Division

Mrs. F. W. Roush,
4689 Lakeview Avenue,
St. Petersburg, Florida.

3. D'Albert-Lake Family Papers.

American Red Cross to Mrs. F. W. Roush[4]

Washington, D.C.
August 26, 1944

Office of Vice Chairman

Dear Mrs. Roush:

Your letter to Mr. Basil O'Connor, Chairman of the Red Cross, arrived during his absence, and since I know how much you must be concerned over the welfare and safety of your daughter, Mrs. Virginia d'Albert-Lake, who was last reported to have been arrested by the Gestapo, I hasten to advise you that while Mrs. d'Albert-Lake is in the hands of the Gestapo the American Red Cross will be unable to be of any assistance.

I advise you to write to the U.S. State Department here in Washington acquainting them with all facts, since they are the agencies which would act in such instances.

We regret that there is nothing at this time which the American Red Cross can do to assist.

Sincerely yours,
Richard F. Allen

Mrs. F. W. Roush
4689 Lakeview Avenue
St. Petersburg, Florida

---

4. D'Albert-Lake Family Papers.

APPENDIX 5

War Department to Mrs. F. W. Roush[5]

Office of the Under Secretary
Washington, D.C.
August 15, 1944

Mrs. F. W. Roush,
4689 Lakeview Avenue,
St. Petersburg 7, Florida.

Dear Mrs. Roush:

I have your letter of August 14th and I am very glad to do anything I can under the circumstances which are very distressing. There will, of course, be nothing that the American Army can do until Germany is defeated and the whereabouts of your daughter can be determined.

So far the German Chancellery has not offered to make any exchange of civilian prisoners or even of military prisoners, unless they are wounded beyond any further participation in the war. I wish I could outline to you some course of action which would be immediately productive of results. If I hear of any turn of affairs which offers any immediate solution or amelioration of her condition, it will give me great pleasure to inform you.

In the meantime, I can only tender my sympathy.
Sincerely yours,

MARION RUSHTON
Colonel, JAGD
Administrative Officer.

5. D'Albert Lake Family Papers.

Headquarters, Army Service Forces, to Mr. F. W. Roush[6]

Office of the Provost Marshal General
Washington, D.C.
15 August 1944

Mrs. F. W. Roush,
4689 Lakeview Avenue,
St. Petersburg 7, Florida

Dear Mrs. Roush:

The Provost Marshal General directs me to reply to your letter of 14 August 1944 written in regard to your daughter, now in German custody.

This matter is being taken up with the Special War Problems Division, State Department.

You may rest assured that everything possible will be done to aid your daughter.

Sincerely yours,
HOWARD F. BRESEE
Colonel, C.M.P.,
Assistant Director,
Prisoner of War Division.

6. D'Albert-Lake Family Papers.

Department of State to Mrs. F. W. Roush[7]

Washington
January 11, 1945

My dear Mrs. Roush:

I have received your telegram of January 6, 1944 [sic] in which you request the inclusion in the forthcoming exchange of Virginia D'Albert-Lake.

The Department appreciates your anxiety and desires to do everything possible to bring about the safe return of your daughter. As explained in the Department's letter of October 13, 1944 we are doing everything possible to assist your daughter. However, to date we have been unable to ascertain her present whereabouts and welfare.

The German Government has indicated that it will not permit the departure of Americans from areas under its control except in pursuance of agreements providing for the exchange of nationals. As the United States Government for security reasons has found it necessary in previous exchanges to withhold certain Germans whose return was specifically requested by the German Government, the Department has not been in a position to insist upon the inclusion of specific Americans in the exchange.

You may be sure that just as soon as some pertinent information concerning your daughter is obtained, you will be informed.

Sincerely yours,

Albert E. Clattenburg, Jr.
Assistant Chief
Special War Problems Division

Mrs. F. W. Roush
4689 Lakeview Avenue
St. Petersburg 7, Florida

7. D'Albert-Lake Family Papers.

Johnny White of MIS-X to Mrs. Edith Roush[8]

February 23, 1945

Dear Mrs. Roush,

I saw Philip [sic] yesterday, and he told me that he had at last had news from Virginia. I cannot give you the source of it, but it seems fairly recent, and says that she is alright and detained at Ravensbruck. Ravensbruck is near Stetin and the Russians may reach it any time now. Philip says that we may still have some anxious moments ahead, but that it is already wonderful to know that Virginia is in good health, and in a definite place.

All is well with Philip here, and the rest of the family is also standing up to it. This is a very short note, but Philip wanted you to have good news at once.

Regards.

Johnny White

---

8. D'Albert-Lake Family Papers.

Joseph Johnson to Mrs. F. W. Roush[9]

4735 York Bld.
Los Angeles #42
California
9-10-44

Dear Mrs. Roush:

I promised Philip that I would write to you when I left him in London.

I was one of the seven boys who was with Virginia when she was caught by the Gestapo. It was thru her efforts that I was restored to my wife and baby son.

I can never tell you how much I appreciate her efforts for my freedom and freedom for fellow Air Men.

When she was caught she was helping 3 Americans, 2 South Africans, one Canadian, and myself. That was besides what she and Philip had taken the days before.

The rest of the boys would like to write to you but I happened to be the only one who had your address.

I thought I had met you and your Doctor Husband when I was in St. Petersburg. I told Virginia and Philip that I thought I knew you and Virginia gave me your address and I have kept it ever since.

I have prayed many times for the end of the war and Virginia's safe return to her husband and family.

I wanted to write to you so I could tell you my admiration for the woman who is your daughter. I only wish I had the cool calm courage that your daughter possesses. It is due to her that 20 to 30 of us American Airmen who parachuted to France thru necessity are returned and reunited with their families.

I always will have a grateful feeling for Virginia. She is one woman I will never forget because only thru her I am able to write this letter, play with my son, and be with my wife.

I always wish to consider her as my friend and I hope she will do the same.

Your Friend

Joseph Johnson
1st Lt. A.C.

9. D'Albert-Lake Family Papers.

Virginia d'Albert-Lake to Philippe d'Albert-Lake[10]

Liebenau, 8 March '45

My own darling, how strange to be able to write to you. Last June seems so far away, that you and my past life seem a dream. I am very happy to have been sent to this camp where I am very well off. It is a charming old convent in the midst of rich farming country not far from the shores of Lake Constance. The food is good and sufficient, and we receive Red Cross parcels on supplement. The rooms are well heated, all sanitary conditions are the most modern. I am warmly dressed too, so you see that you have no reason to worry about me. I made the trip here with Geneviève de Gaulle, niece of the well known leader. We are in a very pleasant room with one French and two English ladies, one of whom is an old friend of Mum's, Miss Gibson. Everyone is nice to us! I will write regularly several times a month. I have the right to three letters and four cards. I'm writing to the family tonight too. How I long for news of you. You must have thousands of things to tell me, and I have as many! You know, Philippe, how I *love* you.

Virginia

10. D'Albert-Lake Family Papers.

Jules D. Miller to Virginia d'Albert-Lake[11]

[ca. 1946]

Julius D. Miller
Gen. Delivery
Lafayette, Ind.

Dear Virginia

If I may be so bold. I wish to take this opportunity again to thank you for all that you did for me while I was in your care. I understand the risk you took for all of my kind and there is nothing great enough we could do to pay you for it.

I have corresponded with Mr. Delanney since the end of the War and they told me that you had been taken by the Germans. I was very much upset for I was afraid that perhaps your efforts on my behalf was the cause. When I heard that you were safe again, I was very much relieved.

After I returned to the states I was stationed at home (Hampton, Va) at Langley field for 16 months. I then decided to go to college under the new Govt. bill whereby veterans can get a free college education. So now here I am at Purdue University in Lafayette, Ind. preparing to enter as a freshman. There are many ex pilots here who were in the 8th Airforce.

By the way if there is anything here in the States I can send you I would be more than glad to do it. Just let me know what it is.

If you should be interested in the details of my trip and if this letter isn't tampered with, let me know, I will give you the story.

With my best Regards,

Jules Miller

---

11. D'Albert-Lake Family Papers.

Charles F. Weis to Virginia and Philippe d'Albert-Lake[12]

1569288 W/o Weis C. F.
M. T. Section 13. 4. 46
R.A.F. Harrogate
Yorkshire
England

Dear Sir and Madame.

I hope you will excuse me for not writing to you sooner by [sic] it was only today that the Air Ministry have sent me your address.

I don't expect you will remember me but I passed through your hands on 26th MAY 1944 as an evader. I was know [sic] as "Jock" by the rest of the boys. I sat on that night in a house and wrote Virginia the words to all the modern music. I was with an American Pilot, Roy Rice and an Australia bombaimer [sic] Jack Lynch.

I can remember it all very clearly. The dinner I had in the cellar under the flower Shop and the little blonde girl who traveled to Chateaudun in the train with us.

I hope you are both in the best of health and resting peacefully on your laurels now. I cannot begin to thank you enough for the risks, and they certainly were risks, that you took for fellows like myself. People my [sic] say that flying is dangerous but I would rather fly than take the risks that you [did]. So I thank you with all sincerity from the bottom of my heart. I am to convey to you my mother's thanks and my father's who unfortunately did not live to see the end of the War.

I am afraid I am not much of a letter writer and now find myself stuck for words. It is not that I have nothing to say but as you will be getting scores of letters from the other blokes this one will probably be boring you so I will close. Hoping to hear from you soon (I also hope to have the pleasure of seeing you too)

I remain
Yours Sincerely

Charles F. Weis

12. D'Albert-Lake Family Papers.

John F. White Jr. to American Embassy, Paris[13]

(Rear) APO 887

10 October 1945

SUBJECT: Attestation

TO: American Embassy, 2 Avenue Gabriel, Paris 8e

1. This letter will serve to introduce Mrs. Virginia d'Albert-Lake, who has the unusual distinction of being one of the few Americans to have endured the experiences of a German concentration camp for political deportees.

2. Beginning in late 1943 Mrs. d'Albert-Lake assisted her husband in the hazardous and most worthwhile endeavor of passing British and American aviators out of German occupied France. Until her arrest in June 1944 she thus devoted all of her time and energies to fighting her country's and her allies' wars in occupied France. She guided around Paris and out of Paris to central France many aviators almost none of whom spoke French and most of whom were illy disguised as Frenchmen by their civilian clothes. Many of these aviators she lodged at her own apartment in Paris or at her house in the country outside of Paris.

3. Mrs. d'Albert-Lake had the misfortune to be arrested by a chance German road control when she was guiding some aviators to a special place of safety in central France. She had the presence of mind to dispose of a list which she was carrying which gave all too accurate indications about other members of the organization. No other member of the organization was arrested because of her subsequent interrogation. The hiding place toward which Mrs. d'Albert-Lake was guiding the aviators when she was arrested was the center of one of the most successful evasion operations of the war, for at it about two hundred allied airmen were safely secured until they were liberated by advancing American forces in August 1944.

4. We have seen a number of the French women who were in the concentration camp of Ravensbruck with Mrs. d'Albert-Lake. Their tributes to her personal generosity and consideration are not for us to detail. But their continual praise of her courage and especially of her inspiration to the morale of her associates requires mention.

5. Needless to say Mrs. d'Albert-Lake richly merits any consideration that may be given her.

For the Commanding Officer
JOHN F. WHITE, JR.
Major AC

13. National Archives and Records Administration, RG 498, Records of Headquarters, European Theater of Operations, United States Army (World War II), MIS-X. A copy of this memo is in the d'Albert Lake Family Papers.

Helen Wickman to Virginia d'Albert-Lake[14]

78120 Pitcher Lane
Cottage Grove, Oregon 97424
March 17, 1993

Dear Virginia

My husband, Alfred Wickman, died on November 16, 1978. He had a heart attack and died quickly in a house we were building in Fresco, Colorado.

The article you wrote for the Readers Digest was brought to my attention by a friend. Alfred would not tell me anything about his experiences in the French Underground or his prisoner of war time for many years. He finally told me what happened to him from the time he left me at Redmond, Oregon until he was separated from the Army Air Corp. in Atlantic City, N.J.

It was difficult for him to talk about your experiences with the German Army. He had heard about your trials and the misery you were experiencing while incarcerated in the German prisons. He had heard of some of the results of your torture. He felt responsible for it and helpless. The time spent in Fresnes Prison in Paris was a difficult time for him. He was threatened with being shot every day and he thought it was because his grandfather was born in Germany that they did not shoot him.

Alfred ended at Stalag Luft I at Barth, Germany where he met some of his friends and where he heard news of you.

He would be pleased to know that you have a son and are happy. Thank you for writing about your experiences so that we will not forget. The world is so miserable now we need help.

Most sincerely

Helen Wickman

14. D'Albert-Lake Family Papers.

Much has been written about France and the French Resistance during World War II. Works that have been particularly useful for this study include Hanna Diamond, *Women and the Second World War in France, 1939–1948: Choices and Constraints* (Essex, Eng.: Longman, 1999); Sarah Fishman, *We Will Wait: Wives of French Prisoners of War, 1940–1945* (New Haven: Yale University Press, 1991); Robert Gildea, *Marianne in Chains: In Search of the German Occupation, 1940–45* (London: Macmillan, 2002); Julian Jackson, *France: The Dark Years, 1940–1944* (London: Oxford University Press, 2001); Julian Jackson, *The Fall of France: The Nazi Invasion of 1940* (New York: Oxford University Press, 2003); and Robert O. Paxton, *Vichy France: Old Guard and New Order, 1940–1944* (New York: Columbia University Press, 2001).

Relevant specialized studies about the role of escape lines in France include M. R. D. Foot, *SOE in France: An Account of the Work of the British Special Operations Executive in France, 1940–1944* (London: Her Majesty's Stationery Office, 1966); M. R. D. Foot and J. M. Langley, *MI 9: Escape and Evasion, 1939–1945* (Boston: Little, Brown, 1979); Airey Neave, *Saturday at M.I.9* (London: Hodder and Stoughton, 1969); and Sherri Greene Ottis, *Silent Heroes: Downed Airmen and the French Underground* (Lexington: University Press of Kentucky, 2001). A very good memoir is George Watt, *The Comet Connection* (Lexington: University Press of Kentucky, 1990). Two other memoirs involving the Comet escape line are William Etherington, *A Quiet Woman's War: The Story of Elsie Bell* (Norwich, Eng: Mousehold Press, 2002), and Raymond Worrall, *Escape from France: The Secret Forest of Freteval* (North Yorkshire, Eng.: Silver Quill Publications, 2004). Thomas Childers, *In the Shadows of War: An American Pilot's Odyssey through Occupied France and the Camps of Nazi Germany* (New York: Henry Holt, 2003), relates the story of a downed bomber pilot, Roy Allen, including his deportation from the Gare de Pantin in Paris to Germany on August 15, 1944, on the same convoy train as Virginia. Also of interest is Peter Eisner, *The Freedom Line: The Brave Men and Women Who Rescued Allied Airmen from the Nazis During World War II* (New York: HarperCollins, 2004).

Information on women in the French Resistance can be gleaned from Marcus Binney, *The Women Who Lived for Danger: The Women Agents of SOE in the Second World War* (London: Hodder and Stoughton, 2002); Elizabeth P. McIntosh, *Sisterhood of Spies: The Women of the OSS* (Annapolis: Naval Institute Press, 1998); Margaret L. Rossiter, *Women in the Resistance* (New York: Praeger, 1986); and Margaret Collins Weitz, *Sisters in the Resistance: How Women Fought to Free France 1940–1945* (New York: John Wiley and Sons, 1995). Memoirs by two American women who were active in the French Resistance include Devereaux Rochester, *Full Moon to France* (New York: Harper and Row, 1977), and Drue Tartière, *The House Near Paris* (New York: Simon and Schuster, 1946). Also useful are Paula Schwartz, "Redefining Resistance: Women's Activism in Wartime France," in *Behind the Lines: Gender and the Two World Wars*, ed. Margaret Randolph Higonnet, Jane Jenson, Sonya Michel, and Margaret Collins Weitz (New Haven: Yale University Press, 1987), pp. 141–153, and "Part II: Gender" in *The Liberation of France: Image and Event*, ed. H. R. Kedward and Nancy Wood (Oxford: Berg Publishers, 1995), pp. 77–141. For a resistance memoir written in the mid-1990s, see Claire Chevrillon, *Code Name Christiane Clouet: A Woman in the French Resistance* (College Station: Texas A&M University Press, 1995) which, written so long after the war, lacks the immediacy of Virginia's narrative.

On Americans interned in German prisoner-of-war, labor, and extermination camps during World War II, see Mitchell G. Bard, *Forgotten Victims: The Abandonment of Americans in Hitler's Camps* (Boulder, Colo.: Westview Press, 1994). A recent and important memoir written by an American prisoner of war in Germany is Angelo M. Spinelli and Lewis H. Carlson, *Life Behind Barbed Wire: The Secret World War II Photographs of Prisoner of War Angelo M. Spinelli* (New York: Fordham University Press, 2004). For a memoir by a Canadian in Paris who was arrested and interned at Besançon and Vittel, internment camps in France for enemy nationals, most of whom held British Commonwealth passports, see Claire Fauteux, *Fantastic Interlude* (New York: Vantage Press, 1961). For an account of the experiences of one Polish Jew at Vittel, see Yitzhak Katznelson, *Vittel Diary*, trans. Myer Cohen (Israel: Hakibbytz Hameuchad, 1972). The best introduction to life at the Ravensbrück concentration camp for women is Jack G. Morrison, *Ravensbrück: Everyday Life in a Women's Concentration Camp, 1939–45* (Princeton: Markus Wiener Publishers, 2000). For a riveting and powerful first-person account, see Germaine Tillion, *Ravensbrück: An Eyewitness Account of a Women's Concentration Camp* (New York: Doubleday, 1975; orig. Paris: Editions du Seuil, 1973). A much shorter memoir by a Ravensbrück internee and the niece of General Charles de Gaulle is Geneviève de Gaulle Anthonioz, *The Dawn of Hope: A Memoir of Ravensbrück* (New York: Arcade Publishing, 1999; orig. Paris: Editions du Seuil, 1998). Also useful is Rochelle G. Saidel, *The Jewish Women of Ravensbrück Concentration Camp* (Madison: University of Wisconsin Press, 2004).

Biographical information on Virginia d'Albert-Lake is included in Rossiter, *Women in the Resistance*, pp. 204–211; Jim Calio, "Resistance and Remembrance," *Philip Morris*, November–December 1989, pp. 36–39; and Thomas Fleming, "'Deliver Us from Evil,'" *Reader's Digest*, August 1991, pp. 115–119. Works in French include Catherine Rothman-Le Dret, *L'Amérique déportée: Virginia d'Albert-Lake de la Résistance à Ravensbrück* (Nancy: Presses Universitaires de Nancy, 1994), flawed by historical errors and inaccuracies as it is; Rémy, La *Ligne de démarcation, XII* (Paris: Librairie Académique Perrin, 1964), pp. 131–173; and Rémy, *Mission Marathon* (Paris: Librairie Académique Perrin, 1974), pp. 137–181.

World War II:

The Global, Human, and Ethical Dimension

G. Kurt Piehler, series editor

1. Lawrence Cane, David E. Cane, Judy Barrett Litoff, and David C. Smith, eds.,
   Fighting Fascism in Europe: The World War II Letters of an American Veteran of the Spanish Civil War.

2. Angelo M. Spinelli and Lewis H. Carlson,
   Life Behind Barbed Wire: The Secret World War II Photographs of Prisoner of War Angelo M. Spinelli.

3. Don Whitehead and John B. Romeiser,
   "Beachhead Don": Reporting the War from the European Theater, 1942–1945.

4. Scott H. Bennett, ed.,
   Army GI, Pacifist CO: The World War II Letters of Frank and Albert Dietrich.

5. Alexander Jefferson with Lewis H. Carlson,
   Red Tail Captured, Red Tail Free: Memoirs of a Tuskegee Airman and POW.

6. Jonathan G. Utley,
   Going to War with Japan, 1937–1941.

7. Grant K. Goodman,
   America's Japan: The First Year, 1945–1946.

8. Patricia Kollander,
   "I Must Be a Part of This War": A German-American's Fight Against Hitler and Nazism.